100% NEW • ALL THE BEST GAMES
AMAZING FACTS • AWESOME SECRETS

GAME ON! 2017

EDITOR IN CHIEF
Ryan King

EDITOR
Stephen Ashby

WRITERS
Luke Albigés, Adam Barnes, Vikki Blake, Ian Dransfield, Ross Hamilton, Oliver Hill, Simon Miller, Dom Peppiatt, Chris Scullion, Drew Sleep, Nick Thorpe, Paul Walker-Emig, Josh West, Alan Williamson, Robert Zacny, Rob Zwetsloot

LEAD DESIGNER
Greg Whitaker

DESIGNERS
Abbi Castle, Steve Dacombe, Andy Downes, Ali Innes, Adam Markiewicz, Anne-Claire Pickard, Andy Salter, Will Shum, Sophie Ward, Perry Wardell-Wicks

PRODUCTION
Sanne de Boer, Ross Hamilton, Hannah Westlake, Rebecca Richards, Philip Morris, Phil King, Carrie Mok, Jon White

PHOTO CREDITS
Riot Games (p.170, p.171, p.173)
Marv Watson (p.172, p.173)
David Pham (p.173)
Blizzard (p.173)

COVER IMAGES
Disney Infinity © 2016. Disney Inc. All rights reserved.

Minecraft: Story Mode © 2016. Telltale Games Inc. All rights reserved.

Plants Vs. Zombies 2: Garden Warfare © 2016. EA. All rights reserved.

SKYLANDERS SUPERCHARGERS © 2016 Activision Publishing, Inc. SKYLANDERS SUPERCHARGERS is a trademark and Activision is a registered trademark of Activision Publishing, Inc. All rights reserved.

SKYLANDERS SWAP FORCE © 2016 Activision Publishing, Inc. SKYLANDERS SWAP FORCE is a trademark and Activision is a registered trademark of Activision Publishing, Inc. All rights reserved.

Star Fox Zero © 2016 Nintendo

Super Mario Maker © 2015 Nintendo

Terraria® is a registered Trademark and © 2011/2016 Re-Logic, Inc. All rights reserved.

ISBN 978-1-338-03272-7
10 9 8 7 6 5 4 3 2 1   15 16 17 18 19
Printed in the U.S.A.   40
First printing, September 2016

Scholastic is constantly working to lessen the environmental impact of our manufacturing processes. To view our industry-leading paper procurement policy, visit www.scholastic.com/paperpolicy.

SKYLANDERS SUPERCHARGERS
TOYS TO LIFE MAYHEM!
This awesome game packs in a whole new selection of cool Skylanders, and adds vehicle-based battles and races for the first time ever!

STAYING SAFE AND HAVING FUN

Always check out a game's rating before you play it. The ratings are there for a reason, not to stop you having fun. If you're playing online with people you've never met, remember that they're not real-life friends. Here are 10 tips for staying safe when you're gaming online:

1 Talk to your parents about your family's rules regarding how long you can stay online, what websites you can visit on the Internet, and what you can and can't do.

2 Don't give out **passwords** to anyone **other** than **your parents.**

3 Never give out **personal** information such **as your** real **name,** phone **number,** or anything about your parents.

4 Never agree to meet **in person** with someone you've met online.

5 Tell your parents or a teacher if you come across anything that makes you feel uncomfortable or scared.

6 When you're online, be nice to other people. Don't say or do anything that could hurt someone else's feelings or make them feel unhappy.

7 Don't respond to any conversations that are mean or make you feel bad. It's not your fault if someone sends you something bad. Let your parents know right away.

8 Don't download or install software or apps to any device, or fill out any forms on the internet, without checking with the person that owns the device you're using first.

9 Remember that any pictures you post might be seen by anyone, and they will be visible for a long time. Don't post pictures that your parents might think are inappropriate.

10 Games are the most amazing things ever! Let everyone know how to have fun playing online, safely.

CONTENTS

FEATURES

THE BIGGEST GAMES

CONTENTS

LISTS

CAPTURE THIS!

SPLIT SECOND

58-59

92-95

24-27

162-163

WHAT A YEAR!

Whether you recently started gaming or have a six-digit gamerscore, there's no doubt that this year has been one of the most exciting *ever* in the world of video games.

The Xbox One and PS4 saw some huge titles taking the stage, from *Star Wars Battlefront* to *Ratchet & Clank*, and there are a whole lot more on the way. Plus some old favorites, such as *Minecraft* and *Sklyanders,* became even more successful.

Of course, Nintendo hasn't been absent from the action in the past 12 months either, with its adorable *Yoshi's Woolly World,* the amazing *Super Mario Maker,* and a little series you might have heard of called *Pokémon,* which made its triumphant return.

PC gamers have had plenty to get excited about, too—there are new games like *Overwatch* to get involved in, along with major updates for favorites like *League Of Legends.*

So join us as we journey through the year's gaming highlights ...

102-103

156-159

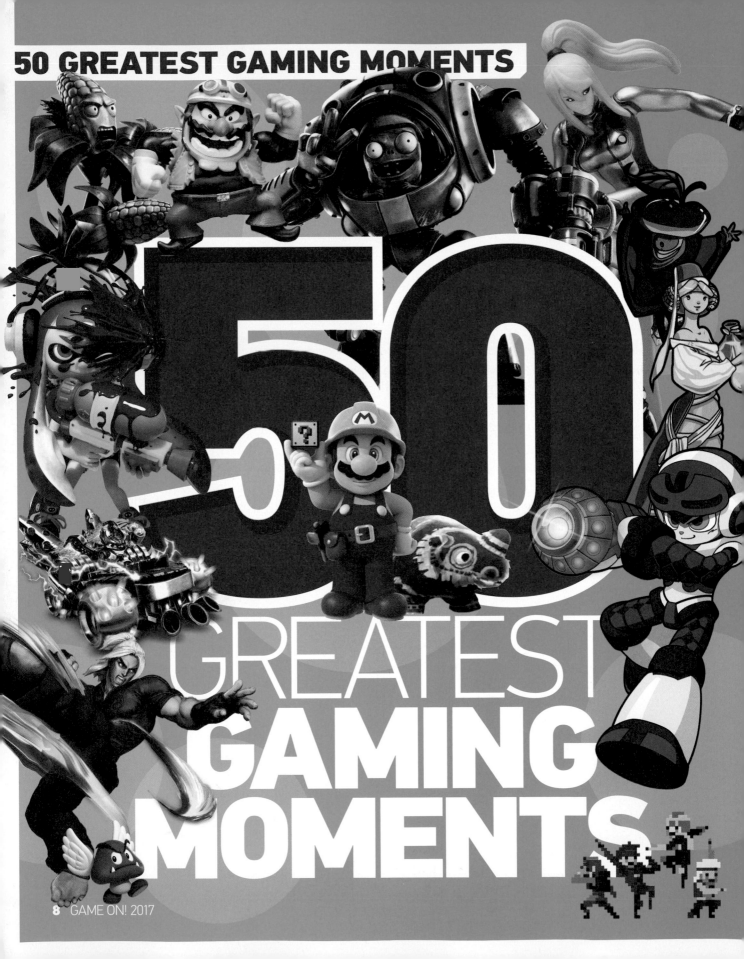

50 GREATEST GAMING MOMENTS

LAUGHING AT THE CRAZINESS OF GOAT SIMULATOR

50 This ridiculous game sees you play as a goat, but you're not quietly grazing... instead you're ramming into pedestrians, climbing cranes, bouncing off mattresses, and causing chaos in what can only be described as *Tony Hawk's Pro Skater* gone wrong!

POKÉMON MEETS TEKKEN IN POKKÉN TOURNAMENT

49 Cute *Pokémon* meets combative *Tekken*, sounds like some kind of crazy dream. Except it's very real as *Pokkén Tournament*—made by the actual *Tekken* developers—brings serious 3D fighting to Nintendo's flagship series for the first time ever.

PARKOUR PERFECTION IN MIRROR'S EDGE CATALYST

48 Most first-person games are shooters, so it's refreshing to play something a little different. *Mirror's Edge* is about running, climbing, and jumping around buildings at high speed to avoid enemies, and *Catalyst* brings an awesome storyline and even slicker visuals to the mix.

DID YOU KNOW?

Transformers Devastation is made by PlatinumGames, the same team behind *The Wonderful 101* and *Star Fox Zero!*

JUMPING INTO A CARTOON IN TRANSFORMERS DEVASTATION

47 It's amazing just how much like the original cartoon series *Transformers Devastation* is—it's awesome to watch, never mind play! With the emphasis on one-on-one combat, this isn't just for *Transformers* fans, but those who want to test their gaming skills too.

50 GREATEST GAMING MOMENTS

SMASHING YOUR HIGH SCORE IN GEOMETRY WARS 3: DIMENSIONS

46 A game that harks back to the days when arcades ruled the world and points were all that mattered is *Geometry Wars 3: Dimensions*. This fast-paced shooter is about combining quick reactions with nerves of steel as you chase your next high score.

GOING OLD-SCHOOL WITH SHOVEL KNIGHT

45 If you've heard gamers talking about the retro platformers on old consoles like NES and Master System and feel like you've missed out ... play *Shovel Knight*! It has all the 2D charm (and tough difficulty) of those retro classics.

WHEN KALIMBA CLICKS AND YOU PERFECT A LEVEL

44 It takes time to get your head around controlling two characters at once in this 2D puzzle platformer, but once it clicks, *Kalimba* becomes a joy. Even better, your newfound skills are constantly tested throughout the game with new and creative obstacles.

BUILDING THE PERFECT DECK IN HEARTHSTONE

43 *Hearthstone* isn't just about cards versus cards battles against your opponents—it's also about chasing that elusive perfect deck. When you finally create one for your playing style? It's bliss, and the *Whispers of the Old Gods* expansion offers even more choice.

BUSTING OUT OF JAIL IN THE ESCAPISTS

42 Busting out of jail isn't easy, as you'll find in *The Escapists*. Patience pays off though, so whether you're collecting spoons to dig a hole in your cell wall or collecting parts to make a screwdriver to get in the vents, you will pull off a perfectly executed plan!

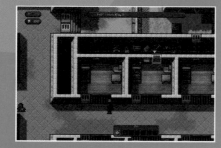

STARDEW VALLEY SURPRISES US ALL

40 Who knew farming could be so much fun? Eric Barone did, which is why he spent four years making *Stardew Valley* by himself. And what a game it turned out to be! Funny, charming, and utterly relaxing, it's something everyone should experience.

JOURNEYING WITH YARNY IN UNRAVEL

41 Has there ever been a game where being tugged apart has been so much fun? Yarny, the hero of *Unravel*, uses his own wool to get around the tricky obstacles in his path and reach secret areas. Cute idea, brilliantly executed.

RATCHET AND CLANK GETS REBOOTED

39 It's great to see the much-loved Ratchet and his robot friend Clank return in this colorful 3D platformer that retells the story of the original game. The fact that the game's got a Hollywood movie to accompany it means we can expect to see much more from this lovable duo!

50 GREATEST GAMING MOMENTS

THE FORCE AWAKENS COMES TO DISNEY INFINITY 3.0

38 We love *Star Wars*, we love *The Force Awakens*, and we love *Disney Infinity*. Combining all three? Bliss. What makes this so much fun is the powers each character has—Rey has awesome moves with her staff, Poe can summon BB-8, and Finn is a great fighter up close. Whoever you use, they're all fun!

PUZZLING THROUGH LARA CROFT GO

37 *Tomb Raider* doesn't just make for great console games, as *Lara Croft GO* has proven. The mobile title isn't really the action-packed adventure that we're used to from our hero—instead, this one tests your brain cells as you seek out an ancient artifact.

BEATING YOUR PERSONAL BEST IN CRYPT OF THE NECRODANCER

36 Who'd have thought that dungeon crawling and catchy music would go together so well? Trying to dodge skeletons to the beat of a pulsating soundtrack is a lot of fun, especially when you manage to better your last attempt in these tricky, random levels.

REVISITING A CLASSIC WITH DAY OF THE TENTACLE

35 If the *Grim Fandango* re-release on PlayStation left you thirsting for another classic adventure brought back, here's one more. Packed full of jokes, this quirky adventure about an evil tentacle trying to take over the world is surprising, clever, and unique.

DID YOU KNOW?
The idea for *The Last Guardian* came from the way players bonded with their horse in *Shadow Of The Colossus*.

THE EXPERT SAYS ...
JAMES MARSDEN
Owner & director of Futurlab, developer of Velocity 2X

DRIVECLUB on PS4 is utterly fantastic; a perfect balance of arcade simplicity dressed up as realism. It has mind-boggling attention to detail on the visual side, beautiful lighting and dynamic weather effects add to the sense of immersion, and a pitch-perfect learning curve/reward system with wonderful, weighty physics makes it stupidly addictive. The thrill of flying around a shallow bend at 150mph to undercut the competition, with camera shaking and controller vibrating in your hands while the engine growls and the tires squeal is unbeatable. Get it!

SHENMUE III GETS BACKED

34 Given that *Shenmue II* came out all the way back in 2001 and was a commercial failure, it seemed very unlikely we'd ever see a third version. That hasn't stopped a cult following campaigning for a new title ever since. Incredibly, they finally got their wish when the series creator announced a Kickstarter to fund a third entry in the critically acclaimed series. $6.3 million later, development is well on its way!

THE LAST GUARDIAN LIVES ON

33 Starting development in 2007, *The Last Guardian* was originally due to be released on PlayStation 3 but news from the team making it went strangely quiet. Fans feared the worst. Fortunately, Sony has revealed this intriguing game is back on track, and we can't wait to play this intriguing tale of a boy and his guardian.

REWINDING TIME IN SUPER TIME FORCE ULTRA

32 In *Super Time Force Ultra* you've got one minute to play through a level, but every time you die you can rewind to any point and continue with a new character. The twist is that all your previous runs will play out on screen too, allowing you to effectively work together with past versions of yourself. It's a brilliant idea that takes an already excellent action game to the next level.

STEALING A WIN IN FORZA MOTORSPORT 6

31 It's always satisfying when you beat your opponent to the finish line in any racing game. So why does it feel better in *Forza Motorsport 6*? It's the combination of the slick graphics and the powerful cars making races feel so much more dramatic.

DISCOVERING THE WORLD OF FINAL FANTASY XV

30 It's been a long time coming, with ten years of troubled development behind it, but none of that matters now that we finally get to play *Final Fantasy XV*. Seeing its stunning wilderness, big cities, and incredible wildlife while traversing the game's huge open world shows exactly what the PS4 is capable of.

TURNING ON A BEAM IN THE WITNESS

29 No game taxes your brain like *The Witness*. That's why it's so rewarding when you finally solve all the puzzles in an area and turn on the beam that points out the next area forward for the next set of puzzles. It's a real moment of celebration after hours of contemplation.

BOSSING THE LEADERBOARDS IN OLLIOLLI2

27 Getting ahead in *OlliOlli2: Welcome To Olliwood*'s leaderboards is all the motivation you need to practice perfect runs in this 2D skateboarding title. They'll come back and beat you of course, but that constant back and forth battle for the top spot is the best part.

SUPERCHARGING YOUR SKYLANDERS

28 *Skylanders SuperChargers* not only offers the chance to drive powered-up cars, it also allows you to supercharge your heroes by pairing them with their own vehicles. The result? A fresh jolt of speed breathing new life into familiar characters we know and love.

FINALLY FINISHING ORI AND THE BLIND FOREST

26 Ori might be a real cutie, but the game that he stars in is pretty tough. With the checkpoints spaced out, there's a real demand on your skill in *Ori and the Blind Forest*, which is why finally completing it feels so satisfying compared to other platforming games.

DID YOU KNOW?

Every background in *Ori and the Blind Forest* is unique— with not a single tree, rock, or mushroom repeated in the entire game.

50 GREATEST GAMING MOMENTS

LEGO DIMENSIONS LETS US PLAY WITH OUR FAVORITE CHARACTERS

25 Whether you're a fan of *Doctor Who* or *The Simpsons*, *Back to the Future* or *Ghostbusters*, the thrill of seeing your heroes in LEGO form is one thing, but then getting them to team up? There's nothing like seeing Homer and Marty McFly working together!

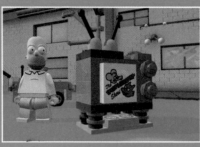

DROPSY REVIVES A LONG-LOST GAMING STYLE

24 It's odd, it's different, it's absolutely bursting with life, and it's strangely brilliant. We love *Dropsy,* and so do other fans of old point-and-click adventures, where you have to collect objects and figure out the best way to use them.

AMIIBO EVERYWHERE!

23 Amiibo aren't a new phenomenon, but now they have really taken off, with over 40 games supporting the cool little figurines. The functionality is awesome, too—scan them in when playing your favorite Wii U games and you'll unlock cool bonuses like new costumes or trainable AI characters!

DID YOU KNOW?

Shovel Knight was the first amiibo of a character that doesn't feature in a Nintendo game. He's still awesome, though!

EXPLORING THE WORLD OF RIME

22 Looking like a cross between *Wind Waker* and a Studio Ghibli film, *Rime* is a spectacularly gorgeous-looking game. No other game makes exploring such a joy thanks to the wide variety of stunning locations, calm atmosphere, and wealth of hidden secrets.

CONTROL GOES ELITE

21 Xbox One already had one of the best controllers out there but Microsoft has managed to improve it even further with its Elite controller, which offers control sticks that you can swap out and triggers you can remove if you wish. We also love the redesigned D-pad.

SETTING THE RESULT RIGHT IN FIFA 16

20 Winning games of *FIFA* against your friends is always a great feeling, of course. But it's made more special in *FIFA 16* thanks to how good the goalkeepers are. You really have to work for your goals now, so no one can accuse you of luck when you win!

PLANTS VS. ZOMBIES GIVES US FLOWER POWER

19 The original had sunflowers and corn-on-the-cobs taking on zombies and somehow, *Plants vs. Zombies: Garden Warfare 2* increases the weirdness factor. There are over 100 characters, from time-traveling plants to superhero zombies. This has it all!

THE BAND GETS BACK TOGETHER

18 Two rhythm-action stars have made a welcome return in the form of *Guitar Hero Live* and *Rock Band 4*, allowing us to pick up our plastic instruments and play along to our favorite tunes. It's the closest thing you can get to feeling like a true rock star!

LIVE STAR WARS: THE FORCE AWAKENS ... IN LEGO FORM

17 We absolutely loved the *Star Wars: The Force Awakens* movie when it was released at the end of 2015, but the one thing we were missing was a tie-in game. That is, until LEGO came along and brought the movie to consoles everywhere. What makes this really special is that the LEGO version brings a unique twist of humor to the film we know and love, making it unpredictable and fun.

BOSSING AN ARENA IN SPLATOON

16 *Splatoon* is a wonderfully unique multiplayer shooter, and no other game lets you make a mess like this one. Winning is one thing, but seeing the multiplayer arena completely covered in your team's ink after the battle is done? That's something you will always take immense pride in.

LEADING A TEAM TO GREATNESS IN FOOTBALL MANAGER 2016

15 As it has become more complex, *Football Manager* has become more difficult. You now need to consider team chemistry, formations, and man management. Becoming successful in *Football Manager 16* makes you feel like you can be a real soccer manager.

SOLVING THE MYSTERY IN HER STORY

14 For older teens and up. In *Her Story*, you have to search an old database of police interviews with a suspect to solve a mystery, pulling out quotes and topics for investigation. Reading the suspect's body language during answers makes you feel like a real detective.

FINAL FANTASY VII REMAKE IS ANNOUNCED

13 As one of the most beloved games ever made—let alone role-playing games—fans have begged creator Square-Enix for a modern version of *Final Fantasy VII*. The developer had resisted the call, but the campaign for a modern update of *Final Fantasy VII* continued, despite the lack of hope or encouragement. So when Square-Enix finally showed the world the debut trailer for *Final Fantasy VII Remake*—of its hero Cloud in glorious HD—fans could hardly believe it. And we haven't even played it yet ...

LAUGHING WITH UNDERTALE

10 Indie hit *Undertale* has won over a dedicated fanbase thanks to its hilarious dialogue, quirky characters, and the way that it pokes fun at video games. It's a unique RPG in that you don't have to defeat enemies in battles, but can befriend them instead!

TELLTALE GAMES PROVES THAT IT 'GETS' MINECRAFT

9 We weren't quite sure how you could take a game that's about creative freedom and make it into something linear and story-based in the Telltale style, but *Minecraft: Story Mode* proved that it can be done and was packed full of *Minecraft* references to delight fans.

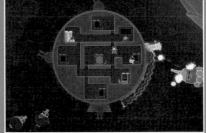

DID YOU KNOW?

Mighty No. 9 is about a small robot who must battle his eight predecessors, who are all infected with a computer virus.

GOING OLD-SCHOOL WITH MIGHTY NO. 9

12 There have been a lot of retro-style games recently, but *Mighty No. 9* shows how to modernize a genre. The creator of *Mega Man* took inspiration from his own series to create a retro platformer with modern elements like time trials, online and leaderboards.

COOPERATING IN LOVERS IN A DANGEROUS SPACETIME

8 While it can be played in single player, *Lovers in a Dangerous Spacetime* shines in multiplayer. Working alongside a friend, you both have to protect your ship by activating its engine, shield, weapons, cannon, and map. Trying to coordinate during the frantic action is hilarious!

PES RETURNS TO ITS FORMER GLORY

11 There's no series quite like *PES* when it comes to replicating the magic of soccer—the speed, the ball physics, the quick passing. Unfortunately, there were a few years where *PES* was *far* from its best but thankfully, *PES 2016* is the game where the magic returned.

EXERCISING YOUR BRAIN IN MONUMENT VALLEY

7 Rightly celebrated as one of the best mobile games of all time is the stunning *Monument Valley*. The game is all about solving puzzles based on mind-bending geometry. It can be tough, but it is also extremely rewarding when you finally work out the solution to a puzzle.

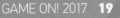

HALO GETS GOOD AGAIN THANKS TO A NEW MULTIPLAYER MODE

6 *Halo 5: Guardians* was under a lot of pressure to do well, and thanks to a brilliant new multiplayer mode called Warzone and an intriguing campaign that saw Master Chief painted as a villain, it returned to the Xbox in style. For those who want a competitive online shooter, this is as good as it gets.

STREET FIGHTER RETURNS

5 Fans were worried *Ultra Street Fighter IV* was the last time we would ever see Capcom's series. Fortunately that wasn't the case, as *Street Fighter V* brought the series back in style, adding eccentric new characters like F.A.N.G. and Rashid.

DID YOU KNOW?

There's a level set on Jakku in *Star Wars Battlefront*—that's the planet Rey lives on in *Star Wars: The Force Awakens*!

BECOMING A JEDI IN STAR WARS BATTLEFRONT

3 There are few things cooler than being a Jedi, hence we love the fact that you can take on the role of Luke Skywalker to battle Darth Vader in *Star Wars Battlefront*, using your force powers to dominate the battlefield. It's even better if your friend is playing as Darth Vader at the time.

ROCKET LEAGUE STEALS THE SHOW

4 Hardly anyone had heard about *Rocket League* before its release, but soon it felt like everyone was talking about the game where you played soccer with rocket-powered cars. *Rocket League* ended up becoming one of the year's most popular games on both PS4 and Xbox One.

NAMING YOUR OWN PLANET IN NO MAN'S SKY

2 How awesome is it to be the first person ever to find a planet and to be able to name it whatever you want? That's precisely what you can do in the mind-blowing *No Man's Sky*—a game with a universe so big that many of its planets will never be seen by human eyes!

MARIO BECOMES NEVER-ENDING

1 In what seems like a logical next step for Nintendo's long-running Mario series, the Japanese developer finally lets you create your own levels with the brilliant *Super Mario Maker*. And honestly, who knew *making* Mario games could be as fun as playing them? We've made high-speed courses, dense platforming mazes, quiz mini-games, and even replicas of famous levels (our best effort has to be recreating *Sonic the Hedgehog*'s Green Hill Zone!). What's more, you can download creations from other players, so you'll never run out of fresh Mario levels. Whether you're playing or creating, this is as good as it gets.

THE EXPERT SAYS ...
STEPHEN ASHBY

Game writer and former Editor of X-ONE magazine

Without a doubt my favorite moment of this year was seeing *Pokémon Sun* and *Pokémon Moon* when they were revealed for the first time. The three new starter Pokémon are totally awesome, and I had a pretty serious discussion with my friends about which one was the coolest! My favorite is definitely Rowlet, the stylish grass and flying type that looks like it's wearing a little bow-tie. And, with the new island of Alola to explore in full 3D, and lots of new Pokémon to catch, the two new games are the best Pokémon titles in years.

CAPTURE THIS!

CAPTURE THIS!

STREET FIGHTER V

FINISH THE MATCH WITH A CRITICAL ART FOR AN EXPLOSION OF COLOR AND SOUND ... AND IF YOU'RE USING THE RIGHT CHARACTER, YOU'LL GET A SURPRISING EXTRA ON TOP OF THAT!

Critical Arts are the huge, one-off moves that do lots of damage, often being the perfect way to end the battle. Try winning with Ken's Critical Art and see what happens next ...

STAR WARS BATTLEFRONT

STATS

9,000,000 players
participated in the beta

29.8 million minutes
played as Boba Fett

1.1 billion
credits earned by community

87.2 million
aerial kills

442 million
vehicles destroyed

THE FORCE AWAKENS

For *Star Wars* fans, it doesn't get much better than this. Not only have a new set of movies arrived, but we also saw the return of *Star Wars Battlefront.* Handled by *Battlefield* developer DICE, who certainly knows how to craft a multiplayer shooter, *Star Wars Battlefront* delivers epic 40-player battles across iconic battlegrounds from the original movie series. It's all here, from the dense forests of Endor to the snowy, blustery fields of Hoth ... not to mention that you can even play as the likes of Luke Skywalker, Leia, and Darth Vader.

Simple but strategic, *Battlefront* is super fast-paced but lets you relive the coolest moments from the movies without feeling like you need Han Solo's trigger finger to survive!

TIPS & TRICKS

SHOOT FROM THE HIP
Not only do you have greater accuracy firing from the hip, but you also have a wider field of vision to spot incoming enemies.

HIGH SCORE ASSAULT
Want to get crazy good points? Play the objective and use vehicles, as this earns you more points than normal kills.

REMEMBER TO FLUSH
When reloading, you can do a "cooling flush"—a well-timed button prompt will reload your weapon faster and get you back in the fight.

TOP 5 GAME MODES

WALKER ASSAULT

1 Looking for the ultimate *Star Wars* video game experience? It doesn't get much better than Walker Assault. It pits 40 players in sprawling, evolving maps that deliver with thrills and moments of pure chaos—recreating some of the most famous *Star Wars* set-pieces from the original trilogy in spectacular fashion.

BLAST

2 Blast is essentially *Battlefront's* take on traditional Team Deathmatch, throwing 20 players into smaller maps designed to heighten tension and get you caught-up in ferocious firefights for leaderboard supremacy (see: bragging rights). While it may be a simple mode, it's definitely great fun.

SUPREMACY

3 It wouldn't be a DICE game without a mode like Supremacy. While it uses the same maps as Walker Assault, it manages to subvert that mode's desperate attack/defend gameplay loop with a drama-intensive battle for capture points. This is full of constant shifts in power; an intergalactic tug-of-war that is rarely stale.

HEROES VS. VILLAINS

4 This is a comparatively small game mode—supporting just 12 players—though it's also one of the most fun. It features all six in-game heroes and villains fighting against one another, and gives you a great opportunity to embody some of the most iconic characters in the *Star Wars* universe.

FIGHTER SQUADRON

5 While we might still be lamenting the decision to remove space battles, Fighter Squadron does a good job of filling the void. 20 players battle it out in awesome dogfights, and it even affords you the opportunity to fly the Millennium Falcon.

"BATTLE ACROSS ICONIC BATTLEGROUNDS FROM THE ORIGINAL MOVIE SERIES

DON'T FORGET ION SHOT

Both the Ion Shot and Ion Grenades, available as Star Cards in your arsenal, are great for taking down turrets and vehicles quickly.

USE TARGETING SYSTEMS

While flying a TIE Fighter or X-Wing, you can hold left trigger (or right-mouse button on PC) to lock on to enemies.

MEET THE SUPERFAN

COOLEST HEROES

LUKE SKYWALKER

Live out your ultimate Jedi fantasy as Luke Skywalker. There's nothing quite as cool as storming the battleground, force-pushing overzealous enemies and deflecting blaster fire right back at the shooter.

HAN SOLO

Who wouldn't want to play as the legendary smuggler himself? With his special Lucky Shot, Shoulder Charge, and Rapid Fire abilities, there are plenty of ways to cause chaos with the rebel hero!

HENRI HUITTINEN

WHO?

Henri Huittinen amassed an impressive collection of 70 *Star Wars* games after falling in love with George Lucas' galaxy far, far away as a child. From the first ever officially licensed *Star Wars* game on the Atari 2600, to the *Millennium Falcon Challenge* on the Tiger R-Zone, to a few rare Japanese oddities; he's got all the coolest games.

WHY?

For Huittinen, he says that "preserving old game culture is important," especially when he considers what his young children will be playing when they grow up. "Sure, there are the classics like *TIE Fighter* and *Knights of the Old Republic*, but I wanted to show everyone that there are quite a lot of other good games as well." One thing is for sure, his children won't have to wait for a *Battlefront* sequel if they want more Star Wars games to play!

AND VILLAINS

BOBA FETT

The community favorite by far; everybody loves playing as the galaxy's deadliest bounty hunter thanks to his jet-pack-assisted movement, powerful rocket barrage, and awesome flamethrower attack.

DARTH VADER

Strike fear into the hearts of your enemies as the Sith Lord himself, Darth Vader. Having the option to use abilities such as Force Choke and Saber Throw are just far too awesome to ignore.

"STRIKE FEAR INTO THE HEARTS OF YOUR ENEMIES AS THE SITH LORD"

THE EXPERT SAYS ...
ANDREW WILLANS
Lead designer, EVE: Valkyrie

There have been a lot of great games recently, but I loved *Battlefront*. A lot of people have made criticisms about the depth, and rightfully so, but it's *Star Wars*, dude! It's easy to pick it up and get in there straight away. It's the sort of game that lets you make and maintain friendships through conflict ... ironically this game strengthens the bonds between friends and siblings. It's just amazing—I think I have sunk more hours in *Star Wars Battlefront* than I have *The Witcher 3: Wild Hunt*, and that's saying something.

DID YOU KNOW?
The free Battle of Jakku downloadable content lets you play through the events leading up to *The Force Awakens*.

ALSO CHECK OUT ...

PLANTS VS. ZOMBIES: GARDEN WARFARE 2
Fast and frantic, it takes familiar gameplay modes and turns them on their head for chaotic results.

DISNEY INFINITY 3.0
Star Wars fan? Then you need to play *Disney Infinity 3.0*; get involved in some of the best scenarios and set-pieces ever to appear in a galaxy far, far away.

STATS

945,000
videos about *Halo 5: Guardians* on YouTube

18.2 million
Number of views on *Halo 5*'s most-viewed video

24 players in *Halo 5*'s new Warzone mode

The number of *Halo* games, including re-releases **13**

4 The number of studios that have handled *Halo*—Bungie, 343i, Ensemble, and Creative Assembly

HALO

15 YEARS, FOUR STUDIOS, STILL GREAT

When you think of Xbox, you think of the *Halo* series. *Halo: Combat Evolved* was in the trenches for Microsoft when it brought Xbox to the console wars in 2001. All these years later, Master Chief remains one of the most dominant heroes in the FPS genre. *Halo 5: Guardians* shows there's plenty of life left in the series too, with huge changes across the board.

For the first time ever, you can aim down iron sights for all weapons, moving *Guardians* closer to fellow FPS games. There are also new abilities, such as Slide and Smart Scope, bringing a "special moves" element to the series. Even so, there's still nothing out there like the slower, considered take on the genre that *Halo* offers, which is strategic in both single and multiplayer.

TIME LINE

HALO: COMBAT EVOLVED 2001
Discovering the "Halo" ring worlds, Master Chief has to stop their destructive power before it destroys the galaxy.

HALO 2 2004
Bringing the fight back to Earth, the sequel sees the Covenant trying to use the remaining Halo rings to destroy everything, apparently.

HALO 3 2007
Picking up where the second left off, Chief finishes the fight, destroys a half-made Halo world, and ends up lost and floating in space.

TOP 5 ENEMIES

ELITES

1 Probably the most iconic enemy in the *Halo* series, but they aren't always your enemy. In fact, in the second *Halo*, part of the game saw you controlling an Elite as he tried to stop those in the Covenant from destroying the entire universe.

GRUNTS

2 You almost feel guilty for offing these little tykes, cute and tiny as they are. But don't cut them too much slack—if you're unprepared and they're in great enough numbers, the dogsbodies of the Covenant forces can and will overwhelm you. That or they'll just run away like cowards.

THE FLOOD

3 Ominous, sometimes downright scary, the Flood is essentially a parasite army that makes zombies of anything it infects. Every side is afraid of them, and with good cause—they can, and will, take out entire armies with ease. They have a harder time with Master Chief, though...

BRUTES

4 Taking the place of Elites in *Halo 3*, the Brutes are rougher than their predecessors. Looking like giant apes and carrying huge power hammers, they're more than formidable and add a whole new element of danger to Chief's adventures whenever they're around.

PROMETHEAN KNIGHTS

5 The Prometheans are from *Halo*'s past—and the Knights are the workhorses of the army. Quick, bizarre, and armed with weaponry Chief and co. have never used before, they offer a unique challenge.

"TO SAY HALO IS A CULTURAL PHENOMENON IS AN UNDERSTATEMENT"

ALSO CHECK OUT ...

DESTINY

The game *Halo*'s creators went on to make has taken on a life of its own and is threatening to become as big and popular as Master Chief and co.

PLANETSIDE 2

Imagine *Halo* but with fewer aliens, in battles involving hundreds of players. There you have PlanetSide 2, and some of the best fun in an FPS.

HALO 4 2012
Four years later, Chief and Cortana wake up in the middle of a new battle—between the Covenant, humanity, and the Forerunners. Cortana ends up sacrificing herself.

HALO 5: GUARDIANS 2015
With Chief's Blue Team on the run, pursued by Fireteam Osiris, the rumor is that perhaps Cortana didn't actually sacrifice herself.

STATS

21 heroes to choose from

68 abilities to explore

411,000 matches played already

An average match lasts **9** minutes

Over **8,300** hours of *Overwatch* footage has been streamed on Twitch

TAKE YOUR HERO TO THE BATTLEFIELD

OVERWATCH

Want to do battle in a near-future Earth? Look no further than *Overwatch*. The game is totally team-based, filled with colorful heroes that each have their own special attacks and abilities to help you on the battlefield. Whether your chosen hero is good in combat, helping your teammates, or even providing defensive cover, to win you will need quick reflexes to attack other players and come out on top.

What we love most about *Overwatch* is just how crazy some of the heroes look. In what other game could you play as an armor-clad gorilla blasting away with a laser rifle, or even a Viking dwarf decked out with his own turret and a gun that shoots out molten metal?

TIPS & TRICKS

KNOW YOUR ROLE
Don't pick a defensive hero if you want to blast away the competition; they don't have the required firepower.

PLAY THE OBJECTIVE
Your abilities will unlock a lot quicker if you continuously play the objective instead of going it alone.

WATCH OUT FOR SNIPERS
Watch out for enemy snipers when in the air. Your movements are easily tracked and you'll have little defense.

TOP 5 CHARACTERS

1 LUCIO

It's all about speed with Lucio, so avoiding attacks is his key to survival. His primary weapon uses the Sonic Amplifier ability, which shouts sound projectiles at enemies, helping knock them back, while you try and find some cover and equip a different weapon to deal more damage.

2 WINSTON

Playing as a gorilla in armor may seem strange, but trust us when we say that Winston is one of the best heroes in the game. Make sure to take his Primal Rage ability for a whirl, as it not only gives him a massive health boost, it also doubles the damage of his melee attacks.

DID YOU KNOW?

You can swap characters throughout a single match, which allows you to utilize their different strengths.

3 BASTION

Not only does Bastion look like a Transformer, some of his best abilities are all robot-based. Use the Sentry ability to put up a defensive wall and begin shooting down enemies from safety, or the Tank ability to switch Bastion into a powerful tank and roll over the competition.

4 SOLDIER 76

Most of Soldier 76's abilities focus in on his visor and the damage it can do to the opposing team. His Tactical Visor ability locks into the closest target and centers them on his crosshairs, letting you blast them off the battlefield in a matter of seconds.

5 MCCREE

Those with a steady hand should definitely play a few games with McCree. His Deadeye ability is great for targeting multiple enemies at once and dealing plenty of damage to them, while his Combat Roll is perfect for avoiding incoming attacks from numerous enemy units.

ALSO CHECK OUT ...

STAR WARS BATTLEFRONT

It's not quite as fast-paced as *Overwatch* but it's far easier to get to grips with *Star Wars Battlefront*!

PVZ: GARDEN WARFARE 2

Who knew that putting plants and zombies together would make such a great game. Definitely worth your time!

BATTLEBORN

This bright and colorful first-person game brings together a range of heroes, all with different abilities, to face off against a hoard of aliens. It's great fun.

BUILD A TEAM

When playing with friends, make sure to have a well-rounded team that takes into account the four hero roles.

ACCOUNT FOR RECOIL

Prolonged fire may look great, but gun recoil is common. Use short bursts to take down the enemy.

TOP 10 TESTS OF YOUR SKILL

BE THE STAR PLAYER IN ROCKET LEAGUE

WHY: Real-life soccer players can rely on their feet, heads, and maybe hands (if the referee isn't looking), but in *Rocket League* all you've got are your four wheels. Bicycle kicks are no use in this game, unless you count flipping your car around. Master reverse aerials and wall hits, and get a strong team together to beat your friends online.

REACH THE BOTTOM OF THE WELL

WHY: It might look simple, but *Downwell* is one of the most challenging games in recent years. As you fall deeper into the catacombs, aquifers, and into another dimension, you'll encounter ever more deadly foes. Learn how to use every weapon and combo your jumps for bonus health, and you might just make it to the bottom.

SAVE THE GALAK-Z ON ROGUE DIFFICULTY

WHY: *GALAK-Z* is a space dogfighting game where you fight aliens among asteroid fields with missiles and lasers. If you're thinking "that sounds awesome," then you'd be absolutely right. Die on the harder "Rogue" difficulty, though, and you'll go back up to five missions! It's so tough, the developers added the easier "Arcade" difficulty for the PC release.

THE EGGPLANT CHALLENGE

WHY: Although it's not necessarily brand new, *Spelunky*'s deadly random dungeons are still incredibly popular with a large number of Twitch streamers. Bananasaurus Rex manages to make a hard task even harder by carrying a fragile eggplant all the way from the mines to the depths of hell, where it becomes an unlikely secret weapon against the final boss Yama.

6 STEPS TO BEATING THE SPELUNKY EGGPLANT CHALLENGE

1 FIND A PRESENT IN THE STORE

To start the challenge, you'll need to find a present in the shop. As *Spelunky* is random every time, this could take a while. Buy (or steal) the present.

2 "SACRIFICE" THE PRESENT TO KALI

Although it's tempting to open your present, instead find a shrine to Kali and give the present as an offering. You will be rewarded with the precious eggplant.

3 REACH THE CITY OF GOLD

Collect the Ankh and Hedjet from the Jungle and Ice Caves, then defeat Anubis to reach the City of Gold – all with the eggplant in tow!

4 COMPLETE THE GAME THE HARD WAY

In the City of Gold, collect the Necronomicon—watch out for Anubis II—and then use it to locate the entrance to Hell within Olmec's lair.

5 TRANSPORT THE EGGPLANT THROUGH HELL

Vampires prefer blood to an eggplant, but that doesn't make the last stage of the journey easier: spike balls and lava pits will turn the eggplant to puree in a flash.

6 THROW IT AT YAMA

Now for the moment of glory – climb to Yama's throne and throw the eggplant at his face to turn him into a giant eggplant and win the fight. Was that really worth it?

FIT YOUR KART WITH GOLDEN WHEELS

WHY: If you thought defeating the cheating computer players in *Mario Kart 8*'s Grand Prix was hard, try beating the Staff Ghost on all 32 original courses and earning gold wheels for your kart. Shells aren't any use against ghosts, and with only three Mushrooms to help you, only those with the best drifting and boosting skills will take the checkered flag.

BECOME A TRUE PACIFIST

WHY: You don't have to kill every monster in *Undertale* to reach the end, but to get the special True Pacifist ending, you can't fight any of them! Every battle becomes a challenge of dodging enemy attacks before asking Vegetron for a healthy meal or patting Doggo until he is tamed. This is seriously one of the toughest challenges you can face in the game—give it a try!

CONQUER BOMB VOYAGE

WHY: Alex Tan—better known as his screen name PangaeaPanga—is famous for using code to complete games really quickly, and for hacking super-hard levels into *Super Mario World*, and now he's on *Mario Maker*. Bomb Voyage took nine hours of play to complete, just so he was allowed to upload it to the internet. Then he made the even-harder sequel "Pit of Panga"!

COMPLETE THE DOTA 2 ALL-HERO CHALLENGE

WHY: There are over 100 heroes in *DOTA 2*; Anti-Mage and Crystal Maiden have been in the game since 2010, while Zet the Arc Warden joined the game at the end of 2015. But can you win a match with all of them and complete the All-Hero Challenge? It's harder than it sounds ...

COLLECT THE DEVIL'S DEBTS IN CUPHEAD

WHY: Although *Cuphead*'s characters look like cartoons, every one of the 30+ bosses packs a unique punch. A pirate who uses an octopus as a rifle, a pair of boxing frogs, a psychic carrot and his hot potato friend ... every level is a unique challenge, requiring you to learn their patterns. Make it easier by teaming up with a friend.

THE EXPERT SAYS ...
MARK BROWN
Creator of Game Maker's Toolkit on YouTube

Super Mario Maker is a fantastic tool for budding level designers: they can study perfect platforming design from 30 years of *Mario* games and then see if they can make a stage as good as the originals. Hopefully you've played my course, Pipeflip Airship (B73D-0000-0047-2D3F)!

This level is about using Mario's spin move to bounce on the heads of spiky enemies. It's not a technique you use a lot in *Super Mario World*, so you'll need to train yourself to use this tricky and precise maneuver when bopping between fast-moving baddies.

Here's a tip for beating it: you don't have to move forward with every jump. Stay on top of the same enemy for a few hops after a tricky leap to regain your composure and ready yourself for the next hop!

SURVIVE THE BLIND FOREST

WHY: *Ori and the Blind Forest* is one of Xbox One's most beautiful games, with a truly touching story, but beneath the artistic surface is a tough and unforgiving platform game that will take skill, quick reactions, and a good memory to survive. Make the most of Ori's Soul Links—you'll need to find energy to create one, but doing so will save your progress so you can respawn if you fall.

SPLATOON

IT'S INK-REDIBLE!

DID YOU KNOW?

Splatoon's squid-like Inklings were first designed as tofu blocks, then humans, then rabbits before the current squid-like design won out!

Nintendo isn't really known for making shooters, but *Splatoon* isn't a shooter in the traditional sense. The Japanese giant has made a game that's every bit as messy as it is fun—look at the pictures here for proof! The idea is that you shoot colored ink at your opponents instead of bullets, but that's not the cool part. What makes *Splatoon* different is you can dive into the ink puddles and swim across the map at high speed. This allows you to pop out of the ground for surprise attacks, making covering the map in ink a tactical move and not just a messy one! With awesome weapons like Splat Rollers, a vibrant community and Nintendo releasing new maps, *Splatoon* is essential for all Wii U owners ... or those after something different!

TOP 5 BEST MAPS

CAMP TRIGGERFISH

1 This lakeside retreat isn't all beach chairs and cold drinks. In fact, the water below the map and the limited number of bridges make this one of the toughest and most dangerous maps to play. That is, until the last minute of the match, when the water drains and the free-for-all begins!

MUSEUM D'ALFONSINO

2 The spinning platforms in this stage make each game much more tactical—get on top of them and you can reach a variety of high points on the map. A path to the left features water, which can be dangerous, but will also lead you to the opposition side of the map.

URCHIN UNDERPASS

3 Although the map itself is fairly simple in terms of design, especially compared to the other maps on this list, you'll find that there are three main routes to the center of the map, allowing you to pick your favorite depending on your weapon choice.

MAHI MAHI RESORT

4 This map floats on top of a swimming pool in a vacation resort; halfway through a match, the water level drops and new platforms appear! At this point, many higher points are also created, letting you quickly access the opponent's base or snipe enemies running around below.

WALLEYE WAREHOUSE

5 Primarily a close-quarters stage, this tight map has a secret. Four side passages—two high and two low—allow players to reach the central battlefield quickly, and can even help you sneak into the enemy base. Players tend to forget they exist, so use them to your advantage!

BEST SPLATOON WEAPONS

N-ZAP '85

This retro zapper isn't too damaging, but we still love it because it looks like an NES light gun, the famous peripheral for Nintendo's first console!

OCTOBRUSH

A heavier but wider take on the classic Inkbrush, the Octobrush has become a favorite because of its increased range (and its cool design doesn't hurt, either).

SLOSHER

Simple but extremely effective when used correctly, the Slosher delivers a heavy dose of paint that, unlike most other weapons in *Splatoon*, deals more damage the further it travels.

.96 GAL DECO

It's big, powerful, and covered in rhinestones. The .96 Gal Deco is among the slowest weapons in the game, but it also packs one of the biggest punches.

SPLATOON

MEET THE SUPERFAN ZONBI

WHO

YouTuber and cosplayer Zonbi has made quite a name for herself thanks to her fantastic array of video game cosplays. Her personality and enthusiasm are infectious, but much of Zonbi's popularity comes from her costume progress videos, as she brilliantly demonstrates the process behind creating her amazing ensembles and props.

HOW

Like many gamers and Nintendo fans, Zonbi was instantly drawn in by the distinctive visual design of *Splatoon*, and the Inklings in particular. Her Inkling cosplay is one of the best we've seen, with fantastically realized tentacles, perfect makeup, and extremely detailed props—including a super cool, custom-made Aerospray MG.

DID YOU KNOW?

Several 8-bit sprites of famous Nintendo characters are hidden in various levels in *Splatoon*, including bloopers and octorocks.

They lost control!!

Mode
Splat Zones
⚙ Rules
Stages

Level 10   1805/11500
0046050

Ranked Battle
Face off in more competitive battles.

Regular Battle

↩ Plaza   🔍 Recon   ⊕ Equip

TIPS & TRICKS

TRY ALL THE WEAPONS
You'll never know which weapon type and combination suits your style of play best unless you've tried them all.

INK FLOORS, NOT WALLS
Inking walls is useful for maneuvering around the map, but remember they don't count toward your final turf area.

CHECK YOUR PERKS
The perks you gain when leveling up gear are completely random, so it pays to mix and match to suit your role.

THE EXPERT SAYS ...
KADEEM TERRELL CARRINGTON-MCKENZIE

Streaming & playing *Splatoon* competitively

Splatoon is an amazing game and extremely unique compared to other games in this genre in terms of mechanics. This is what has drawn me to the game and why I love it so much: because it's not like your average team multiplayer game where you aim, shoot, and repeat—it's much more than that. It's fun no matter what type of gamer you are, and whether you're competitive or casual you can play the game however you want! I'm one of the more competitive players because it's a lot of fun being able to play in tournaments.

Splatoon is great fun, and this is coming from a person who has been playing games competitively for years!

ALSO CHECK OUT ...

SUPER MARIO SUNSHINE
Dig out your Wii and this GameCube game—there's no better paint-based game than tropical island adventure.

DE BLOB 2
Splatoon's visuals owe a lot to this series, where you're a paint-spreading Blob. This creative puzzle-platformer deserves a re-release.

JET SET RADIO
Sega's classic found a new home on mobile, which means you can enjoy acrobatic grinding and spray-painting from the comfort of your phone/tablet.

WATCH THE MAP
The Wii U GamePad gives you an overview of the action at all times—use it to plan your approach. *Splatoon* is a game of tactics, not smashing buttons.

DON'T DIE!
Knowing when to retreat in *Splatoon* is absolutely crucial, especially in Turf War. Learn to back off and live to fight another day.

SUPER MARIO

GAMING'S BIGGEST STAR!

STATS

Over 260 million blocks have been used in levels

Over **3.3 million** levels have been uploaded so far

Designers have given out a generous 14 million super stars

You can choose **4 different** game styles for your level

The Super Mushroom is the most popular mushroom, used 13.3 million times

For more than 30 years Mario has jumped from one amazing platform game to another, accompanied by his iconic theme song. But this wasn't enough for some fans, they wanted more—crazier puzzles, insanely hard jumps, new concepts! Some fans even thought they could make up their own levels, so Nintendo finally gave them what they craved—*Super Mario Maker*.

If you're more of a fan of Mario's other interests, *Mario Tennis: Ultra Smash* sees the world's most popular plumber take to the court with his friends and foes. As you would expect, it's not a standard game of tennis as you'll have to deal with power-ups and powerful Chance Shots, so prepare to return some rather crazy shots!

DID YOU KNOW?

Mario Tennis: Ultra Smash is the first game in the series to not offer a tournament mode for players to challenge.

TOP 5 THINGS TO BUILD IN MARIO MAKER

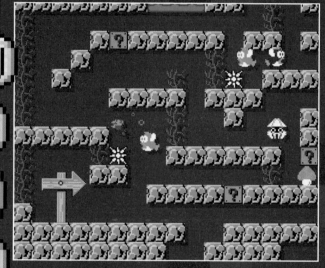

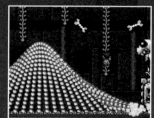

THE FIREWALL

3 One of the trickiest obstacles in *Super Mario Bros* was the spinning fire barrier, and now you've got access to as many of them as you want. So why not make something really devious and line up a whole bunch of them, creating a deadly no-go area for players?

BLOCK MESSAGES

4 If you need to get a message to your players, writing it in blocks or coins is a good way to do it. We've seen some weird and wonderful things, from instructions to strange questions about the meaning of Mario's life. Why not try your own?

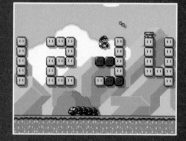

CRAZY MAZE

1 There aren't too many *Mario* levels out there that really stretch a player's ability to find a path, so a tightly-packed maze level will really stand out. Just make sure that you give other players time to find the exit—or if you feel evil, make the time limit short!

PRETTY PICTURES

5 One of the things we often see from Japanese creators is lovely art made out of blocks—some of it visible in stages, some only in the menu preview screens. If you're feeling nasty, you can make these enticing stages deadly too—this one here is pretty tough.

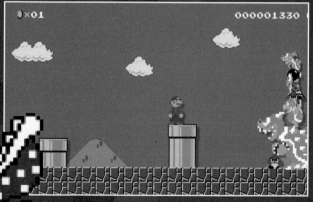

TOWER OF DOOM

2 What's worse than a Goomba? A stack of Goombas. What's worse than that? How about a mini-Bowser on top of a Bob-Omb, on top of a Koopa and a Hammer Bro, with a full-size Bowser at the bottom.

ALSO CHECK OUT ...

RAYMAN LEGENDS

There's no level creation, but if you're hankering for classic 2D platform game action after *Super Mario Maker*, this is an enjoyable game.

ORI AND THE BLIND FOREST

If you want a more modern take on platform games, *Ori* will give you everything you need.

SUPER MARIO

DID YOU KNOW?

Mario's first tennis game came out in 1995, and was the only long-running series to start on the Virtual Boy console.

THE EXPERT SAYS ...
KEIJI INAFUNE
Developer on the *Mega Man* series, *Mighty No. 9*, and more

[The *Mario* games] are all great! I love them all. But actually, the very first game is the most important to me. I played it at a time when I was still unemployed, before starting out somewhere. Playing this, I realized for the first time, "Oh, there is a game industry. This is something I could realize being creative, and actually conceive works of art." *Super Mario Bros* would be my favorite because it actually pushed me into this industry. Otherwise, possibly, without this I wouldn't even have ended up there.

DID YOU KNOW?

The hardest *Super Mario Maker* level, *Pit Of Panga: U-Break*, took 11 hours to make and 39 hours to beat!

MITSUGU KIKAI

WHO?

Mitsugu Kikai was born in 1985, the same year that the original *Super Mario Bros* was released for the NES, and he grew up loving the series. In 2010, he was awarded the Guinness World Record for the world's largest *Mario* collection, with over 5,400 items in his hoard!

WHY?

Mitsugu didn't intend to build a record-breaking collection, but just kept getting *Mario* merchandise as it became available. He has a room in his house dedicated to his *Mario* memorabilia, but even that isn't enough—he's had to store some of his collection at his parents' house!

40 GAME ON! 2017

TIPS & TRICKS
MARIO TENNIS: ULTRA SMASH

UNLOCK MORE CHARACTERS

To get more characters, play ten Mega Battles, plus ten standard matches and ten simple matches in Classic Tennis mode.

GET MEGA MUSHROOMS

Just like in other *Mario* games, they'll make you huge. That gives you a wider reach, as well as major shot power.

GET SPRIXIE PRINCESS

To get this elusive character, you'll need to hit 100 consecutive shots in Mega Ball Rally. This might take practice!

USE YOUR AMIIBO

Not only can you train up a special amiibo partner, you can use it to gain a major advantage in two-on-one games!

PERFORM CHANCE SHOTS

Move to color-coded areas of the court and input the right command, and you'll perform a powerful Chance Shot.

FOUR DEADLY ENEMIES

LAKITU

This guy's a real coward—he won't face off with Mario directly, he just hovers above the level dropping Spiny enemies. Take shelter underneath blocks to avoid them.

THWOMP

Getting past a Thwomp is all a matter of timing—not a problem, you'd think. But in *Super Mario Maker* they can break the floor too, making life harder.

HAMMER BRO

One Hammer Bro isn't a problem, but when you get lots of them together, the hammers they throw can be hard to track. One wrong move and you've lost a life.

BOWSER

There's a reason that he's Mario's nemesis—his fireballs are deadly and his jumping patterns are unpredictable. To make players suffer, ensure you include him in your level.

SPLIT SECOND

BATTLEBORN

A HOST OF HEROES ...

This sci-fi/fantasy adventure drops you into a world of heroes and pits you against hundreds of alien enemies in a colorful extravaganza of lasers, swords, and explosions. It's an FPS crossed with a MOBA and the results are chaotic and completely awesome.

BATTLEBORN

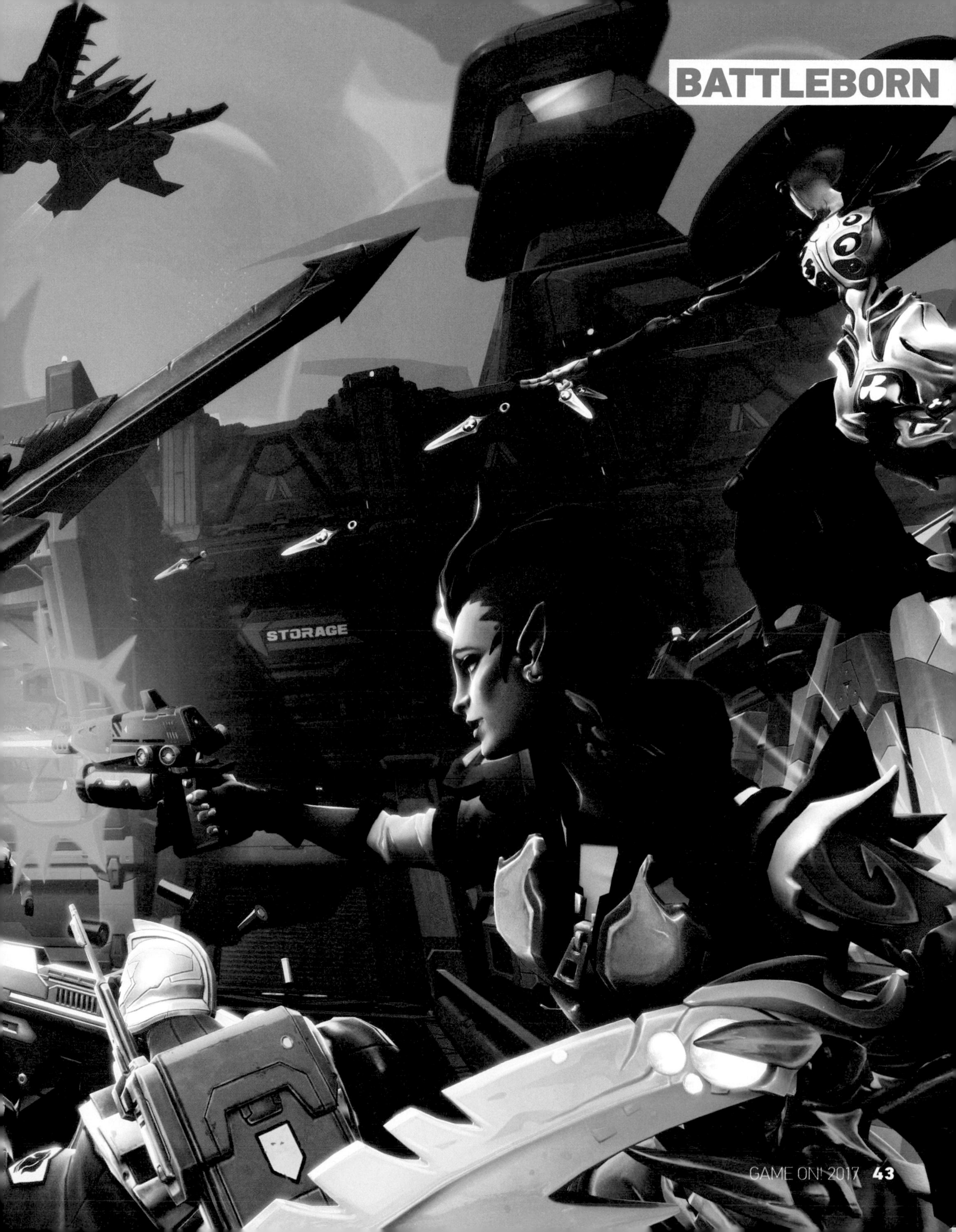

TOP 10 SPECIAL EDITION CONSOLES

PS4 20TH ANNIVERSARY EDITION

Released to celebrate the 20th anniversary of PlayStation, this console's design is inspired by the original PlayStation, using a gray color scheme and the old iconic PlayStation logo. You can still buy the 20th Anniversary controller separately from the console.

XBOX ONE FORZA MOTORSPORT 6 1TB CONSOLE

This special edition *Forza 6* Xbox One kind of looks like a sports car. It has a sleek and stylish design, and the colorless buttons on the pad and the unique version of the Xbox One logo on the main unit look really classy.

ANIMAL CROSSING NEW NINTENDO 3DS

Nintendo loves its special edition consoles, which is why there are so many game-themed 3DS consoles that you can pick up. One of the best is the *Animal Crossing Happy Home Designer* version of the New 3DS – it is packed with color and detail.

SUPERCHARGE YOUR CONSOLE

1 CONTROLLERS

A few online sites can make custom controllers, designed to your unique specifications. You can also buy different sticker sets to lay over your controller and give it a cool new look.

2 CONSOLE DECALS

Some limited edition consoles can be expensive, so you could customize the one you already have. Whether you're just looking for a cool color scheme, or a retro theme, there are plenty of options.

3 TURN IT UP

A good headset makes a big difference, even giving you a competitive edge in multiplayer. For some games it will allow you to hear where your foes are coming from quicker.

4 VIRTUAL REALITY

The ultimate accessory right now has to be a virtual reality headset. PlayStation VR is a great option, but we're excited to see what Microsoft can do when Hololens comes to Xbox One.

5 ONLINE GAMING

Being able to connect to the internet easily is essential for online gaming. Get a parent to help you make sure you've set up your connection correctly and safely.

6 GET ACCESSIBLE

If you have special needs that mean you find a standard pad difficult to use, a custom controller could be just what you need. Many companies can adapt consoles to suit any gamer.

THE LEGEND OF ZELDA PREMIUM Wii U

This special version of the Wii U that comes with *The Legend Of Zelda: Wind Waker HD* packed in isn't as crazy and colorful as some of the other special edition consoles on this list, but it does still look amazing. The detailed gold *Zelda*-themed bordering laid around the edge of the Wii U gamepad stands out beautifully against the black of the pad and adds a touch of class to the console.

SUPER SMASH BROS. NINTENDO 3DS XL

This special edition of the XL version of the 3DS, celebrating *Super Smash Bros.*, really stands out. The inclusion of the black and white character art featuring the likes of Mario, Pikachu, Samus, Link, and Kirby, really makes the bright red background pop. If you're a Nintendo fan, you can't do much better than a console that features so many iconic characters!

PS VITA DRAGON QUEST METAL SLIME EDITION

Built to tie-in with the release of *Dragon Quest Builders*, this special edition Vita is themed around the *Dragon Quest* series' iconic Slime. The brilliance is in the detail with this one, such as the cute little Slime clinging on to the underside of the console and the replacement of the Up symbol on the d-pad with yet another Slime!

LIMITED EDITION HALO 5 XBOX ONE

A treat for any *Halo* fans out there is this *Halo*-styled limited edition Xbox One. There's plenty to enjoy, such as the cool blue coloring spread across the primarily black and gray unit, plus all the tiny details. You'll find UNSC lettering, a hexagon theme carried over from the console onto the controller, and it's a great special edition that really embraces the *Halo* ethos.

XBOX 360 STAR WARS LIMITED EDITION

The game it was created for— *Kinect Star Wars*—wasn't the best *Star Wars* game, but you can't deny that the console itself is a thing of beauty. The limited edition *Star Wars* Xbox 360 is designed to look like R2-D2 and it comes with a golden controller inspired by his robot companion, C-3PO.

DID YOU KNOW?

Rare limited edition consoles like the *Panzer Dragoon Xbox* can sell for as much as $1,500.

FINAL FANTASY XIII-2 LIGHTNING EDITION

Lightning, the star of *Final Fantasy XIII* and *XIII-2*, appears on this striking special edition of the PS3, which just has a dash of hot pink to set off the cool black and white art splashed across the console.

STAR WARS LIMITED EDITION PS4

We've got some more *Star Wars* love with the limited edition PS4 released alongside *Star Wars Battlefront*. The Darth Vader image on the console looks great, and the controller takes it to the next level. With a deep red d-pad and a red lightsaber-style circle button, this controller is completely different to any other PS4 pad you can get.

THE EXPERT SAYS ...
PAUL WALKER-EMIG
Games Writer at NowGamer

Though they remain rare individually, the practice of releasing special editions of consoles is becoming increasingly common. In the process, they've become a lot less crazy—gone are the days where Sega would release a special edition Divers 2000 Dreamcast that was essentially a weird shaped TV with a Dreamcast built in, or when Nintendo worked with Panasonic to release a DVD-playing GameCube that looked like a Hi-Fi. Instead, we now get more practical special editions with the same functionality and shape, but with a cool design that sets them apart from standard editions.

TOP 10 STUNT GAMES

FIFA 16

WHY: *FIFA 16* may not be the first game you think of when it comes to stunts, but some of the skills you can pull off are incredible. Want to chip a soccer ball up into the air, over someone's head, catch it on your foot, and then thump it into the back of the net past a despairing goalkeeper? How about take on an entire defense with Lionel Messi and bamboozle them all? *FIFA* is waiting …

MINECRAFT

WHY: Have you seen some of the things people have built in *Minecraft*? They're epic! One such structure is "The Stunt Rollercoaster", an actual theme park ride you can sit in and ride. It's crazy, too, rocketing you up into the sky before plummeting back down to earth. Get this on a big screen and you might actually feel like you're riding it for real around a huge theme park. Very impressive.

NEED FOR SPEED

WHY: In true open-world fashion, *Need For Speed* is desperate for you to play around within it. More specifically, it wants you to find epic jumps to fly over. Rewarding you with a "Perfect Moment" splash onscreen, it not only looks great, but will make you feel like a driving superhero as you send your car zinging across the city, past bewildered cops.

MARIO KART 8

WHY: *Mario Kart* doesn't hope you perform stunts by accident—it actively encourages them. A quick tap of the R trigger the moment you leave a ramp will activate your chosen character's stunt and give you a speed boost when you land. You can abuse this technique too, by repeating the method every time your kart leaves the ground for a sweet speed boost. You'd be crazy not to.

»»»»» 6 STEPS TO STUNT SUCCESS »»»»»

① GO FAST!
No good stunt was ever achieved by going slow! So whether you're trying to successfully land a huge jump, or flip your car upside-down and then back onto its wheels, you'll need some serious speed!.

② IMPROVISE
A search of YouTube for "gaming stunts" will show you hundreds of stunts that were pulled off by mistake. If you're looking to try something new, wiggle the stick, mash all the buttons, and see what happens.

③ HIT THE RECORD BUTTON
How can you execute a successful stunt if no one else knows you did it? Anytime you're trying to show off, just make sure to record your actions.

④ TRY AGAIN
Unless you're incredibly lucky, few people carry out a successful stunt on their first try. The key, as always, is to keep practicing. The satisfaction will be all the more sweet when you finally succeed.

⑤ THINK OUTSIDE THE BOX
Everyone has flipped a car, owned a jump, or loop-the-looped! However, only an original and creative gamer can pull off the perfect stunt.

⑥ DON'T COPY OTHERS
The internet is awash with stunts from games everyone knows. While there's nothing wrong with this, why not find a new game and become the master of it?

FORZA MOTORSPORT 6

WHY: *Forza's* main objective is to portray driving in the most realistic way possible. That means whatever you could do in an actual car, you can do in-game. Handbrake turns, flips, jumps, skids, spins. You name it and *Forza* gives you the tools to make it happen. It's a stunt-person's dream.

DRIVECLUB

WHY: Anything is possible when you're driving at speeds of up to 200mph, but learning how to flip a car on its roof, sliding along the road for a while, then flipping it again takes some doing. But that's what *DRIVECLUB* is all about; giving you the tools to have some serious fun in some of the world's most powerful and beautiful supercars. And when you pull off that perfect flip, it's so satisfying that it'll keep you coming back for more.

DIRT RALLY

WHY: Unlike some games in the *Colin McRae Rallly* series, *Dirt Rally* is a simulator. It's incredibly hardcore as well, which means that even the slightest mistake can send your vehicle crashing into the environment. It also allows amazing control over your car, however, which opens up the opportunity to do some truly incredible stunts. We challenge you all to see how many times you can roll your car in the dirt and then keep on driving.

TRACKMANIA TURBO

WHY: If you're looking for a game where you can loop-the-loop until you can't loop-the-loop anymore, *Trackmania Turbo* is for you. Each individual course has some form of stunt ramp to try, with many asking you to keep the loop going for what seems like an eternity. This is the appeal, though, and the reason why you'll keep coming back for more. Just how good can you get?

SKYLANDERS SUPERCHARGERS

WHY: It seems very likely the main reason for the addition of vehicles in *Skylanders Superchargers* was to allow for stunts. Driving upside down in tunnels, performing huge jumps, flying through the air (quite literally in some contraptions). You can even head to the water for more stunt-based action, and combine land, air, and sea together. It's amazing to see what stunts you can pull off.

THE EXPERT SAYS ...

KORNEL JASKULA

Producer on Xbox One/ PS4 game Dying Light

I love to make difficult games easy for myself. I'll look for little holes or stunts that I can pull to make the game go easier for my character. Since I design games, I like to see what other developers didn't think about when making their own games. If I can jump through to areas I shouldn't be allowed to. If I can make a lot of cash super-fast. If there is a weapon combination that is very overpowered. It may sound a bit cruel or silly, but this is what makes games fun for me.

LEGO BATMAN 3: BEYOND GOTHAM

WHY: What would you do if you had an open world to play around in as well as all your favorite superheroes and their vehicles? We think you know where we're going with this. *LEGO Batman 3*'s lack of restrictions means you can pull off some ridiculous stunts, including loop-the-looping the Batwing!

PLANTS VS. ZOMBIES

DID YOU KNOW?

Plants vs. Zombies: Garden Warfare players can transfer nearly all of their unlocked characters to this sequel.

OH HOW YOUR GARDEN GROWS

PLANTS VS. ZOMBIES: GARDEN WARFARE 2

There's something utterly endearing about *Plants vs. Zombies: Garden Warfare 2*. Perhaps it's because it doesn't take itself too seriously, or that it's incredibly fun ... maybe it's because it lets us pummel cosplaying zombies as an ever-beaming Sunflower. *Garden Warfare 2* is chaos connected to a controller and we wouldn't want it any other way. This spin-off of the ever-popular *Plants vs. Zombies* tower defense game sees PopCap building on the breakout success of 2014's *Garden Warfare*, with a sequel that's bigger and better in every way imaginable. Don't let its cartoony looks fool you. *Garden Warfare 2* is surprisingly robust and enjoyable; there's nothing else out there that's quite like it.

TIPS & TRICKS

FIND YOUR CLASS
With 14 character classes to choose between, make sure you sample them all to dominate this all-out botanical battle.

SAVE YOUR COINS
Don't go wasting your coins on the cheap sticker packs; save them up for the expensive ones—bigger rewards await you.

PAY ATTENTION TO UNLOCKS
As you unlock new character abilities, a skippable cutscene will play to detail the move. Make sure you watch these for tips and tricks.

TOP 5 NEW CHARACTER CLASSES

CITRON

1 If you're looking for ways to surprise your enemies, look no further than Citron. He's a world famous time-traveling bounty hunter that, yes, also happens to be an orange. He is also able to transform and roll into battle faster than any other Plant, before instantly launching into an attack mode.

CAPTAIN DEADBEARD

3 We've got rampaging cobs of corn and bounty-hunter oranges, so why not a zombie pirate from the past? Captain Deadbeard might look a little crusty, but he's packing enough tricks up his sleeves to lay waste to Suburbia. And if you really get in a tight jam, Deadbeard can even call on his trusty Parrot Pal for aid.

KERNEL CORN

2 We love the weird sense of humor of *Garden Warfare*, and this is massively realized in Kernel Corn. This Plant packs some serious firepower with his dual Cob Busters (yup) and can quickly take down Zombies with his Butter Barrage and Shuck Shot ... we just don't even.

SUPER BRAINZ

4 This super-powered Zombie has enough hero powers to see you through any and all altercations. Attacking from a distance? Well, his hand can transform into a laser gun. He's also pretty handy up close too, in fact, he's able to dish out a swift three-hit punch; for justice!

"GARDEN WARFARE IS CHAOS CONNECTED TO A CONTROLLER"

ROSE

5 This is one rose you wouldn't want a kiss from. A powerful sorceress from the future, Rose is able to utilize her mystical plant powers to ensnare enemies from afar, beat them around with arcane artistry and, well, even turn particularly annoying enemies into goats.

ALSO CHECK OUT ...

PLANTS VS. ZOMBIES
The crazy idea that started it all; you'll need a level head to make it through this tower-defense game.

OVERWATCH
Another third-person shooter with distinct individual abilities and an awesome cartoon style, *Overwatch* is fast, furious, and frantic!

DUNGEON DEFENDERS
A similar game to *Garden Warfare*, but with a dungeon setting and a focus on (you got it) defense over offense.

BE DEFENSIVE
Yes, it's fun to run riot, but the best offense is a good defense. Use the Cactus and Peashooter to spot enemies from afar and plan a trap.

HOT-SWAP BETWEEN CHARACTERS
Don't forget you can jump between the other members of your team at a moment's notice—great for unleashing combos.

YOSHI'S WOOLLY WORLD

YOSHI'S WOOLLY WORLD
NINTENDO'S CRAFTIEST GAME SO FAR!

Welcome to Yoshi's adorably woolly world! At the demand of his master, Baby Bowser, evil magikoopa Kamek has turned all the unsuspecting yoshis into bundles of wool.

Well ... almost all. Just two escaped the curse, which means it's up to you—and a friend!—to jump, bounce, explore, and stomp your way across the world in search of Kamek, rescuing all the cursed yoshis as you go.

Yoshi's Woolly World is the latest and greatest side-scrolling adventure for Mario's trusty dino-shaped sidekick. It packs all the things we've come to expect from a Nintendo platformer—simple controls, beautiful graphics, and super-secret secrets—and finishes it off with extra dollops of yarn-charm, making it the perfect game for the young and young-at-heart to play together!

TIPS & TRICKS

HAVING A LITTLE TROUBLE?
If you're struggling to time your jumps and hit hard-to-reach places, switch to Mellow Mode for an easier time.

BAG THOSE BEADS
Beads act as *Yoshi's Woolly World*'s in-game currency. Try to collect as many as you possibly can so that you can stock up on ...

BUY BADGES
... badges! Make sure you build up a good collection so that you can redeem them and make exploration a little easier!

TOP 5 AMIIBO SKINS!

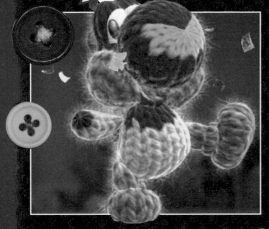

YOSHI SAMUS

1 If you thought Yoshi was already super cute in green, just wait until you see it dressed up in Samus' costume! Use a Samus Aran amiibo to transform Yoshi into Nintendo's most beloved intergalactic bounty hunter. Sadly, you won't get her blaster—just her awesome suit!

YOSHI SONIC THE HEDGEHOG

2 As champions of Nintendo and SEGA respectively, Mario and Sonic are often thought to be sworn enemies. But if you have a Sonic the Hedgehog amiibo, you can celebrate Sonic by dressing Yoshi in Sonic's iconic blue, red, and white colors!

"IT'S THE PERFECT GAME FOR THE YOUNG AND YOUNG AT HEART"

MARIO YOSHI

4 There are plenty of Mario and Luigi amiibos to experiment with as you build your amiibo collection, but we have to admit that the standard Mario variation is probably our favorite. Yoshi looks surprisingly good in blue dungarees, a red shirt and hat, and Mario's huge black mustache!

YOSHI LINK

3 It's hard to imagine any other character dressed up in *The Legend of Zelda*'s Link's trademark outfit, but when it comes to Yoshi, we'll make an exception (we particularly love that cute tunic). Just use your Link amiibo to turn Yoshi into Zelda's everlasting hero!

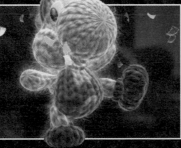

YOSHI DONKEY KONG

5 Mario's original enemy was Donkey Kong, the giant ape with a penchant for drumming and eating bananas. Don't worry, though—they're best buds now, and Yoshi can don Kong's famous red tie, along with his furry appearance, by popping his amiibo on the Wii U gamepad.

DID YOU KNOW?
When Nintendo's Emi Watanabe knitted a Yoshi plushie just for fun, she didn't realize it would inspire the cuddly amiibo.

ALSO CHECK OUT ...

KIRBY'S EPIC YARN
Developed by the same team behind *Yoshi's Woolly World*, *Kirby's Epic Yarn* is another crafty Nintendo platformer. Check this out on Wii!

LITTLEBIGPLANET
If you love the idea of *Yoshi's Woolly World* but don't own a Wii U, give Sackboy and his friends a try! Available on PS3, PS4, and PS Vita.

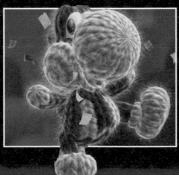

DARN YARN!
If you're struggling to reach a sneaky Smiley Flower, don't forget you can sometimes reach collectibles with a well-timed yarn ball!

KEEP AN EYE OUT!
Every level has secrets and secret passages—don't be afraid to explore and sneak around for bonus flowers and wool!

CUTE CHARACTERS

DID YOU KNOW?

There are 114 variations of Yarn Yoshi in *Yoshi's Woolly World*, unlocked by playing the game and using your amiibo!

YARNY
Unravel

WHY: While he could easily have looked like a little woolen demon, Yarny from the platform game *Unravel* fortunately fell on the right side of "super sinister or actually cute". While many associate the Xbox console with shooting and racing games, *Unravel* proves that, actually, it can surprise you and make you go "aww" as well.

BEEFALO
Don't Starve

WHY: You can use beefalo for meat in *Don't Starve*, but they're just so adorable you probably won't want to do that. Instead just wait until they fall asleep and shave them—not only will they thank you for it (maybe), you'll also get a bunch of useful wool from them! And friendship plus wool outweighs steak every day.

TEMMIES
Undertale

WHY: The adorable denizens of the hidden Temmie Village through the waterfall can actually be a tough enemy to beat in *Undertale*... or you can just befriend them. We'd suggest the latter, as they're just too cute to bother fighting with, from their cat-in-a-shirt looks to the endearingly unique way they "speak."

LINK(S)
The Legend of Zelda: Tri Force Heroes

WHY: When one cute Link isn't enough, add another. If that's not good enough, make it three! Yes, *Tri Force Heroes* features three of our favorite heroes of the Zelda series, looking his most adorable this time around. The fact you can also dress Link up just adds to the cute factor.

6 WAYS TO DESIGN A CUTE CHARACTER

1 HEAD AND FACE
Give your character a big head, with eyes wide apart, a small nose and mouth, and what do you have? Well, something that should look weird, but actually looks really cute. Who knew?

2 ARMS AND LEGS
Short and stubby with big fingers is the accepted wisdom, but it's not a rule set in cute-stone—just look at BUD. Generally, though, if you make a character who waddles, you're set.

3 SHAPE
One word: round. If not a sphere, then your character at least needs to be rounded. No sharp, painful edges. Even if they're a robot, softening parts of them makes them adorable.

4 SIMPLICITY
Complexity is the enemy of cute—cute is something that appeals to young and old alike, so something that isn't difficult for the brain to process. Too many fine details don't make a character cute!

5 SIZE
Giants can be cute, but generally speaking, if you make a little, squat character they're going to immediately set off the "aww" klaxons. Short, squat, and squidgy? You've got yourself a winner.

6 COLOR
Colors can make a character look warm and friendly—pastels, pinks, light blues, yellows, for example. Avoid stark contrast and too many dark or bold, primary colors.

INKLING
Splatoon

WHY: In human form they're pretty cute, but in squid form the inklings are on a whole other level of adorable. Trust Nintendo to make something as inherently strange as the cephalopod and turn it into something you want to shout "aww" at before clawing at the screen and trying to hug its tentacled little body.

NARU
Ori and the Blind Forest

WHY: It's not just small and childish that makes something cute, as Naru proves. She is older, wise, and quite large, but still manages to be utterly adorable both in how she looks and in how she acts, becoming like a mother to Ori, the tree spirit. Her selflessness is the cherry on top of the already-cute cake.

SUNFLOWER
Plants vs Zombies: Garden Warfare 2

WHY: Sunflowers are already pretty, so *Garden Warfare 2* ramps up the cuteness factor—a smiley face with freckles!—and then makes the sunflower a badass to boot. In the war against the shuffling zombie hordes, you could do a lot worse than inviting this big-faced, adorable flower onto your team.

"SHORT, SQUAT, AND SQUIDGY? YOU'VE GOT YOURSELF A CUTE WINNER"

BUD
Grow Home

WHY: Standing for Botanical Utility Droid, BUD is not just adorable, he's also useful around the garden! The little fella is great at making the green stuff grow, and while it might be due to his programming, we can't help but be taken in by his non-traditional cuteness. If only we had our own BUD for spring and summer!

THE EXPERT SAYS ...

MR. MEOLA
Australian YouTuber with over 140,000 subscribers!

The cutest character in gaming is definitely, without a doubt, Yoshi! I mean, what's cuter than a green dinosaur that gobbles up his enemies and pops them out as eggs!? Exactly! Every single little thing about our cute little dinosaur friend just increases his cuteness! Everything from his big googly eyes to his big cheerful smile, his tiny red shell to his oversized boots! And don't get me started on his voice! Always letting out a cute little squeal or his squeaky little "YOSHI!" Yoshi was the video game character I grew up with since I was very young. He was the loyal partner of Mario in *Super Mario World* on the SNES! Whenever you saw that green Yoshi egg appear, you knew you were in for a good time!

YARN YOSHI
Yoshi's Woolly World

WHY: Sure, Yoshi was always cute, but this woolen version of him has the potential to be not only the cutest he's ever been, but the cutest any character ever has been. The fact you can pick up actual yarn amiibo of Yoshi in this form makes it even harder to bear—and we only say that because *we want to buy all of them.*

CAPTURE THIS!

ELITE: DANGEROUS

DISCOVER AN UNEXPLORED SYSTEM

There are more than 100 billion star systems in *Elite: Dangerous*, and while many of the closer systems have already been explored by other players online, there are still *loads* that haven't yet been visited. We flew almost exactly 1,000 lightyears to reach this one, then sold the data for credits—but can you go further?

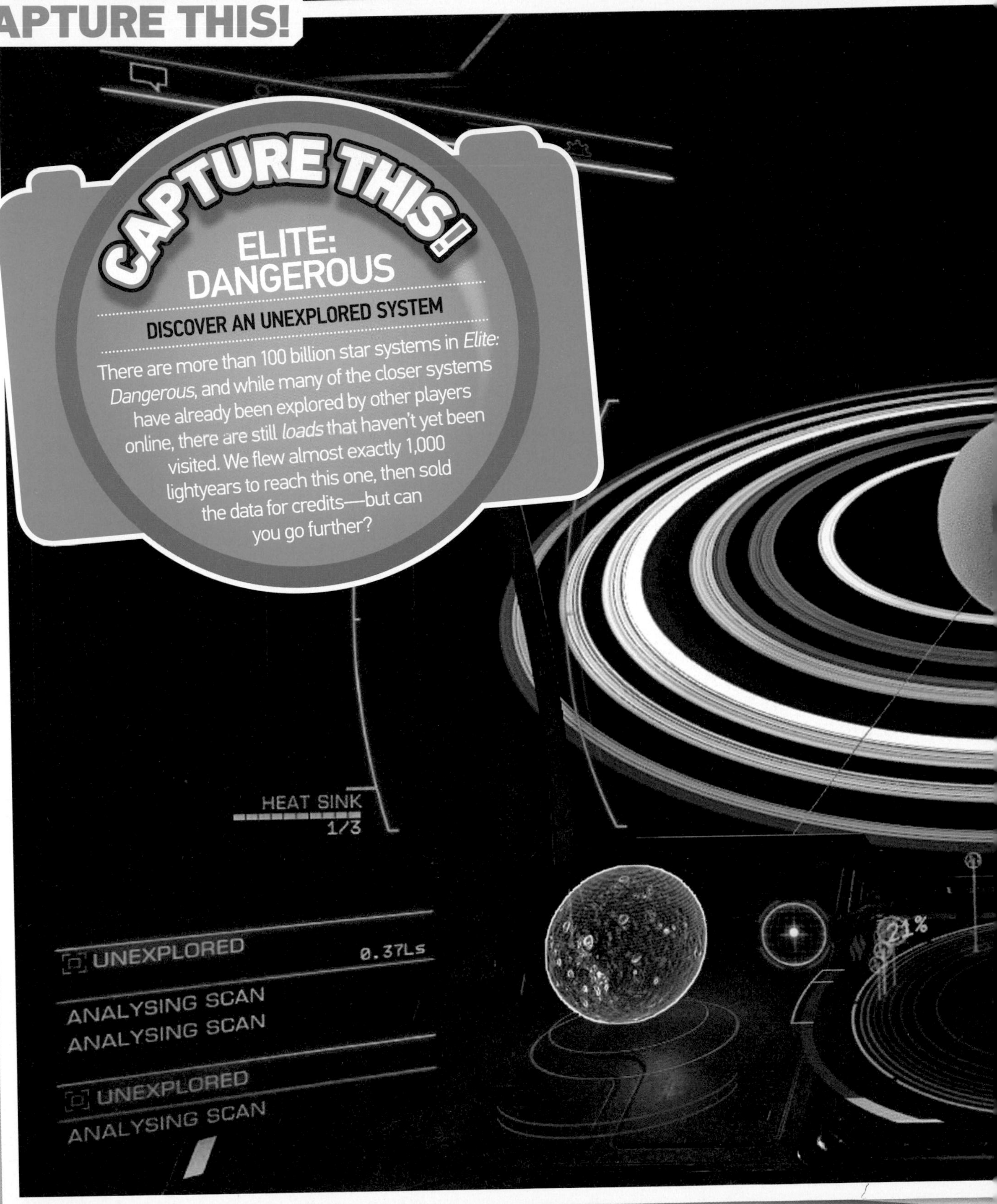

HEAT SINK
1/3

UNEXPLORED   0.37Ls

ANALYSING SCAN
ANALYSING SCAN

UNEXPLORED

ANALYSING SCAN

21%

MINECRAFT

STATS

70 million copies
of the game have been bought

$2,500,000,000
the amount Microsoft paid to acquire developer Mojang and *Minecraft*

651
The number of different types of blocks and items

47 billion
YouTube views

256
layers from the top of *Minecraft* to the bottom

MINECRAFT

A WORLD APART

Is *Minecraft* the biggest game in the world? We'd say so, as it's hard to think of any game that has dominated YouTube, Twitch, and every console it has ever been released on in the way that *Minecraft* has. And all this was started by one person! Created by Markus "Notch" Persson under the name "*Cave Game*" in 2009, it was later rebranded as *Minecraft* and launched in 2011—quickly becoming one of the most influential games of all time. You start off in a randomly generated world (it's never the same world twice), and then you build using raw materials you find. You can be artistic in Creative mode or tackle Survival mode, where enemies and hunger are introduced. It's a game you can play at your own pace, in any way you want. How many games let you do that? No wonder *Minecraft* is so popular.

TIPS & TRICKS

SURVIVE UNDERWATER
Did you dive too deeply in the unknown? Torches can create handy little temporary air pockets, letting you get a quick breath in before it's too late.

TORCHES ARE KING
Running low on certain blocks? You can actually build off of the side of torches, making them the perfect scaffolding tool.

LADDER TO SAFETY
Looking to create a pathway through lava or water? You can use a ladder to stop the flow. This is also useful for building deeper underground.

TOP 5 SCARIEST ENEMIES

CREEPER

1 Without question one of the scariest monsters you will encounter, in any game, ever. Not only does Creeper have a tendency to sneak up on you, but it'll make a spine-tingling hiss before exploding—scaring the life out of you and likely destroying your carefully-crafted constructions in the process!

DID YOU KNOW?

It's estimated that up to 10,000 copies of *Minecraft* are sold on PC every 24 hours. Sales are already well past 22 million.

ZOMBIE

2 Eventually you are going to need to venture into *Minecraft*'s deep and dark caves to find rare materials, and that's when you'll really start to get the heebie-jeebies. Make sure to bring a sword and a spare pair of pants, you'll need them to fight the walking dead.

ENDERMAN

3 Let's put it this way, if you see something out in the world that doesn't look like it could be easily defeated and cooked, it's probably offering some seriously negative vibes. Enderman is a towering, frightening creature that'll rush you if you dare look it in the eyes. Our advice? Stay clear!

GHAST

4 Entering the Nether can be scary enough as it is, but of course there's more to fear than a few creepy colored blocks. These ghostly, ghastly foes will freak you out with their weird jellyfish shuffle and then totally decimate you with a fireball. Grab your pickaxe and run for your life!

ENDER DRAGON

5 It's rare that *Minecraft* is a real challenge, but you'll need to go on a grand adventure to meet this foe. Technically, Ender Dragon is *Minecraft*'s toughest boss—a huge, flying beast—and you'll need all of your wits (and swords) to get past this encounter.

"MINECRAFT SHOULD BE EXPERIENCED BY EVERYONE AT LEAST ONCE"

ALSO CHECK OUT...

TERRARIA

Terraria is essentially a 2D version of *Minecraft*—letting you build wild structures and venture deep into the underground—though it features a heavier emphasis on story and adventure.

LEGO WORLDS

This is what happens when a game gets so big it can no longer be ignored. LEGO has unleashed *LEGO Worlds* upon us, its take on *Minecraft* that lets you build truly impressive worlds with the familiar colored bricks.

CREATE AN INFINITE WATER SUPPLY

Creating a three-block trench and filling it with a bucket of water will create an infinite source of water.

GENERAL MAINTENANCE

Want to quickly clean up the area around your house? While it may seem illogical, you can chuck a bucket of water over long grass to quickly mow it down.

MINECRAFT: STORY MODE

MINECRAFT: STORY MODE

STATS

heroes to find

Choose from **6** character designs for Jesse

5 Major decisions in *Episode 1*

30 Achievements to unlock

6 chapters in *Episode 1*

A NEW ADVENTURE!

Minecraft has always been great for gamers wanting a huge adventure, or for those that just want to build a really massive castle. But there's one thing that it has never had: a proper story to play through. That all changed with the release of *Minecraft: Story Mode*, a game devoted entirely to the story. You take on the role of Jesse, a new player in the world of *Minecraft*, who sets out with his/her friends to find the legendary Order of the Stone—five adventurers who defeated the Ender Dragon and saved the *Minecraft* world. You don't choose your own path through the world with your own two feet, but with the storyline decisions you make. Each decision changes the story down the line and what happens to your favorite characters ... it's really tense! If you want something different to do in *Minecraft*, give this clever game a try.

TIME LINE

EPISODE 1—THE ORDER OF THE STONE
Jesse and the gang enter a building competition, but it's disrupted when the evil Ivor creates the Wither Storm.

EPISODE 2— ASSEMBLY REQUIRED
The adventure leads Jesse and friends into the Nether. Once they escape, the team looks for the heroes.

EPISODE 3—THE LAST PLACE YOU LOOK
The group's journey takes them to The End where they search for another of the four heroes.

TOP 5 CHARACTERS

JESSE

1 Jesse loves all things *Minecraft*, and is desperate to win the Endercon Building competition with his friends. But when a series of unfortunate events results in the spawning of a Wither that threatens to consume everything, Jesse and his friends must search for the Order of the Stone—five heroes that have saved the *Minecraft* world before. Along the way he'll face all kinds of scary threats and difficult choices—but he is ready for the adventure of a lifetime …

PETRA

2 Petra is a real tough cookie, and is always the first one to defend her friends. She's very protective of those she loves, but is also very shrewd, spotting things that her friends have missed. She's a valuable asset to Jesse's team as they seek for the Order of the Stone.

OLIVIA

3 She can be a little impatient at times, especially when others can't keep up, but she's also very smart. Her brains can help the group out of some sticky situations, and her assertiveness can benefit the team when they're not sure of the best way to solve a problem.

AXEL

4 Axel is the strong one of the group, and isn't scared to speak his mind or pull pranks on his friends. He can be impulsive at times, but he is also fiercely loyal to the gang. All of these qualities make him one of the most dependable members of the squad.

REUBEN THE PIG

5 Reuben is Jesse's best friend as well as pet pig. Sometimes you have to make tricky decisions on whether to put the search for the Order of the Stone ahead of your friendship with Reuben, however …

"YOU TAKE ON THE ROLE OF JESSE, A NEW MINECRAFT PLAYER"

ALSO CHECK OUT …

MINECRAFT
Obviously. It might not have a scripted story, but with infinite worlds and countless skins, the possibilities for exploration and building are endless.

LEGO DIMENSIONS
If you've played *Story Mode* but miss the creative aspect, why not try a game all about bricks and building? *LEGO Dimensions* ticks all the boxes.

EPISODE 4—A BLOCK AND A HARD PLACE
Time is running out for the Minecraft world—can Jesse save it from the approaching Wither Storm?

EPISODE 5— ORDER UP!
A new Order of the Stone is formed, and Jesse and friends must protect the world from new enemies rising around them.

TOYS TO LIFE

(BUT NOT IN A SCARY WAY)

Toys to life are a relatively new phenomenon, only really coming to prominence in the last five years or so. It's strange to consider that in the time before we had the likes of *Minecraft* and *LittleBigPlanet*, nobody tried the seemingly obvious thing of "making toys that you can use in your video games."

Since the meteoric rise of *Skylanders: Spyro's Adventure* in 2011, we've seen the big-hitters coming out from Disney, LEGO, and even Nintendo, all keen to capitalize on this brand-new area of gaming. And it's not just the big companies making the most of their characters—us gamers are happy to buy into the toys and figures, collecting them in their millions. We don't just buy them to use in the games, tapping on NFC pads and portals to enter into the titles we're playing—we also buy them just for the sake of collecting; to complete a set; to customize and make our own. It's only been five years, but in that time everyone seems to have realized: toys to life are exactly what we all wanted all along.

STATS

$3 billion
The amount of money *Skylanders* has made since it started in 2011

44
characters planned for *LEGO Dimensions'* first five waves

$500
The cost of buying everything for *Disney Infinity 3.0*

4 years
The time between Anki hiring its first employees and *Overdrive* releasing

31 million
amiibo sold by the end of 2015

TOP 5 TOYS TO LIFE TITLES

AMIIBO

4 Nintendo's amiibo—that's the plural of amiibo, fact fans—bring together a mix of classic Nintendo (and some other) characters for you to tap into your Wii U and 3DS games. They are absurdly popular, and with good reason: they look amazing, and include some legendary characters, like Mario, Link, and even Sonic.

DISNEY INFINITY

1 When one of the biggest companies in the world starts bringing out toys to life, you know you're in for a treat with characters like Spider-Man, Elsa, Rocket Raccoon, Woody, and Lightning McQueen. And yes, Disney did eventually bring out some *Star Wars* figures along with a game, and yes, it was amazing.

ANKI OVERDRIVE

5 Created by a tech/robotics firm favored by Apple, you would expect *Anki Overdrive* to be impressive. It is. Scalextric controlled by iPhone, *Overdrive* adds driver stats and a real sense of progression to a type of game that has already been proven fun for decades.

SKYLANDERS

2 The old hand in the world of toys to life, *Skylanders* now has five main games in its series and dozens of figures to use in and around its colorful worlds. Originally a *Spyro The Dragon* sequel, the game soon developed into the all-conquering beast we love today—Activision is probably happy it dropped that sequel idea ...

DID YOU KNOW?
The biggest-selling toys to life series is currently *Disney Infinity*, squeezing just ahead of the *Skylanders* series!

COLLECT 'EM ALL!
Once you've bought one figure, the bug bites. You have to get more and more until you have an entire shelf dedicated to them. Some think you're crazy—you know it's just cool.

LEGO DIMENSIONS

3 Offering probably the broadest selection of worlds, LEGO's toys to life offering includes the likes of *Jurassic World*, *Ghostbusters*, *Batman*, *Doctor Who*, and so many others it's easy to lose count. Plus it has the added bonus that in traditional LEGO fashion, you get to build the figures yourself!

STATS

44 playable characters in wave 1

269 individual pieces in the starter pack

14 franchises brought together

It would cost over **$600** to own every single wave 1 character

480 Gold Bricks to collect

LEGO DIMENSIONS

BREAKING DOWN THE WALLS ...

Is this the coolest LEGO game we've ever played? Almost certainly, and there's one major reason for that: building! Like other games in the toys-to-life genre, *LEGO Dimensions* lets you put real, physical toys onto the Gateway and have them appear in the game. In this game, though, you also have to build the characters and vehicles before they can be used—and even better, the vehicles can be rebuilt into different forms with different abilities! Better still, the plot of this game brings together characters from all kinds of different stories, so prepare to see Batman and Gandalf leaping past Homer Simpson, Doc Brown, and Marty McFly in Oz, and the Ghostbusters in the TARDIS. It's a game that breaks down the barriers between franchises, and lets you build your own awesome universe.

TIPS & TRICKS

SMASH EVERYTHING!
Like most LEGO games, punching every item around you is well worth it to collect studs ... and work out any anger.

GET RED BRICKS
Red Bricks are really helpful, increasing the number of studs you collect or pointing out hidden secrets. Find them all!

COLLECT THE STUDS
Pick up every stud you can find— you'll need them if you want to unlock all the vehicles and characters in the game.

TOP 5 COOLEST MINIFIGURES

DID YOU KNOW?

TT Games has hinted that the game will be updated with new levels and story for three years after launch!

PETER VENKMAN

1 This *Ghostbuster* is probably one of the most challenging minifigures to build, simply because of the Proton Pack he has strapped to his back. In the game, the biggest bonus to dropping Dr. Venkman on the Gateway is the option to access the extra *Ghostbusters* level that is otherwise locked away.

NYA

2 This LEGO Ninjago warrior not only moves faster than most other characters in the game, she also looks totally awesome. Her spin move in the game makes her a fearsome teammate—especially when you pair her with her devastating Samurai Mech vehicle.

CHELL

3 This silent *Portal* protagonist has one of the coolest accessories in any video game—a gun that fires portals. In *LEGO Dimensions*, this weapon allows her to travel across huge gaps simply by stepping through a hole in reality. Thankfully, there's a whole *Portal*-themed level to explore with Chell, too.

UNIKITTY

4 This cheerful little cat is always handy to have around—she's the only character who can use the Rainbow LEGO sections, so she's essential to unlocking every hidden section of the game. She's great fun to build, too. Oh, and she can turn into a giant rage monster and destroy everything. Cute!

GOLLUM

5 There isn't much building involved with this guy because of Gollum's hunched figure! But in the game, he's really useful—he's agile, so can leap higher and farther than most characters. And that fish he carries is more useful than it looks—it activates boomerang switches!

"NYA'S SPIN MOVE IN THE GAME MAKES HER A FEARSOME TEAMMATE"

ALSO CHECK OUT...

LEGO MARVEL'S AVENGERS

None of Marvel's heroes appear in *LEGO Dimensions*, instead they get their very own game featuring over 200 characters.

LEGO STAR WARS: THE FORCE AWAKENS

You've seen the movie, now you can relive it in LEGO form as the cutesy characters offer their comedic take on *Episode VII*.

TEMPORARY UNLOCKS

If you don't own a specific character, you can 'hire' them with studs for 30 seconds and use their abilities.

READ THE INSTRUCTIONS!

You can access vehicle building instructions at any time from the character wheel.

MEET THE SUPERFAN 1

JOSEPH ZAWADA
Creator of a LEGO Hyrule Castle build

WHO?
Talented LEGO builder Joseph created his own version of Hyrule Castle from *The Legend of Zelda: The Twilight Princess*. "An official LEGO *Zelda* theme is the dream for many people," he said. "I got tired of waiting and took the matter into my own hands."

WHY?
The castle took more than two years to finish, and Joseph credits his father for pushing him to finish the incredible creation. "About three-quarters of the way through the building process I wanted to throw in the towel. My dad gave me the much-needed motivation to finish the castle. I couldn't have done it without his support."

MOST AWESOME VEHICLES

TARDIS
The Doctor pops up in all of his various regenerations in *LEGO Dimensions*, so it's only right that his trusty time machine is here as well. Remember, it's bigger on the inside!

DID YOU KNOW?
Major actors including Chris Pratt, Gary Oldman, and Michael J. Fox recorded all-new voice audio for *LEGO Dimensions*.

DELOREAN
Who doesn't love the coolest time machine ever? This incredible motor is useful for activating time-travel switches, while simultaneously looking and sounding absolutely awesome.

GYROSPHERE

The ultimate cool vehicle from *LEGO Jurassic World* makes a return here, and just like in that game it's the only thing that you can use to power the gyrosphere switches.

WINGED MONKEY

One of the few vehicles that grants you the ability to fly without any alterations, the Winged Monkey is a really cool option to have in your arsenal.

MEET THE SUPERFAN 2

DAYTON LOVELOCK
Built a model of Arkham Asylum out of LEGO

WHAT INSPIRED YOU?

"I have been a fan of Batman for as long as I can remember. I've always wanted to try building my own version of Arkham Asylum, and even more so after reading Grant Morrison's 1989 classic *Batman Arkham Asylum: A Serious House on Serious Earth* a couple of years ago. Playing the video game by Rocksteady Studios kept the idea alive and had me planning and designing in my head until about a year ago, when I really started planning in detail and began to source the parts I would need."

WHAT WAS THE MOST DIFFICULT PART OF THE BUILD?

"I think the most difficult part was getting the balance of the interior and exterior right. I wanted to ensure there wasn't anything that blocked out the windows or didn't fit design-wise. Physically, the building went great and I fortunately didn't have any collapses or breakdowns during the process."

WHAT IS YOUR FAVORITE PART?

"My favorite part of the build has to be the building itself. I love how the exterior turned out and I especially like the roof with the skylights. Killer Croc's cell is close in second, that's the one thing I really wanted to include."

SKYLANDERS: SUPERCHARGERS

STATS

350+ different figures

240 million+ toys sold

22 million+ copies sold

2011 The year the original *Skylanders* was released

12th biggest selling franchise of all time in Europe

BRINGING TOYS TO LIFE

Skylanders: SuperChargers is, in many ways, the ultimate gaming experience. Bringing you many different forms of entertainment—the game itself, the toys that are digital characters that you play with in the game and real figures you can play with in reality—you couldn't really ask for much more.

SuperChargers summed this idea up perfectly, adding in vehicles to the series for the first time, adding a new super high-speed element. Plus, Activision went a step further by bringing in famous faces from other franchises. Those who opted for the Wii U version could get Donkey Kong and Bowser Skylanders as part of the package, as an extra bonus.

Given that 20 brand new SuperCharger vehicles are available regardless of what console you play it on, it's easy to see why the game has such huge appeal.

TIPS & TRICKS

LEVELLING UP
It's important to keep levelling up in *Skylanders: SuperChargers* and a great place to do this is Battle Brawl Island. There are loads of enemies!

MIX AND MATCH
While we all want the latest *SuperChargers* characters, don't forget you can use your old Skylanders, too. A mixture of both is best.

CHOOSE WISELY
Even if you have a big Skylanders collection, don't just stick with your favorite. Pick the right type for the right battle.

TOP 5 SKYLANDERS

SPITFIRE

2 The leader of the SuperChargers team, Spitfire drives "Hot Streak", a vehicle that helped him become one of the fastest drivers on the Super Skylands Racing Circuit. After a devastating accident, everyone thought Spitfire would never drive again, but he returned to the track before falling under the rule of Kaos.

ASTROBLAST

3 Another debut entry, Astroblast drives the Sun Runner and is never more than a few seconds away from shouting his catchphrase, "Ready. Steady. Glow!" After crashing on an island, he found the legendary Rift Engine. Returning it to the Skylander Academy, he soon became an official Skylander.

DID YOU KNOW?

During its development phase, *Skylanders* wasn't going to be a "toys-to-life" game. At one point special hats were going to be the focus instead.

DIVE-CLOPS

4 Dive-Clops sadly lost his wings when they were shot off by pirates. This attack saw him sink to the bottom of the Swirling Sea before he was saved by the Jelly Dwarves. After they built him a diving suit so that he could explore the ocean, Dive-Clops was able to regain the sense of adventure he once had!

HAMMER SLAM BOWSER

5 Exclusive to the Wii U, this version of Mario's greatest enemy is also one of the game's finest toys. Using the Clown Cruiser to fly around the skies, Bowser is on the side of good here, trying to stop the evil Kaos.

SPYRO THE DRAGON

1 If it weren't for *Spyro The Dragon* there would be no *Skylanders*, so this list wouldn't be complete without the young purple dragon! With numerous different versions that can be transported into the game and a constant present throughout, he's arguably Skylands' biggest hero.

"SKYLANDERS SUPERCHARGERS IS THE ULTIMATE GAMING EXPERIENCE"

ALSO CHECK OUT ...

LEGO DIMENSIONS

LEGO Dimensions takes the brick-based toy and brings it to life in a video game. Furthermore, you can play with *The Simpsons*, *Doctor Who*, and lots more.

AMIIBO

Amiibo can be used throughout numerous Nintendo games as well as being cool toys. If you're a fan of Mario and co., this is definitely for you.

EXPLORE EVERY LEVEL

While you can finish the game without collectibles, getting these will help you on your journey. Search each level to find as many as you can.

GET RICH

In-game money is important when leveling up your Skylanders, so make sure you get a lot. Look out for treasure chests.

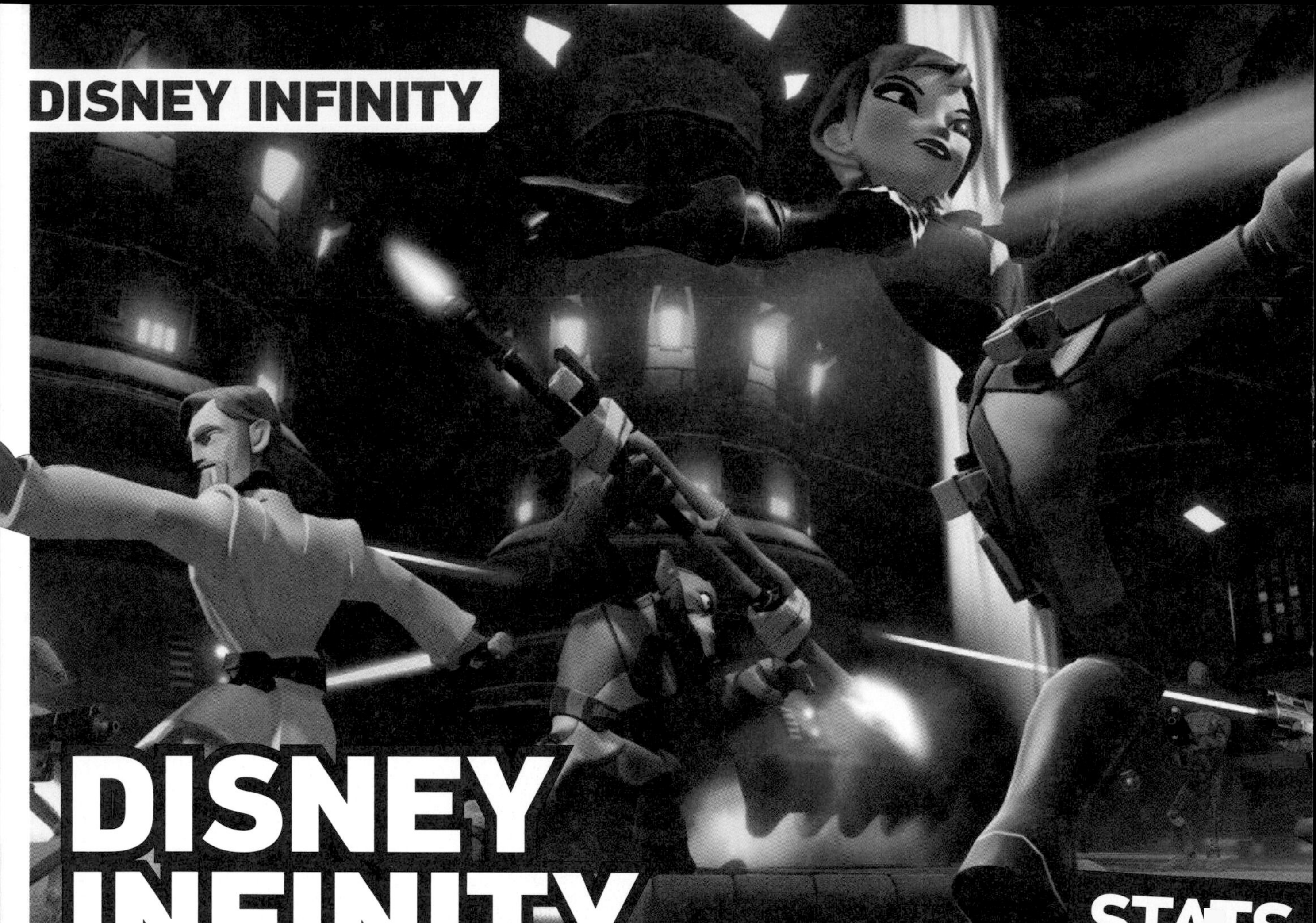

DISNEY INFINITY

TO INFINITY... AND BEYOND!

Imagine you had all your favorite Disney, Marvel, *Star Wars*, and Pixar toys in a big toy box, and could just get them out and play with them whenever you liked. Imagine if each toy had its own home, its own levels, its own set of abilities and funny remarks, its own history, its own unique way to play with. Awesome, right? That's *Disney Infinity*: the biggest toybox in gaming!

Play Sets are the stories set in specific universes where you can only use those characters— Elsa in *Frozen*'s world, for example—but the real fun comes from the Toy Box creator when you can mix and match anything you want, even designing new universes and games for others to enjoy. For those of you who want to become a games developer, this will teach you lots of cool skills that actual developers use.

STATS

The game went through over

100

art styles before setting on the current direction

More than

3 million

copies of the game have been sold

90 playable heroes and villains

The game is available on

nine platforms

Disney spent over

$100 million

making the game and all its base figures

DISNEY INFINITY

TOP 5 TOY BOXES

EPIC MICKEY

1 YouTuber DizExplorer03 based this level on the video game of the same name. In this toy box (read: custom level), you play as Mickey as he jumps, fights, and flips his way through everything forgotten in the Disney universe. You use the diffuser to defeat enemies, but in the original game, this was called "the magic brush."

DARTH VADER: RESURGENCE ON MUSTAFAR

2 This is a puzzle/platformer toy box made by KingOfTheTunas, and it's tough! The idea is that surviving generals of the rebellion have come together to take down Vader and his Empire, and it's your job to solve the puzzles, take these generals down, and make sure *nothing* stands in the way of your galactic domination.

RAPUNZEL'S BIRTHDAY TRADITION

3 This one was created by MightyGitis and here you have to engage your brain a little bit more. You need to mix paint to unlock new areas, and find lanterns to see them light up before you can progress. It's tough, and a good box to play through in single player!

DID YOU KNOW?

The Disney Interactive crew were inspired to make this game after seeing all the toys come to life at the very beginning of *Toy Story*!

SAM FLYNN: INTO THE GRID

4 Based on the film *Tron: Legacy*, you actually play through the journey Sam Flynn takes in the film (to find his father). You've got to fight your way through the arena *and* race on a bike to finish this level. It's presented in a genuinely cinematic way by SonicPhoto, too—which is very impressive!

OLAF: A FROZEN ADVENTURE

5 An absolute nightmare for some Disney fans, a dream come true for others, this adventure—created by Erdadi3—has "Let It Go" playing in the background constantly as you progress through the *Frozen* world, playing as an Olaf that's *just* been created by Princess Elsa. Save the mountain village and prevent the earthquakes!

DISNEY INFINITY

CADEN YURK

WHO?

Caden Yurk's channel is dedicated to family gaming—he creates gaming videos, unboxings, vlogs, and more with his wife and son. The channel focuses on toys-to-life games, and has a really friendly, approachable tone—it's ideal if you're after creative ways to play with your family.

WHY?

"I started *Disney Infinity* on its initial release," he explains. "Upon getting home and opening up the Starter Pack Box, I noticed how detailed the figures were. My love and passion for *Disney Infinity* grew and so did my character collection. My main draw to the game is the variety of characters to choose from, and the Disney Infinity Toy Box. I make daily YouTube videos for *Disney Infinity* because I love the game, the characters, the stories, and the franchise. The developers are wonderful, and listen to their fans, and that's what makes a good game great!"

THE EXPERT SAYS ...
JONATHAN GORDON
Editor, games™ magazine

I've been a fan of the art style of *Disney Infinity* from the beginning, but getting to see my favorite *Star Wars* characters recreated for the most recent update was a particular joy. I don't think Luke Skywalker, Darth Vader, or Boba Fett have ever looked better in a video game.

More importantly though, *Disney Infinity 3.0* greatly improved the Toy Box system. Creating your own levels and races in the game is both easier and packed with more features, so you can make some amazing play sets. I'm not sure I'll ever stop being delighted by seeing Jack Sparrow face off against Iron Man.

It's a real shame that there won't be any more play sets being added to the game to expand the world, but I have been really impressed with how good these titles have been.

TIPS & TRICKS

YOU CAN TRIPLE JUMP!?
Unlock the hover board in *The Incredibles* play set, hit the hoverboard button after a double-jump and—hey!—you get a third hike!

STACK POWER DISCS
If you open a pack of power discs and get repeats in there, don't worry! You can use the same disc *on top of* another to trigger a whole new effect!

EASY ACHIEVEMENT
This works on PlayStation or Xbox: connect a second controller and walk off the edge in any level—do it for a quick achievement!

DID YOU KNOW?

Most of the characters from Disney—including Elsa's Idina Menzel—came back to voice their characters in *Disney Infinity!*

TOP 4 CHARACTERS

LIGHTNING MCQUEEN

If you want to turn *Disney Infinity* into an easy-to-place, fun-to-win racing game, we recommend picking up the *Cars* play set: you can do cool flips and stunts with the cars' turbo boosters!

MR. INCREDIBLE

Disney Infinity might have the full roster of Marvel heroes at its disposal, but there's just a charm to Mr. Incredible that can't be overlooked (also his Super Ground Pound attack is super powerful!).

JACK SKELLINGTON

The Nightmare Before Christmas leading man is frightfully useful in the game—his ranged exploding pumpkin bombs are especially handy when dealing with tough enemies that need dispatching from a distance.

WRECK-IT RALPH

If you want to get a bit of retro-gaming action in your game, get a Wreck-It Ralph set—he's good at building *and* destroying, and his villain-turned-hero persona is always a refreshing change to those other do-gooders.

ALSO CHECK OUT ...

SUPER SMASH BROS. 4

If the idea of collecting figures and training them appeals to you, you'll *love* Nintendo's take on the craze and the most action-packed fighting game out there!

SKYLANDERS: SUPERCHARGERS

The original "toys-to-life" game started off the trend for a reason: it's fun, challenging, and the models are made to a high quality!

LEGO DIMENSIONS

All the best parts of *Disney Infinity*, but with all the other movies and characters you love— *Batman, The Simpsons, Back To The Future, Portal* ... all with that wonderful LEGO look.

"SUMO" ADVENTURE

The "Sumo" level is known for being tough, but if you've got *The Incredibles'* Violet or *Monsters, Inc's* Randy, just turn invisible and the enemies will get confused.

LEVEL UP QUICKLY

The *Toy Story, Monsters University,* and *Cars* play sets allow you to play side missions—just do this a few times and you'll max out figures in no time!

AMIIBO
STATUES OF PURE NINTENDO POWER

When *Skylanders* first came out, the idea of actually having real-life toys that you could play with both digitally and in real life was undeniably cool. Awesome little statues that could be used in a game? What's not to love? And once it proved a success, it was almost inevitable that others would eventually soon follow suit.

It was really exciting, then, when Nintendo announced its own statues that would use the same idea. Nintendo-made premium figurines are good enough as it is, but now your Luigi can fight in *Smash Bros* as well! Nintendo has released well over a hundred amiibo now and while some are more collectible than others, it's always fun to have a selection of the characters you like. Amiibo can now also unlock new levels and costumes in certain games, so it's worth picking up a few to make your games better!

STATS

400+ *Animal Crossing* amiibo cards to collect!

There are six Mario amiibo, if you count Dr. Mario

Super Smash Bros has the most amiibo at **55**

40+ games support amiibo

Over **21.1** million amiibo have been sold worldwide

TIPS & TRICKS

TRAIN YOUR AMIIBO
In *Super Smash Bros* you can train your amiibo to fight a specific way. Use your best character against it to make it tougher.

AMIIBO TACTICS
Fight your amiibo with a character you want to beat, and your amiibo will learn to defend against those attacks.

TRAINING BUDDY
Have your amiibo fight against other high level amiibo or level nine computer opponents so it can learn new defensive techniques.

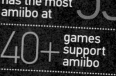

TOP 5 AMIIBO

YARN YOSHI

1 The most adorable amiibo in existence is this knitted yoshis from *Yoshi's Woolly World*, available in three colors. Very limited and slightly more expensive than normal amiibo, these yoshis are soft, huggable, and when you tap them into *Woolly World* you can play with your friends! And, if you like these cute amiibo, you should know there's also a giant version ...

"NINTENDO HAS RELEASED OVER A HUNDRED AMIIBO!"

GOLD MARIO

2 This limited golden version of everyone's plumber (unless you prefer Luigi, of course) is as rare as they come. Selling very briefly in America, it's the ultimate collectible amiibo and it looks fantastic as well. Use it in *Super Mario Maker* and you can get an extra-special gold costume to show off.

INKLING SQUID

3 Are you a kid or a squid? In *Splatoon* you can be both, and the excellent squid amiibo shows your Inkling mid-jump in one of the fast-paced matches you can find in said game. The squid amiibo looks cool and also unlocks a lot of challenging levels that give you awesome costumes at the end.

SHOVEL KNIGHT

4 *Shovel Knight* is an awesome (if tricky) platform game you can download to your 3DS and Wii U, however it's not made by Nintendo! It's very surprising that the game got an amiibo for it but it unlocks a cooperative mode and also looks really great on a shelf guarding your games.

PIXEL MARIO AMIIBO

5 To celebrate Mario turning 30 and the release of *Super Mario Maker*, this special 3D voxel Mario was created, coming in original or new colors. Tap it in to *Super Mario Maker* and a giant mushroom appears, allowing Mario to crash through walls.

DID YOU KNOW?

Amiibo can be used in *Mario Kart 8* to unlock secret costumes for the Mii racer—give it a try!

ALSO CHECK OUT ...

THE LEGEND OF ZELDA: TWILIGHT PRINCESS HD

The Wolf Link amiibo allows you to access a brand-new area.

MARIO & LUIGI: PAPER JAM!

Some *Mario* amiibo work in *Paper Jam* to give you special attack cards if the fights are getting too hard.

CODE NAME: S.T.E.A.M.

Scan in *Fire Emblem* amiibo to get them in-game. You'll need to re-scan each time they're defeated, though.

CUSTOM MOVES

Really confuse human opponents by giving your amiibo a custom move set; you can edit it in the options.

FEED YOUR AMIIBO

Feed your amiibo items to make it stronger, faster, and have greater defense. Now it'll be a real challenge to beat!

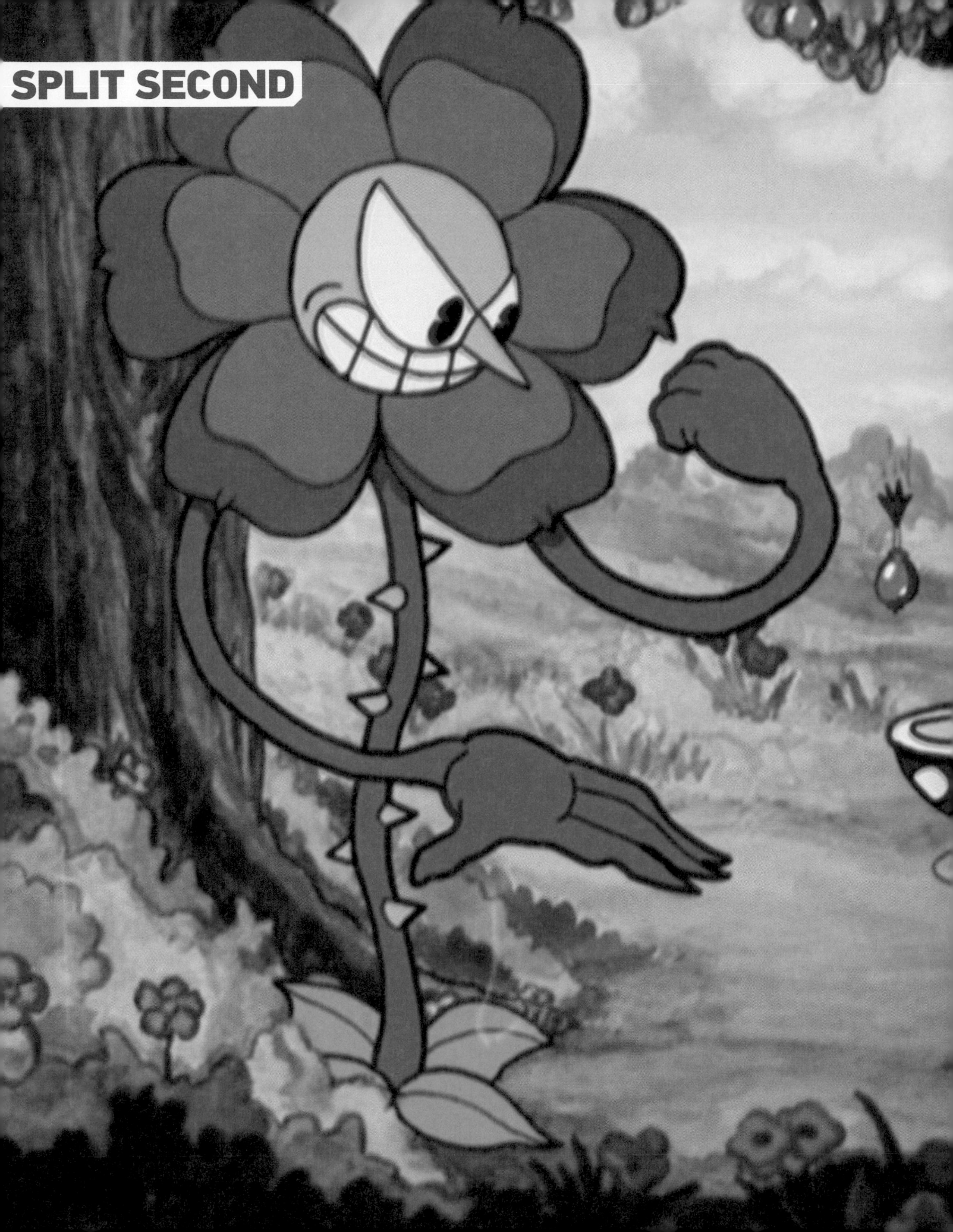

SPLIT SECOND
CUPHEAD
BATTLE THE BOSSES
·

A lot of games include *boss battles, but* Cuphead *is only* boss battles. *The whole game is a series of big fights against giant, screen-filling enemies —and they're all styled in a beautifully retro cartoon way. It's pretty, fast, and really tough: prepare for a proper fight.*

50 UNMISSABLE MOBILE GAMES

SHRED IT!
AVAILABLE ON iOS/Android/Windows

50 Take to the slopes and snowboard your way through this endless runner game, watching for hazards and trying to make it to the top of the leaderboards. Collect extra points to unlock cool power-ups that can help you move faster, jump higher, and perform amazing tricks in the air.

DOTS HERO
AVAILABLE ON Android

49 You'll need to conjure up an unstoppable army of heroes as you face off against hordes of the undead. Special attacks will stop their progress and upgrades like new armor and weapons will make you stronger than ever before. With over 100 levels to conquer, how far can you go?

SCRIBBLENAUTS UNLIMITED
AVAILABLE ON iOS/Android

48 This puzzler has a clever system that lets you create all kinds of objects to help you solve the puzzles. Type whatever you want into the in-game notepad and it'll appear for you to use, no matter how crazy it is!

FRANK THE DILLO

AVAILABLE ON iOS/Android/Windows

47 Mini golf has never been so fun! Watch out for obstacles and collect gems as you and Frank putt your way through tough levels. It even has some great platforming parts, where you'll need quick reflexes to master the toughest parts of the course.

MAGIC: PUZZLE QUEST
AVAILABLE ON iOS/Android/Windows

46 This game will test your brain as much as your skill. Build a deck of cards and challenge rivals in a match-3 game mode, piece together icons to banish your opponent's monsters from the battlefield and reduce their life to zero. You collect more cards as you play, making your deck stronger and keeping you fully engaged!

MONSTER AND COMMANDER
AVAILABLE ON iOS

45 Command your armies of monsters, ghouls and ghosts and defend the wall from oncoming hordes of enemies. There are plenty of amazing RPG elements to explore that help you add new weapons and armor to your army. Plus, you can connect with your friends to create the ultimate monster army.

PRUNE
AVAILABLE ON iOS/Android/Windows

44 Okay, so growing a tree may not seem like fun, but trust us, *Prune* proves to be an experience like nothing else out there. Swipe to cut off branches, guiding your tree into the sunlight, while avoiding the dangers of the world around you. There's a hidden story that you'll unlock as you play.

50 UNMISSABLE MOBILE GAMES

THE PRINCE BILLY BOB
AVAILABLE ON iOS/Android

43 Billy Bob wants to be a hero—and he can be if you help him get through the deep and dark dungeon he's found. What makes this game brilliant is that there are *so* many weapons and items available to upgrade Billy Bob's skills and to banish the huge dragons you'll encounter. Phew!

INTO THE DIM
AVAILABLE ON iOS

41 If you love working out puzzles and exploring mythical worlds, then you must download *Into the Dim* right now. There are loads of dungeons to explore, mysteries to try and solve, and pesky enemies that need to be defeated in order to uncover the truth behind your hometown's deadly secrets.

DID YOU KNOW?
Nope, there isn't something wrong with your screen; *Into the Dim* is played completely in black and white!

DOCKIT ROCKET
AVAILABLE ON iOS

42 There are seven ships to try in *Dockit Rocket*, and each one has their own set of weapons and special abilities that can help you blast through the levels. Make sure you collect all the power-ups that appear as you play to help improve your ship in different ways, and be prepared for some seriously tough missions as you progress through the game.

PAC-MAN 256
AVAILABLE ON iOS/Android

39 Imagine PAC-MAN, but with lasers ... exciting, right? Well, *PAC-MAN 256* brings back the retro coin gobbler with a host of weapons in tow. Collect as many coins as possible, before using your weapons to fight back against the ghouls that want to capture you once you've got a power pellet.

TOON CLASH CHESS
[AVAILABLE ON] Android/Windows

40 Chess isn't just a boring board game that your grandparents might play, it's actually really fun! Hundreds of cool characters bring the chess pieces to life, and there are various boards and worlds you can play within. Don't know the rules? No worries, the game has a helpful tutorial for you to follow and get you up to speed.

POKÉMON SHUFFLE MOBILE
AVAILABLE ON iOS/Android

38 More of a puzzle game than your typical *Pokémon* adventure, this is just as much fun. Battle wild Pokémon by lining up Pokémon heads and clearing your board before your foe. It gets tough as you progress, but you'll be able to capture your favorite Pokémon and level them up!

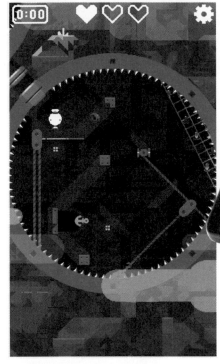

BENEATH THE LIGHTHOUSE
AVAILABLE ON iOS/Android

37 Can you reunite a boy with his missing grandpa? Venture beneath his lighthouse to explore a hidden world filled with puzzles and mysteries waiting to be solved. Stick with it, and you'll be rewarded with one of the best mobile game endings we've ever played through.

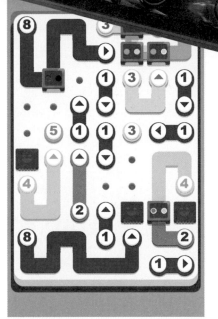

SHOOTY SKIES
AVAILABLE ON iOS/Android

35 Enter the crazy world of *Shooty Skies* and soar like an eagle as you try and dodge colorful enemies that want to halt your progress. Find epic loot crates as you weave through the sky to upgrade parts of your airplane and create the ultimate flying machine.

LITTLE BROKEN ROBOTS
AVAILABLE ON iOS/Windows

34 The wires of all these robots have been scrambled, and it's your task to piece them back together again. You can fix each robot by tapping on a number and dragging the wire to the correct dot ... it sounds simple, but the later levels will tie your brain in knots! One for budding scientists and inventors.

MARVEL FUTURE FIGHT
AVAILABLE ON iOS/Android/ Windows

36 Create your squad of awesome Marvel superheroes and fight the supervillains that threaten the world. The action is fast, so get ready to mash onscreen buttons to defeat foes and tackle gigantic bosses head-on at the end of each level.

BATTLETIME
AVAILABLE ON iOS/Android

33 This thrilling action game tasks you with choosing your General, raising an army, and capturing your enemies' castles. Each General brings their own special skill to the table, with some great at killing enemy soldiers, while others find hidden power-ups dotted around the map. A fantastic mix of skill and speed!

DREII
AVAILABLE ON iOS/Android

32 In *Dreii* your mission is simple; build a massive tower and try to keep it upright for as long as possible. To stop you building higher there are thunderstorms, explosions, and other annoying things that you need to stop to keep your tower intact. Play with friends to see who can build the biggest tower!

TRAFFIC RIDER
AVAILABLE ON iOS/Android

31 If you feel the need for speed, then you'll want to get behind the wheels of a motorbike in *Traffic Rider*. Play through various missions by overtaking traffic and keeping a close eye on other drivers around you. With over 40 missions, there's a lot of racing to do. On your marks, get set ...

TWO DOTS
AVAILABLE ON iOS/Android/Windows

29 With well over 550 levels to complete (and more being added all the time through free updates), *Two Dots* is probably the biggest puzzle game out there. The idea is simple—connect dots of the same color to remove them and meet your mission quota—but with different blocks, dot types, and other mechanics standing in your way, it's more complex than it looks at first!

BLADE: SWORD OF ELYSION
AVAILABLE ON iOS/Android

30 *Blade: Sword of Elysion* is an epic action RPG that puts you in charge of a band of heroes whose only goal is to banish all evil forces. Slash your way through countless dungeons and enemies to reach your goals, or venture online and take on other players to find out who is the ultimate hero.

DID YOU KNOW?
Any character in *Crashlands* can become your sidekick. Hatch any egg and grow your own hideous bundle of joy.

CRASHLANDS
AVAILABLE ON iOS/Android/ Windows

28 Become Flux Dabes, a space trucker whose latest load of goodies has been stolen by an alien menace. To track him down you'll need to create weapons and tools from various items you stumble across, and even build your own series of bases for any characters who join you on your quest.

A GOOD SNOWMAN
AVAILABLE ON iOS/Android

26 If we've learned anything from this game, it is that building a snowman is harder than you might think. Puzzles are plentiful, as you try and build the perfect snowman by rolling up layers of snow until they stack on top of one another. Watch out, though—run out of snow and you'll need to start again!

JETPACK FIGHTER
AVAILABLE ON iOS

23

One of the things that make *Jetpack Fighter* so fun to play is how simple it is to control. All you need to do is swipe the screen at the correct moment to speed past enemy robots, smash down walls, and face-off against bosses as you glide through Mega City with your jetpack.

GOPOGO
AVAILABLE ON iOS/Android

27 In a grim future where using a pogo stick has been made illegal, you play as a gang of misfits who are fighting back and showing what the mighty stick can do. Pogo over hazards, buildings, and the police in increasingly hard levels that will put your reflexes to the ultimate test.

AIRATTACK 2
AVAILABLE ON iOS

24 With fully destructible levels to blast through, *AirAttack 2* is one of the most fun (and best-looking) shoot-em-ups we've ever played. Deck your plane out with flamethrowers, bombs, and more as you tackle enemy planes, conquer powerful tanks, and battle your friends in a high score challenge.

AGE OF WUSHU DYNASTY
AVAILABLE ON iOS/Android

25 Martial arts are cool, right? Well, in *Age of Wushu* you'll learn exactly how cool. The game is played solely online, meaning you can put your karate or kung fu skills to the test against players all around the world. Climb up the leaderboard to unlock new moves and skills.

SKY CHASERS
AVAILABLE ON iOS/Android

22 Your imagination, and the crazy controls, are the only limits that you'll face in *Sky Chasers*. Players control Max and his magic cardboard box through a series of levels, attempting to grab keys and coins to serenely progress. Max wants to become the world's best Sky Chaser—can you help him?

GNOMIUM
AVAILABLE ON iOS

21 This clever word game plays like a fast-paced arcade game, where you mine coins and gems in a magical letter grid in the sky. Switch tiles around to make words and clear the grid completely before the timer runs out. Spend your hard-earned coins on booster items to help you get further.

OCTODAD: DADLIEST CATCH
AVAILABLE ON iOS/Android

20 Somehow Octodad (an octopus) has managed to convince his family that he's actually human, and he wants it to stay that way. You need to use clever tactics to master everyday human tasks and keep his nautical secret from his wife and kids through 20 levels of fun.

GODS OF OLYMPUS
AVAILABLE ON iOS

19 Command the *Gods of Olympus* as they battle evil forces through ancient Greece. Build an army of trusted soldiers to battle the enemy, take over cities, and use each God's special powers to get the upper hand on the battlefield. Check out the co-op mode to play the game with a friend.

QUICKBOY
AVAILABLE ON iOS/Android

18 You play as the *Quickboy* squad, a group of guys and girls who like to deliver mail—fast. Help them deliver their mail by smashing your way through zombie-filled cities and using agility to dodge oncoming enemies. Make sure that you use the drones feature to clear more advanced obstacles.

CANDY CRUSH JELLY SAGA
AVAILABLE ON iOS/Android/Windows

17 We hate to admit it, but we absolutely loved the original *Candy Crush* game. Actually, we're not that ashamed at all. It was great! The *Jelly Saga* is pretty much the same as the original, but there are more levels than ever before, an array of new boosters available and fun boss battles against the evil Jelly Queen. If it's half as addictive as the original, you're in for a real treat. Bring it on, Jelly Queen!

SWING
AVAILABLE ON iOS/Android

16 Swinging from platform to platform is easy, right? Well, not exactly. Getting from platform to platform in *Swing* requires you to measure out your rope and attempt to land perfectly on the next platform to continue on your merry way. There's a lot of trial and error, but do your best to set a high score.

DUNGELOT
AVAILABLE ON iOS/Android

15 How fast can you escape from a dungeon? *Dungelot* wants to put you to the test. Flip over tiles that can reveal amazing treasure to help you on your journey, or deadly monsters who want to stop you. The quicker you escape, the better your rewards!

STAR WARS: GALAXY OF HEROES
AVAILABLE ON iOS/Android

14 *Star Wars* excitement is at fever pitch as new movies keep coming, and now you can live your fantasy of becoming a Jedi with *Galaxy of Heroes*. There's a campaign for both the light and dark side of the Force, and if you complete both, you'll unlock some classic characters.

NEED FOR SPEED NO LIMITS
AVAILABLE ON iOS/Android

13 If you've never played any of the classic *Need for Speed* titles, then you're missing out! *Need for Speed No Limits* is the first mobile port of the world's greatest driving series, and it brings with it all the excitement of racing, drifting, and customizing some of the coolest cars out there to drive. There are around 1,000 races for you to take part in, but to access the later ones you need to be driving with some serious style.

DID YOU KNOW?
There are over 2.5 million possible custom combos to make a car your own in *Need For Speed*. That's a lot of options!

NAMASTE SPACE BUFFALO
AVAILABLE ON iOS/Android

12 For something weird and wacky, you can't look past *Namaste Space Buffalo*. Take control of the mythical flock of Spuffalos, who are trying to reach the end of the galaxy. To do so, players need expert timing to dodge obstacles and collect power-ups to transform their Spuffalo herd.

THE INCORRUPTIBLES
AVAILABLE ON iOS/Android

11 In this tactical title, you must save your homeland by building your own empire of heroes to fight off the evil Corrupted. To do this, you'll need to craft recipes to improve the abilities of your army, and use clever tactics on the battlefield to outwit your enemies and claim victory.

CIRCA INFINITY
AVAILABLE ON iOS/Android

10 Be warned, if you get dizzy easy, then stay well clear of *Circa Infinity*. This confusing platformer requires you to run around the outside of a circle, trying to figure out the best way to get to the center. Each time you reach the center, a new circle will appear. Your head will be spinning!

LOST IN HARMONY
AVAILABLE ON iOS/Android

9 Music-based games are fairly uncommon, but *Lost in Harmony* is a rare hit. Tap along to the music and keep the rhythm to guide Kaito and Aya around their city, dodging vehicles as you go. You can even add your own music to change up the game whenever you like.

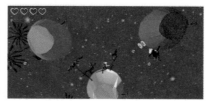

MOMOKA
AVAILABLE ON iOS

7 Control Momoka as she flies around the solar system in this brilliant platforming adventure. Blast your way past obstacles and deadly traps to reach the end of the level, but don't forget to look for hidden items to give Momoka new powers.

CUT THE ROPE MAGIC
AVAILABLE ON iOS/Android

6 Om Nom is back to recover more stolen candy, in his best adventure yet. What makes this version so great is that you can now transform Om Nom into magical creatures that help to solve some of the more difficult puzzles. Even *Cut The Rope* veterans will struggle with this!

THE DEER GOD
AVAILABLE ON iOS/Android/Windows

8 *The Deer God* is a gorgeous 3D art adventure that's all about survival and learning about nature. The levels are completely different each time you play, although the puzzles you find are always the same. Dedicated players might even unearth some of the cool secrets hidden away, such as a train you can ride or hidden bosses to be fought!

BADLAND 2
AVAILABLE ON iOS

5 As you can guess, Badland isn't a nice place to live in; so much so that our hero is looking to escape for good. Roll, fly, and guide him through dangerous levels packed with an endless number of dangers that can stop you in your tracks. Can you escape the Badlands?

LARA CROFT GO
AVAILABLE ON iOS/Android/Windows

4 Lara Croft is back for another mobile adventure, and what an adventure it is! Explore the ruins of an ancient tribe and uncover the myth of the Queen of Venom in this iconic brain-testing puzzler.

PLEASE, DON'T TOUCH ANYTHING
AVAILABLE ON iOS/Android

3 When asked not to push the big red button, you'd obviously press it, right? Well that's the question asked in this game; if you don't follow the rules, you could blow up the world. Any slip up as you follow instructions could lead to failure, so be careful and do as you're told!

RAYMAN ADVENTURES
AVAILABLE ON iOS/Android/Windows

2 Embark on a quest with Rayman to jump, swim, and punch his way through mythical worlds and rescue the Incrediballs—the special eggs that bind the world together. Each Incrediball you unlock will give Rayman a new ability to use to overcome obstacles and enemies; ranging from minotaurs, bandits, and even monkeys! With so many worlds to explore and secret items to discover, *Rayman Adventures* is a story you really can't miss.

THE EXPERT SAYS ...
LUKE WHITTAKER
Co-founder of State of Play Games (Lumino City)

I had the most fun I've ever had working on a game with *Lumino City*, and maybe the most stress, too. We had to develop prototypes before going ahead and building "cardboard sketches" of the city and characters from grey cardboard and masking tape.

I think people have really connected with the world we created. It's all handcrafted and because of this, you can really connect with the artists behind it. But by itself that wouldn't be enough; perhaps, like many games, it's the blend of design, music, and story that work alongside the environment to create a world people really want to explore and interact with.

When you create something you always hope someone else will like it, but it's always a surprise when accolades come from places you couldn't guarantee interest from. Winning a BAFTA was definitely the highlight of our year for this reason.

LUMINO CITY
AVAILABLE ON iOS

1 Not only is *Lumino City* one of the best-looking mobile games *ever* (every level was hand-made and photographed!), it also has the best story of any mobile game we've ever played. You play as Lume, who is desperate to uncover who has kidnapped her beloved grandpa, and you must go on an epic journey to find out the truth. There's a bunch of people to meet and puzzles to solve, and as you get deeper into the story, you'll find hidden sections. It's not a rollercoaster ride of action but it's emotional, it's unique, and it's brilliant.

SCORE 0

S.D. HIGH SCHOOL

17,9

. . . + Heelflip + Man
+ Manual + Tailg
+ No Comply + Pop Shov

CAPTURE THIS!

TONY HAWK'S PRO SKATER 5

SMASH OUT A MONSTER COMBO

The ultimate test of skill in any *Tony Hawk* game isn't completing the objectives, it's linking together a dizzying array of moves as you chase the highest combo possible. We managed a 3.1 million combo on the School III level—can you beat that?

43

Leap of Faith! + Judo
Revert + Manual
Manual + Varial Heelflip

MOST EVIL BOSSES

DID YOU KNOW?

Angry Birds has been downloaded over 2 billion times and around 200 million people are playing it a month.

BOWSER
Mario & Luigi: Paper Jam Bros.

WHY: Bowser is certainly one of the most famous evil-doers, if not the brightest. Causing havoc since 1985, the King Of The Koopas was still up to no good in the 2016 3DS game *Mario & Luigi: Paper Jam Bros*. Intent on capturing Princess Peach for good, Bowser's only other wish is to vanquish Mario.

DARTH VADER
Star Wars Battlefront

WHY: Darth Vader is as terrifying in the new *Star Wars Battlefront* as he was in the *Star Wars* movies. As ever, he's focused on wiping out the Rebels and letting The Empire reign supreme. The difference this time, however, is that you can choose to actually play as him!

EMPEROR KAOS
Skylanders: SuperChargers

WHY: Emperor Kaos has proven his credentials evil time and time again throughout the *Skylanders* series, including in *SuperChargers*. Unleashing his most evil weapon yet—The Doomstation Of Ultimate Doomstruction—he wants to collapse the Skylands completely!

THE MOON
The Legend Of Zelda: Majora's Mask 3DS

WHY: It's odd to think of The Moon as good or evil—it's just The Moon. In *The Legend Of Zelda: Majora's Mask 3DS*, The Moon decides it wants to crush the world in three days, and you've got to work against the clock to save humanity. But if anyone can save the world, it's Link.

6 WAYS TO DEFEAT ANY BOSS

1 LEARN THE PATTERNS

Most bosses you come up against will have an attack pattern you can learn. Pay attention to what they do before an attack, so you can make your own moves.

2 DON'T STRESS YOURSELF OUT

Everyone gets stuck on a boss sometimes. The key is to give yourself a break and chill out for a bit; you're more likely to notice something useful with a rested brain.

3 CHANGE THE DIFFICULTY

If you're genuinely stuck and finding it impossible to slay a boss, don't let pride get in the way. If you can, just switch the difficulty level to easy.

4 GET LOADS OF HEALTH

Make sure whenever you go to an area where you're expecting to find a boss that you're loaded up with health potions or whatever the game uses to heal.

5 ASK YOUR FRIENDS

Friends can be a great resource for boss fighting tips! Or if you're the right age, you might find some good advice on social media like YouTube.

6 DON'T STOP MOVING

No matter what challenge you face, if you stay on your toes they're going to struggle to inflict any damage. So stay quick, stay safe, and be victorious!

THE GREEN GOBLIN Disney Infinity 3.0

WHY: Spider-Man and The Green Goblin have been enemies for years, so it's no surprise to learn that the two tangle yet again in *Disney Infinity 3.0*. With The Green Goblin desperate to take over the world and have absolute power, you can turn the tables here and actually take charge of him.

THE JOKER LEGO Batman 3: Beyond Gotham

WHY: The Joker and Batman are destined to battle for all time. Without a doubt one of the most evil bosses in any game, The Joker sets out to destroy the Dark Knight in *LEGO Batman 3* so he can let his madness reign Bat-free. Thankfully there's a whole host of heroes ready to stop him.

M. BISON Street Fighter V

WHY: Supported by his corrupt criminal organization known as Shadaloo, and helped by *Street Fighter* characters Vega and Sagat, M. Bison wants to rule the world and is willing to do whatever is necessary to make that happen. This is why he enters the Street Fighter tournament, and this is why it's so important to ensure he doesn't win.

MEGATRON Transformers: Devastation

WHY: It's no surprise that you're up against Megatron for the final showdown in *Transformers: Devastation*. What is a surprise is how difficult it is to triumph. Megatron mixes up close-range assaults with distant attacks and in the meantime, the ground is erupting with flames around you.

THE EXPERT SAYS ...
LUKE WILLIAMS
Designer of I Am Bread and Surgeon Simulator

"The most evil boss that I know of is Mizar from 1999's *Jet Force Gemini* on the N64. He enslaved little teddy bear people called Tribals with his army of modified drone ants and made them mine for him. Not only that, but he was the hardest boss that I ever had to beat. It became doable due to the fact that player two could just control a little robot that followed the main character, so I spent the time just trying not to get hit while my brother shot him every chance that he had! Even listening to the boss music now gives me flashbacks of the hours and hours of having Mizar beat me! That might be why my games are so hard now..."

THE PIGS Angry Birds 2

WHY: You'd be pretty mad if someone took your stuff, right? This is why the angry birds are so upset and why the Pigs—who are responsible for the theft—have to be considered the purest of all evil. By taking the birds' eggs, the Pigs have basically tried to steal their children! Time for the birds to take their revenge.

"THE JOKER AND BATMAN ARE DESTINED TO BATTLE FOR ALL TIME"

STATS

12 million
the highest number of subscribers

13 different playable races

2 factions
Horde or Alliance

14 crafting professions to choose from

The game is 10 years old

YOUR NEW LIFE AWAITS

WORLD OF WARCRAFT

There is just so much to do in the *World of Warcraft*. You'll get to create a character of your own design, picking from different types of characters and classes. You might be a strong, powerful warrior, a sneaky rogue, or a mage capable of flinging fireballs at foes. Also, as you explore the realm of Azeroth, you'll see new areas, defeat a vast range of beasts and baddies, and gradually level-up your character to make them more and more powerful. What's especially cool is that you can team up with your friends to take on tough challenges together, and maybe even defeat some of the legendary bosses in the game! There isn't just fighting, either, since you can collect dozens of pets, craft interesting new items, and take part in fun mini-games throughout the world.

TIME LINE

WORLD OF WARCRAFT (2004)
World of Warcraft makes its debut and millions of people start playing for the first time.

THE BURNING CRUSADE (2007)
The first expansion pack for the game is released, letting players explore the space-like environment of Outland.

WRATH OF THE LICH KING (2008)
The third expansion pack adds the icy landscape of Northrend as the Horde and Alliance try to defeat the Lich King.

TOP 5 ZONES

STORMWIND

1 As the capital of the Alliance faction, it's no surprise Stormwind is so popular. It has everything you might need, but the castle walls and classic medieval buildings make it a nice environment to visit. You'll find players of every class visiting this huge city as they ride around on horses, elephants, and even dragons!

DID YOU KNOW?
World of Warcraft is based on the *Warcraft* series, strategy games about building a base and an army.

ORGRIMMAR

2 The main city for the Horde faction couldn't be any more different from Stormwind. Despite being set in what should be desolate rocky mountains, it's packed with players. It's probably the busiest place in the whole *World of Warcraft*, so you're bound to meet lots of players.

GRIZZLY HILLS

3 After marching through the frozen wastes of the north, you'll come to Grizzly Hills. Full of natural wonders, this woodland area is especially nice due to the music that plays.

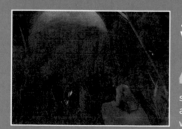

SHADOWMOON VALLEY

4 In Draenor there's an area called Shadowmoon Valley where it's always night. That might sound scary, but it's lit by the moon and stars, and filled with animals and huge trees with blue leaves. It's really quite magical!

HELLFIRE PENINSULA

5 The Dark Portal is an intimidating structure, teleporting you away to another realm, Hellfire Peninsula—a scary place with red rock and devilish monsters, but also exciting to explore.

"MEET OTHER PEOPLE AND TAKE ON TOUGH CHALLENGES WITH THEM"

CATACLYSM (2010)
This expansion pack is huge–not only because of the new areas it introduces, but because a destructive force changes the entire world!

MISTS OF PANDARIA (2012)
The fifth pack adds the Pandaren, a race of panda-like warriors that are as strong as they are wise.

ALSO CHECK OUT ...

STAR WARS: THE OLD REPUBLIC
It's another online-only game. You can explore the many planets of the *Star Wars* universe.

TROVE
Mixing the online gameplay of *World of Warcraft* with the blocky graphics of *Minecraft*, *Trove* has cool classes like Neon Ninja and Candy Barbarian.

STATS

The Zelda series is now **30** years old

There are 3 alternate timelines in Zelda

13 incarnations of Link in the main story

Ocarina of Time can be beaten in **20 mins**

There are over 2 million Let's Plays of Zelda games on YouTube

THE LEGEND OF ZELDA

TALES OF COURAGE, WISDOM, AND POWER

This classic game series, inspired by creator Shigeru Miyamoto's childhood exploration of woods and caves, chronicles the events of heroes called Link throughout the ages. Making use of magic, swords, and bombs in the shape of mice, these heroes need to stop the evil Ganondorf's plans and make sure the current Princess Zelda can seal him away—maybe one time for good.

The Legend of Zelda is known for its focus on exploration, solving puzzles, and finding amazing new weapons to help rid Hyrule of nasty monsters and moblins. So grab your pointy green hat, find a fairy to help you out, and sit down for an epic adventure across a sea, time, seasons, and through the sky.

TIME LINE

FOUNDING A LEGACY
SKYWARD SWORD
After saving Hyrule, Zelda and Link are cursed, ensuring their descendents will have to fight against this evil forever.

A BROKEN TIMELINE
OCARINA OF TIME
The wicked thief king Ganondorf attempts to claim the Triforce to conquer Hyrule, but is stopped by Link.

TROUBLED WATERS
THE WIND WAKER
Although defeated by the Hero of Time, Ganondorf is resurrected. The Kingdom of Hyrule is flooded to try to stop him.

TOP 5 ITEMS

HAMMER

1 Appearing in many *Zelda* games, such as *A Link Between Worlds* and *Phantom Hourglass*, these powerful weapons squash enemies flat. The best hammer is *Ocarina Of Time*'s Megaton Hammer, used for smashing Ganon's tail during the climactic battle atop his castle. Be careful, though—Link is vulnerable to attack as he picks it up.

GORON MASK

3 Inhabited by the spirit of the proud Goron warrior Darmani, Link uses this in *Majora's Mask* to gain enormous strength and the ability to roll around at great speeds. He also gains a set of amazing drums that can put even the most upset Goron children to sleep.

DID YOU KNOW?

The "legend of Zelda" is that all princesses of Hyrule must be named Zelda after one Zelda is cursed to sleep for eternity.

HOOKSHOT

2 A multi-purpose tool used primarily to traverse dungeons and obstacles in entries like *The Wind Waker* and *Majora's Mask*, the hook shot can also kill weak enemies out of reach of your swings, or bring stronger ones to you to meet the pointy end of your sword.

SPIRIT TRAIN

4 Link's ancient locomotive from *Spirit Tracks* is the finest and most luxurious transportation Link can obtain. Able to steam through forests, volcanoes, and even underwater, it's a durable machine with a cannon attached just in case you try and bother it. Oh, and it also has a steam whistle.

DID YOU KNOW?

Not every *Zelda* game has a different Link; *A Link to the Past*, *Oracle of Ages*, *Oracle of Seasons*, and *Link's Awakening* all star the same hero.

BOMBCHU

5 An uncommon item in the series that seems to have a mind of its own, the bombchu will race away from Link and climb any manner of obstacles ... usually leading back to Link for an explosive headbutt. Be careful of the real versions that run toward you with nothing to lose in *Majora's Mask*.

A DARK DESTINY
A LINK TO THE PAST
In this timeline—where the Hero of Time is defeated—Ganon is finally vanquished by the Seven Sages.

A BRIGHT NEW DAY
TWILIGHT PRINCESS
The Hero of Time is sent back in time to warn Zelda of an evil plot; the bad wizard Zant brings Twilight to Hyrule.

THE SWORDS OF ZELDA

© Cosplay.co.uk

LITTLEGEEKY

WHO?

Littlegeeky is a UK cosplayer who is also a videographer—she makes awesome cosplay videos at conventions and expos. It was her love of *Zelda* that introduced her to cosplay; searching for information on *Twilight Princess*, she came across people dressed as Link. Since then, she herself has done a Link cosplay.

WHY?

Littlegeeky was introduced to *Zelda* on the SNES, specifically *A Link to the Past*. She spent hours looking through the instruction manual to get every last drop out of the game. She's been playing games from the series ever since, as well as attending concerts of the music and creating a sizeable collection of *Zelda* merchandise.

FIERCE DEITY SWORD

When Link wears the Fierce Deity mask he wields a powerful blade, able to focus his magical power into a disc of light and release it during an attack.

GODDESS SWORD

Crafted by the goddess Hylia, the Goddess Sword is inhabited by the spirit known as Fi, who guides Link on his path to be hero. Later, Link tempers it into the Master Sword itself.

THE LEGEND OF ZELDA

RAZOR SWORD

The coolest looking sword in all of Termina is forged from your Kokiri Sword to make it twice as powerful. Although, after 100 swings, it turns back to normal.

DID YOU KNOW?

Three *Zelda* games were made for the ill-fated CDi console but it's not worth tracking these rare games down—they're all terrible!

MASTER SWORD

The Blade of Evil's Bane, the Master Sword is a legendary sword used to slay and seal away the greatest of evils to attack Hyrule before being laid to rest.

"THE MASTER SWORD IS LEGENDARY"

THE EXPERT SAYS ...
SUPERMCGAMER

Organizer of Zeldathon, a charity marathon of the Zelda game series that has raised over $250,000

The Legend of Zelda is a series that has grown with me. This series has followed me through every part of my life, both in happy and sad times. The games have made me understand what it means to be a hero, and see the world in a different light. It is thanks to *Zelda* that I make videos online and live in my own house right now. It is thanks to *Zelda* that my friends and I have been able to change the world and help hundreds of people worldwide. *Zelda* is more than a game; it helped me through tough times, and was there to laugh with me in the good. *The Legend of Zelda* is a friend, always there to welcome you back into the Kingdom of Hyrule, and make you feel like the hero you always wanted to be.

ALSO CHECK OUT ...

FINAL FANTASY XV
A huge story and quest, although in this game you have a horse instead of a car and there are way fewer boomerang puzzles to figure out.

OKAMIDEN
With its wonderful mix of fantasy, magic, and exploration, *Okamiden*'s creator has stated his game was inspired by *The Legend of Zelda*.

EASIEST GAMES

ALL LEGO GAMES

WHY: Fun as they are, these pretty much always follow the exact same template and it's impossible to actually die. Aim for Red Blocks (which unlock cheats and multipliers) as soon as possible to help speed the process along, and you should be able to hit 100 percent in no time.

POKÉMON

WHY: Sure, there's a lot of depth and complexity to *Pokémon* battling, but you can pretty much just ignore it if you'd rather. By grinding against strong trainers for ages (you only lose cash if you lose, so spend it all first!), you can write off strategy altogether and just bang your head against trainers until you win!

RATCHET & CLANK

WHY: There are usually one or two relatively tricky sections in these cute platform shooters but at the same time, there are also usually a couple of weapons that make even these trivial. Smash everything, purchase and upgrade all your gear, and nothing will be able to stand in your way.

MAKING HARD GAMES LOOK EASY

1 DARK SOULS
Some people spend months just trying to finish the game, but speed-runners have figured out how to use glitches to skip huge areas and bypass difficult fights, getting to the end credits in just 20 minutes!

2 GUITAR HERO
DragonForce's gruelling epic *Through the Fire and Flames* is one of the hardest songs in history. Few players have managed to hit all 3,722 notes flawlessly.

3 SUPER MARIO WORLD
By using shortcuts and accessing Star World early, you can actually beat Bowser in under *ten minutes*!

4 POKÉMON
Not up for hundreds of hours of training to beat the Elite Four? Then just don't bother! Glitches in several of the games make it possible to beat them in under five minutes, but they're *really* technical...

5 DESTINY
Once upon a time, the Flawless Raider Trophy was a symbol your team was among the best. After The Taken King, though, Guardians are so powerful that it's actually possible to beat Crota and get this alone!

6 PORTAL
Given that we spent *hours* over some puzzles, it blew our minds that record times come in under 20 minutes—without glitches! Using glitches, players have broken the ten-minute barrier!

DID YOU KNOW?

Avatar: The Burning Earth is the quickest 1,000G completion ever: under a minute! Achievements are earned in the tutorial.

THE EXPERT SAYS ...
LUKE ALBIGÉS
Editor, Play Magazine

Although a look at the insanely demanding Trophy lists might suggest otherwise, Omega Force's *Warriors* games – from *Dynasty Warriors*, which started it all, to themed spin-offs like the *Zelda*-themed *Hyrule Warriors* and *One Piece: Pirate Warriors* – are among the simplest games I've ever played. Although every character has loads of different moves and unique skills available, you'll quickly find the one or two that do everything you need, and just mashing one button is usually enough to see off entire armies of onrushing enemies. They're great fun, allowing you to just turn off your brain and enjoy the action with just a few button presses. But once you start earning new weapons and more powerful moves, don't expect any kind of challenge!

TEARAWAY UNFOLDED

WHY: The *LittleBigPlanet* team only seems to make adorable games and *Tearaway*, while never exactly challenging, is worth playing just to enjoy its lavish papercraft world. If you want the Platinum trophy, there's a fair bit of back-tracking and clearing up to do, but otherwise, just enjoy the colorful and entertaining ride.

"BY GRINDING AGAINST TRAINERS YOU CAN WRITE OFF STRATEGY ALTOGETHER"

MOST TELLTALE GAMES

WHY: *Minecraft: Story Mode* is dead easy. You can't really fail—messing up a QTE puts you back where you started and the games are more about what you do along the way than actually getting there...

KIRBY GAMES

WHY: Everyone's second favorite floaty *Smash* character (behind Jigglypuff, obviously!) comes from games that are notoriously easy. The Game Boy original can be finished in under an hour by flying over most of it, and newer games like *Epic Yarn* are rarely much more of a challenge.

VIVA PINATA

WHY: Rare's gardening games are brilliant for winding down as there's no fail state. Even on the off chance your garden gets messed up or your best animals move away, just chill and have fun with all of the crazy critters that will visit your garden!

SKYLANDERS

WHY: If you're starting from scratch then sure, the *Skylanders* games might take a little more work. But if you've already got a cupboard full of powered-up toys, they're usually incredibly easy. Should one hero fall, simply replace them on the portal with another healthy maxed-out character and you can basically retry any challenge until you run out of toys.

TOP 10 FREE-TO-PLAY GAMES

HEARTHSTONE: HEROES OF WARCRAFT

WHY: While *Hearthstone* might not look like the most exciting game to play, it's actually really addictive—there's a lot of strategy involved here. That's where the fun comes from and when you've built a deck of cards that is unbeatable you can feel so powerful! It's definitely one to put some practice into.

HUSTLE KINGS

WHY: Learning the skills (and science) to become good at pool is really rewarding, especially since it's a game you usually play against other people. Put enough time into *Hustle Kings* and you'll soon find yourself pulling off some really tricky and impressive shots.

WORLD OF TANKS

WHY: *World Of Tanks* is easily one of the most popular free-to-play games out there for gamers, and for good reason. You're able to ride around in huge tanks, firing explosive shells at other players as you battle across towns and villages.

WHEN "FREE" DOESN'T MEAN FREE

1 BUYING CONTENT
Some free-to-play games will try and get you to buy items or currency to carry on playing, or get access to new things. Always check with your parents before making any purchases.

2 UNLOCKABLE CHARACTERS
There are a lot of games that try to get you to pay for extra characters, but quite often you'll be able to unlock these for free—it's completely up to you.

3 DIFFERENT SKINS
Additionally, some characters will have unique skills too, and usually you can only buy these with real money. Don't waste your money on all of them; just buy ones for characters you like.

4 ITEM RENTALS
If you have to pay real money for an item that you only get access to for a short while then it's probably not worth doing. Only buy things that you can use permanently.

5 MYSTERY PACKS
Some games—like card games—only work through mystery pack purchases, but if you don't know what you're going to get you should think hard about whether it's worth paying for.

6 NEW THINGS TO DO
If some content is being restricted until you pay for it, then consider how much time you've already played it. If you've put a lot of hours in, then it might be nice to pay to play a little bit more.

STAR WARS: THE OLD REPUBLIC

WHY: Everyone wishes they could be a Jedi, and while that might not happen in real-life, at least you can play *Star Wars: The Old Republic*.

SNOW

WHY: There aren't many big snow games these days, so it's great that *Snow* is free. Here you're free to explore the different mountains and courses across a huge open world, with the only charge being the option to buy different clothes and equipment from the world's biggest brands.

WAR THUNDER

WHY: Much like *World Of Tanks*, *War Thunder* has a very clear reason to be a popular free-to-play game. Instead of on the ground, however, you'll spend your time flying through the air. It's a high-speed thrill as you spin to try and evade gunfire.

MARVEL HEROES

WHY: There are so many Marvel characters that it's impossible to pick a favorite. Do you love Iron Man? Thor? Well, thankfully it doesn't matter with *Marvel Heroes*—because you can play as practically any of the Marvel universe superheroes and villains.

SMITE

WHY: *Smite* is a little more complex to learn than some other games, but it's fun to put the time in because every character plays differently. This team-based MOBA gives you control of a god and tasks you with destroying the enemy Crystal. This will keep you coming back over and over again!

THE EXPERT SAYS ...
CRAIG TING AKA HAMMEH
Twitch streaming and YouTube videos for Failcraft

Free-to-play games are great for gamers as you can try a bunch of different titles to see what you like, and don't have to pay a penny if one's not for you! Many games such as *Hearthstone*, *Heroes of the Storm*, and *League of Legends* have a huge depth of gameplay, and hours of skills to learn and challenges for you to get stuck into. Many F2P games are also popular eSports, so if you've got the skills, you could even be a pro gamer or broadcaster! Be sure to look out for daily challenges, quests, and bonuses you can get for being referred by or playing with your friends—with free items, characters, and boosts, they're a great way to get a head start.

ROBOCRAFT

WHY: The core gameplay of *Robocraft* is pretty simple. However you can also design and build your own robotic vehicle, which you can customize to control in any number of ways. This is interesting because it means that it's less about being the most skillful and instead about crafting the most powerful robot-slaying machine!

TROVE

WHY: Though *Trove* might look like *Minecraft*, it's not just a cheap rip-off. Instead, it's an MMO, with a huge world, monsters to slay and friends to meet. Of course you can still build, but with this you can also create your own game modes and maps for multiplayer. It's all about expressing your creativity.

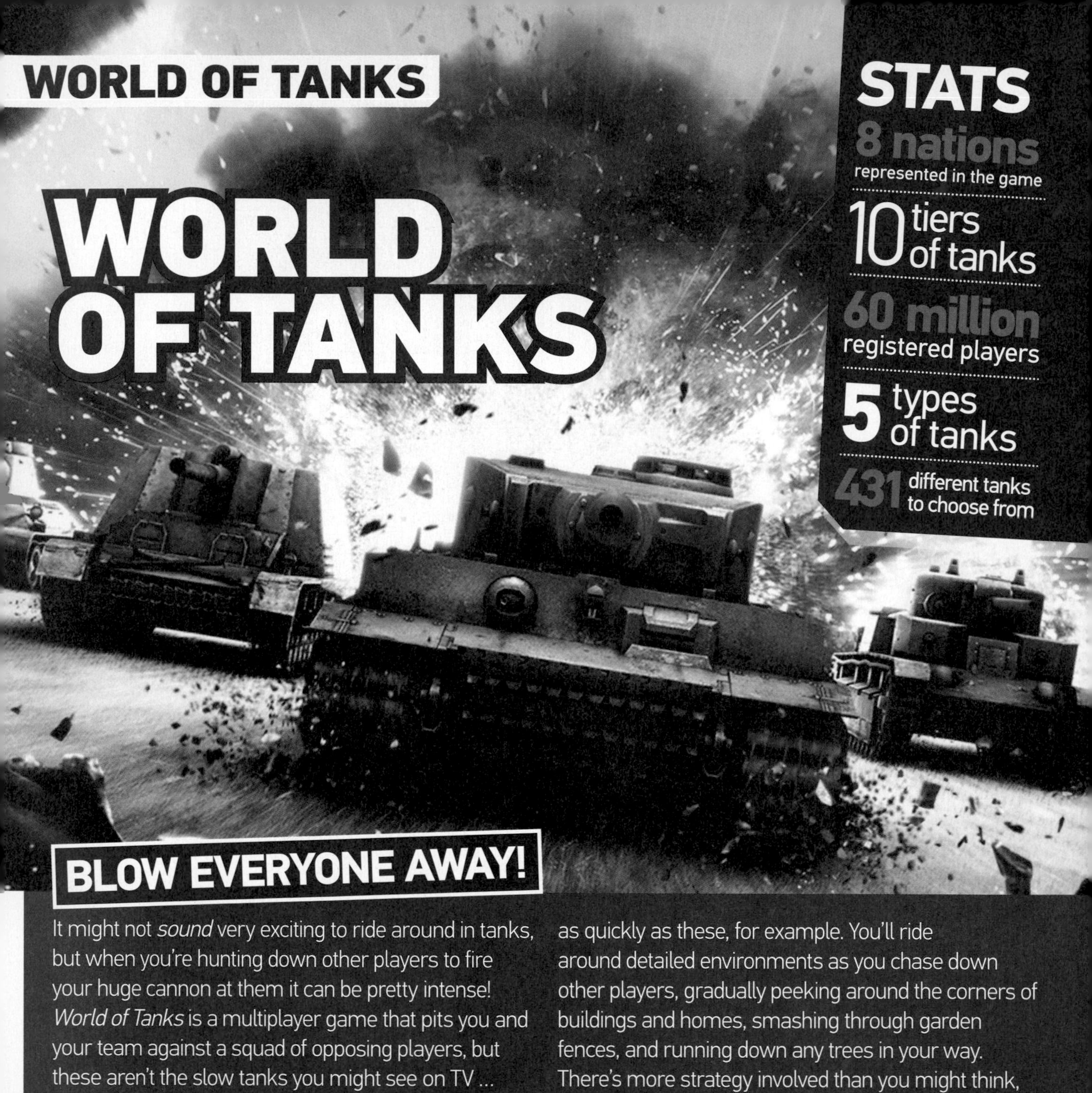

WORLD OF TANKS

STATS

8 nations
represented in the game

10 tiers of tanks

60 million
registered players

5 types of tanks

431 different tanks to choose from

BLOW EVERYONE AWAY!

It might not *sound* very exciting to ride around in tanks, but when you're hunting down other players to fire your huge cannon at them it can be pretty intense! *World of Tanks* is a multiplayer game that pits you and your team against a squad of opposing players, but these aren't the slow tanks you might see on TV ... they've been modified and simplified to make them a lot more fun to play with! Real tanks can't fire nearly as quickly as these, for example. You'll ride around detailed environments as you chase down other players, gradually peeking around the corners of buildings and homes, smashing through garden fences, and running down any trees in your way. There's more strategy involved than you might think, and *World of Tanks* is rightly one of the most popular free-to-play games around.

TIPS & TRICKS

SCOUT FIRST, SHOOT LATER
Rushing into a fight will only draw attention to yourself. Play it stealthily, at least at first.

USE COVER
The more visible you are, the easier you are to hit—thankfully there are a lot of places to hide. If you're in a fight, try to find cover.

SET UP AMBUSHES
If you know where the enemy is or where they're heading, wait for them to pass—then shoot them from behind.

TOP 5 TANKS

DID YOU KNOW?

There is also a mobile and tablet version of the game called *World of Tanks Blitz*, which uses the same tanks.

T49

1 The T49 is one of the best in the game with a respectable number of total wins worldwide. It's an American light tank with a powerful gun attached to it. It's pretty quick, too, making it a great vehicle for setting up ambushes.

M18 HELLCAT

2 It's another American tank, but this one is a destroyer. It's great at long-range fire, as well as a very capable vehicle to scout out the enemy's locations. It has quite thin armor, though, so you'll need to watch out for explosive rounds. Definitely one for those who like playing tactically.

TIGER I

3 Here's a German heavy tank, and a great sniper tank to go for. The penetration on its top gun is impressive, smashing through most opponents' weak points with ease. Its armor is the tank's downfall, however, so be smart with positioning.

S35 CA

4 This French tank destroyer has a very unique design to it, which is why it's commonly referred to as the "Bathtub". It's a tall tank, which can make it an easy target, but it's also powerful—a great defensive tank, rather than an aggressive one.

T40

5 As a prototype American tank, the T40 was never actually used in a real war, which makes this one all the more exciting to play with in-game. It's adaptable, too, so the weapon you choose to use will affect the way you play.

"REAL TANKS CAN'T FIRE NEARLY AS QUICK AS THESE"

ALSO CHECK OUT ...

HARDWARE: RIVALS

Hardware: Rivals is similar, but it's much more colorful, quicker, and includes vehicles other than tanks.

WORLD OF WARPLANES

This is made by the same company as *World of Tanks*, but it's all about taking to the skies in classic warplanes!

HIT WEAK POINTS

Though weak points differ from tank to tank, try and target these rather than shooting blindly. You'll do more damage that way.

SMART SHOOTING

You may notice that when you aim your target reticle begins to get smaller—that means that your shot will be more accurate.

STATS

19 games in the entire series

200+ characters in *LEGO Marvel's Avengers*

60 Over **million** games sold

2-player co-op in every game

BLOCK AND LOAD

LEGO GAMES

DID YOU KNOW?

LEGO Marvel's Avengers has team-up moves where two characters work together to attack enemies. There are nearly 800 moves in total!

For funny, action-packed games you just can't beat the LEGO series. Ever since the first *LEGO Star Wars* game in 2005, British developer Traveller's Tales has been taking some of the best movies and comic book heroes and turning them into small LEGO versions—and the results are some of the most awesome video games you'll ever play! There are a number of elements that give LEGO games their unique feel: their drop-in and drop-out co-op multiplayer, their massive rosters of playable characters, their beautifully detailed worlds full of breakable objects and secret collectibles, to name just a few. There's so much to love, but the one thing that makes a LEGO game stand out from all the other adventures games is its brilliant sense of humor. Good luck trying to play one without bursting into fits of laughter!

TIME LINE

LEGO STAR WARS (2005)
The first LEGO game based on a movie lets you play through *Star Wars Episodes I-III*.

LEGO INDIANA JONES (2008)
The first non-*Star Wars* LEGO game lets you play through the first three movies of everyone's favorite whip-cracking hero.

LEGO ROCK BAND (2009)
LEGO teamed up with MTV for this music game, which let you control LEGO versions of David Bowie, Queen, and Blur.

TOP 5 RECENT LEGO GAMES

LEGO MARVEL'S AVENGERS

1 *LEGO Marvel's Avengers* takes parts from *eight* different Marvel movies, as well as classic Marvel comic book stories. From Iron Man, Hulk, and Captain America to Thor and Black Widow, they're all in here to make the ultimate superhero game! Battle it out against Ultron, and save the world from destruction.

LEGO JURASSIC WORLD

3 *Jurassic World* was the biggest summer movie in 2015 and it's no wonder; it was brilliant. *LEGO Jurassic World* not only lets you play through a LEGO version of that, but also the first three *Jurassic Park* movies. And yes, you even get to play as the dinosaurs, too.

THE LEGO MOVIE VIDEOGAME

4 If you still can't get *Everything is Awesome* out of your head after all this time then you might as well play *The LEGO Movie Videogame*. It retells the story of *The LEGO Movie* and lets you play as over 100 different characters! It's shorter than most other LEGO games, but it's still great fun.

LEGO BATMAN 3: BEYOND GOTHAM

2 If you're crazy about the Caped Crusader, then *LEGO Batman 3* is the one for you. Although you'd think it's just a Batman game from the title, it's actually packed with lots of DC Comics characters, including Superman, the Flash, Green Lantern, and Wonder Woman. You can even play as baddies like the Joker or Lex Luthor.

LEGO THE HOBBIT

5 A few years ago there was *LEGO The Lord of the Rings*, which covered all three of those amazing films. This follow-up is based on the first two *Hobbit* films, *An Unexpected Journey* and *The Desolation of Smaug*. If you're a fan of all things Middle-earth, you'll love it.

ALSO CHECK OUT ...

LEGO DIMENSIONS
This brilliant toys-to-life game plays just like the other LEGO adventures, but crosses over lots of different movies and TV shows.

BIONICLE HEROES
Bionicle Heroes is an awesome action game that plays like the LEGO games, but changes the view so it's over your character's shoulder.

LEGO CITY UNDERCOVER
This Wii U exclusive isn't based on any media, but is a funny new story about the adventures of a cop called Chase McCain.

LEGO HARRY POTTER: YEARS 1–4 (2010)
The first of two *Harry Potter* games, this covered the first four movies. The sequel, using movies 5–7, came out a year later.

LEGO PIRATES OF THE CARIBBEAN (2011)
The adventures of Jack Sparrow and Will Turner were retold in this game, which included levels from all four movies.

POKÉMON

POKÉMON

STATS

- Over 270 million games sold worldwide
- Over 55 million views on Twitch
- **722** Pokémon to catch!
- 906 TV episodes and 18 movies
- *Pokémon Sun & Moon* mark the start of generation

DID YOU KNOW?

Pokémon was invented by Satoshi Tajiri because he wanted to share his love of collecting insects with children around the world!

GOTTA PLAY 'EM ALL

There are few games out there that want you to make friends as much as *Pokémon* does—since the first games came out in 1996, the series has always wanted you to trade with people, battle with people, give items and monsters away to friends. The game's famous motto—"Gotta catch 'em all"—is impossible to achieve if you don't trade with different versions.

We caught all the Pokémon once when there were only 151 of them (yes, we even got Mew!) but now, with well over 700 of the monsters out there, that's a much more difficult task! And that's not forgetting the recently introduced Mega Evolutions of certain Pokémon. *Sun* and *Moon* marks the seventh generation of *Pokémon* games to be released—and there is a healthy number of spin-offs such as the recent *Pokkén Tournament*. Despite being over 20 years old it doesn't look like the *Pokémon* craze is going to go away any time soon.

BEST GAMES

POKÉMON RED AND BLUE (1998)
Our hero ventures out into the Kanto region and experiences 150 wild Pokémon for the first time!

POKÉMON RUBY AND SAPPHIRE (2002)
The third major entry in the series included the first double battles as our hero explored the islands of Hoenn.

POKÉMON DIAMOND AND PEARL (2006)
The Nintendo DS gets its first proper *Pokémon* game, with the second screen being used as a digital smartwatch.

TOP **5** POKÉMON GAMES

POKKÉN TOURNAMENT

1 You'd have thought a fighting game with Pokémon in it would have been made as soon as the games got popular, right? Well, it's taken 20 years to get here, but it was certainly worth the wait: the *Tekken/Pokémon* crossover is colorful, fun and packed with Easter eggs that'll make all Pokémon fans grin from ear to ear.

POKÉMON HEARTGOLD AND SOULSILVER

2 The Nintendo DS remakes of the Game Boy Color games are a fantastic reimagining of the Kanto/Johto regions, and perfectly recapture the original magic of earlier games. With new Pokémon thrown into the mix and even easier ways of trading, these are the definitive main-series *Pokémon* games.

You are challenged by Passerby Boy!

POKÉMON SNAP

3 An N64 game where you take pictures of Pokémon instead of capturing them doesn't sound *too* fun, but *Pokémon Snap* was a surprise no one was expecting. It was a brief window into what a fully 3D *Pokémon* game would look like—people all over the world are still clamoring for a sequel to this day!

POKÉMON GO!

4 This is basically *Pokémon* in the real world—using satellite technology, your smartphone can figure out where Pokémon would live on Earth. You've then got to find them, battle them, and catch them—in all kinds of real locations near you: fields, mountains, forests, and so on. Pokémon can live anywhere, and you've got to work out where to locate them all!

POKÉMON SUN AND MOON

5 The all-new game in the series takes us to the new region of Alola, a Hawaii-like island filled with new monsters to catch! It uses similar 3D graphics to *Pokémon X* and *Y*, but the map is bigger and there's so much to do and explore. The game also introduces some awesome new monsters, like the three starters—Rowlet, Litten and Popplio.

ALSO CHECK OUT ...

DIGIMON STORY: CYBER SLEUTH
The PS4/Vita game proves that long-running *Pokémon* rival *Digimon* stands well on its own.

YO-KAI WATCH
As another monster-collecting game available on 3DS, *Yo-Kai Watch* offers a different slant on *Pokémon's* familiar gameplay mechanics.

MONSTER HUNTER 4: ULTIMATE
The more beasts defeated in *Monster Hunter*, the more powerful you get. It's hard to master but definitely worth it.

POKÉMON BLACK AND WHITE (2010)
This is where the graphics really stepped up, putting players in 3D and showing proper animated battles for the first time.

POKÉMON X AND Y (2013)
Pokémon goes 3D on the 3DS, with Mega Evolutions and over 720 Pokémon to collect!

FASTEST GAMES EVER

BURNOUT 3: TAKEDOWN

WHY: Any *Burnout* game would be perfect on this list, but we're going for *Takedown* as the quintessential entry. Developer Criterion managed to create a rare sense of blistering speed, heightened by gratifying and completely over-the-top crashes.

CRAZY TAXI

WHY: Sega's classic arcade game is all about getting from A to B in as little time as possible, and few games have managed to re-create this completely manic sense of speed. The original version of *Crazy Taxi* still delivers thrills and spills today, but a smartphone version was also released for Android and iOS if you want to try a different platform.

F-ZERO GX

WHY: We're still waiting for a new entry to Nintendo's futuristic, supersonic, and wickedly fun racing series, but despite being released back on the GameCube in 2003, *F-Zero GX* holds up brilliantly. The multiplayer is as intense as it gets, and the game features some of the best graphics of its generation.

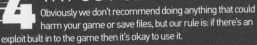

6 WAYS TO MASTER FAST GAMES

1 LEARN THE GAME
Whatever game you're playing, mastering it is going to require you to have an in-depth knowledge of the way that it works—try to familiarize yourself with every single thing: whether that's the racetrack layouts or enemy movement patterns.

2 DON'T OVERTHINK IT
With fast-paced games, your best bet is often just to play using instinct. Don't let yourself get caught thinking too far ahead—that's when you're likely to slip up and make a mistake.

3 TAKE BREAKS
Sometimes in games that require lightning-fast reflexes you can easily get stuck in a rut. If this does happen it's often best to just put down the controller, step back, and take a few deep breaths.

4 TRY OUT GLITCHES
Obviously we don't recommend doing anything that could harm your game or save files, but our rule is: if there's an exploit built in to the game then it's okay to use it.

5 WATCH STREAMS
There are few better ways to improve your gaming than by watching other players online. If you're old enough, check out streamers on YouTube or Twitch to pick up some tips.

6 PRACTICE, PRACTICE, AND PRACTICE SOME MORE
Ultimately, practice makes perfect—or at the very least, improvement. Keep plugging away at your favorite fast games and eventually your lap times, high scores, and overall skill level will all get better and better.

"EXPERTS CAN NOW BLAZE THROUGH OCARINA IN MINUTES"

DID YOU KNOW?

The current world record time for completing *Sonic The Hedgehog 2* stands at an incredible 15 minutes and eight seconds.

THE EXPERT SAYS ... ZFG (JAYSON ESPOSITO)

Holder of the 100% speedrun record for Ocarina Of Time

I love speedrunning. It lets you explore games in completely new ways. Instead of playing the game as intended, you now have to think about every movement you do, why you're doing it, and what you could do to make it faster. *Ocarina Of Time*, my favorite game both casually and for speedrunning, is amazing for this. The game has a ridiculous amount of tricks and glitches, which leads to so many possibilities—it's the job of the speedrunner to figure out how to go as fast as possible and execute it. *Ocarina Of Time* is also a game that is always evolving with things being discovered all the time.

TEMPLE RUN 2

WHY: An App Store sensation, *Temple Run 2* takes the chase sequence from *Raiders of the Lost Ark* and streamlines it into one of the most brilliantly frantic touch-screen games played. Taking control of the game's many avatars, you'll have to time every tap and swipe to perfection if you want to avoid perilous cliffs and terrifying beasts.

THE LEGEND OF ZELDA: OCARINA OF TIME

WHY: *Ocarina* is a game that takes dozens of hours to complete on a normal playthrough. But gamers have managed to master the N64 adventure, and experts can now blaze through *Ocarina* in minutes.

SONIC THE HEDGEHOG 2

WHY: No list of fastest games would be complete without the blue blur. Sonic has lent his speedy skills to countless games over the years, but his second outing on the Sega Mega Drive/Genesis is arguably his best, adding some whirlwind 3D stages to go along with the rapid 2D platform action.

WIPEOUT HD

WHY: One of the games that first sold us on the power of the PS3, *WipEout HD* is still an absolutely stunning racer to this day. You'll be hurtling your antigravity ship around deviously winding tracks and hairpin bends, while the sound of techno music pumps in your ears.

Don't drop it!

WARIOWARE: SMOOTH MOVES

WHY: A game made up entirely of dozens of individual microgames, *WarioWare: Smooth Moves* is rapid-fire Nintendo weirdness at its best. Make a sandwich! Balance a broom! Fly a paper airplane! Zip up a panda suit! Do it all in three seconds or less.

ANNOYING ONLINE PLAYERS

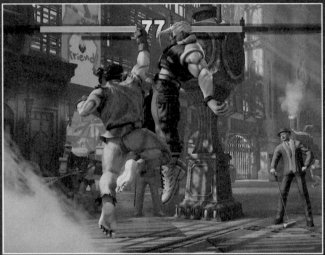

REPLAY WATCHER

WHY: There's nothing more likely to make you go almost completely crazy than *FIFA* players who insist on watching replays of their goals, as though they have just won the FIFA™ World Cup! It's twice as infuriating when players do this after scoring a penalty.

ESPORTS PRO

WHY: Whether it's in a shooter like *Gigantic* or a fast-paced brawler like *Super Smash Bros.*, it can be genuinely annoying to be up against someone who's just so unbelievably *good* at the game. When every move is punished and every mistake is fatal, it quickly becomes incredibly dispiriting.

MOVE SPAMMER

WHY: When someone picks Ryu in *Street Fighter V*, there's always a worry you'll be up against a spammer, which is someone who uses the same moves over and over again. They're easy to beat but no fun to play against, and they're the worst kind of online opponent because it dumbs the game down for both players.

HOW TO BE A GREAT ONLINE PLAYER

1 RIGHT AGE
Don't play games or with other people that aren't the right age for you. See page 3 to remind yourself what's ok and what's not for you and your family.

2 WATCH & LEARN
Even if you're losing badly, stay calm and look at *why* you're losing. Watch the more experienced, dominant players and you'll pick up plenty of cool techniques and awesome secrets.

3 NEVER QUIT
Some games will punish you for abandoning the match if you're losing but more importantly, it's crucial that your team sticks together through good times and bad.

4 BE PATIENT
Whether it's being patient with yourself for not doing as well as you'd like, or with new players who are learning the ropes, it's important not to let frustration throw you off your game.

5 KEEP PRACTICING
The more you play, the more advice you'll have to give to new players and naturally, the better you'll be at the game! Soon you'll become the player others look to when they want to learn.

6 HAVE RESPECT!
Treat others as you want to be treated when you play online—this will create a friendly environment for all and make the whole game far more enjoyable for everyone.

PERFECTIONIST

WHY: It's never fun when you're on the same team as one of those players who constantly criticizes you for everything. "What are you doing, idiot? Shoot his legs. HIS LEGS. Shoot his legs! Where are you going? Jump over him. JUMP. OVER. HIM. Are you even listening? Why are you playing this game?"

THE EXPERT SAYS ...
JOSH WEST
Writer, games™ magazine

There's always one player that causes me to launch my controller into the wall. Is it a childish reaction? Of course, but they can materialize in any game I dive into—and they are impossible to fight against. It's the soldier that's sitting on an unreachable ledge, sniping gleefully under the cover of flickering, glitching shadows. It's the driver careering around the track backwards, destroying a perfect lap as Adele blares through their headset and invades my otherwise serene living room. It's the player taking advantage of my terrible connection to slam 40-yard screamers into the back of my net while I'm still, inexplicably, waiting for kick-off. Sometimes, it's simply the player that votes against my favorite map in a lobby, just because I mentioned over chat that I really wanted to play it next. Sportsmanship died a long time ago on Xbox Live. I mourn its loss deeply.

"THERE'S ALWAYS ONE PLAYER THAT CAUSES ME TO LAUNCH MY CONTROLLER"

HEADSET NOISE

WHY: Sometimes it's people breathing into their microphones, sometimes it's people singing, or sometimes it's the sensitivity being turned too high on the headset. Whatever it is, no one wants to deal with headset noise and *Rocket League* attracts more of this type of player than most.

GAME LEAVERS

WHY: Sometimes the odds start to slide in the enemy's favor. If you're playing *Battlefront*, that means you're suddenly dealing with the likes of Vader. You know what makes life harder? Your team rage quitting on you, making it even harder to fight back as your numbers are whittled down.

ACHIEVEMENT & TROPHY HUNTERS

WHY: Games like *Plants vs. Zombies: Garden Warfare 2* are stuffed with fun achievements and trophies for using weapons a certain number of times. This is all well and good ... until your teammates start using ineffective weapons for the sake of achievements, leaving you exposed. Stop working on your gamerscore and shoot!

STATS

$ Over 100 million copies sold

FIFA 16 has **650** playable teams from over 30 leagues

♀ FIFA 16 first to include women's soccer

🏆 **24** Mainline games in 23 years

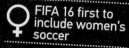

FIFA 16 sold almost 1 million copies in its first week on sale

FIFA
THE BEAUTIFUL GAME

There's one day that soccer fans look forward to every year almost as much as the start of the real soccer season; the day that the latest *FIFA* is released. Who can blame them? With its brilliant commentary, amazing match day presentation, and realistic recreations of the most famous players and stadiums, it makes it easy for us soccer fans to pretend that we are taking our favorite teams to victory! Of course, it's also great fun to play, especially with friends. That's why since the release of the first game in the series—*FIFA International Soccer*—in 1993, *FIFA* has gone on to become the best-selling sports video game series of all time. And with regular updates and refinements of the hugely popular FIFA Ultimate Team (FUT) player trading mode, we don't think *FIFA* is going to lose its top spot any time soon.

TIPS & TRICKS

TWEAK YOUR TACTICS
If you're struggling to break a team down, try changing your approach, whether that be with a formation change or new attacking strategy.

MIX IT UP
Playing the same way all the time makes you predictable. Mix up short passes, crossfield balls, through balls, and dribbling.

PLAY ONE-TWOS
Hold down L1/LB while making a pass and the passer will then make a run after releasing the ball, key to breaking down defenses.

TOP 5 ULTIMATE TEAM PLAYERS

94 RW

MESSI

92 PAC	95 DRI
88 SHO	24 DEF
86 PAS	62 PHY

BASIC

LIONEL MESSI

1 Any Ultimate Team manager is going to want the best player in the world leading their attack. Goals; dribbling; assists; skills; creativity: the Barcelona star gives you it all! You can play him anywhere across the front three, but we prefer to have him cutting in off the right with that left peg!

88 CB

SILVA

74 PAC	73 DRI
57 SHO	90 DEF
73 PAS	79 PHY

BASIC

THIAGO SILVA

4 In front of our goalkeeper, we're going to need a leader in the center of defense. Silva's high stats for defending, interceptions, heading, marking, and tackling make him great to stop the opposition, but decent passing stats mean he is also good at starting attacks from the back.

CRISTIANO RONALDO

2 We can't imagine Ronaldo ever lining up alongside Messi in real life, but the beauty of Ultimate Team is that we can make that happen. Ronaldo brings the physicality and heading ability to the attack that Messi lacks. His high attacking stats make him a great option, whether on the left wing or as a center forward.

93 LW

RONALDO

92 PAC	90 DRI
93 SHO	33 DEF
80 PAS	78 PHY

BASIC

87 CM

KROOS

56 PAC	82 DRI
81 SHO	66 DEF
88 PAS	69 PHY

BASIC

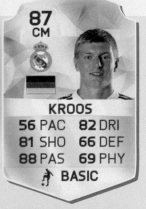

DID YOU KNOW?

Manchester City's Samir Nasri and Chelsea's Eden Hazard have complained about their stats being too low in *FIFA* games!

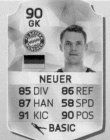

90 GK

NEUER

85 DIV	86 REF
87 HAN	58 SPD
91 KIC	90 POS

BASIC

MANUEL NEUER

3 Before we get carried away with our goal scorers, let's remember we need to stop the other team scoring as well! There's no one better to put between the goalposts than the highest rated goalkeeper in the game: Bayern Munich and Germany's 6'4" shot-stopper Manuel Neuer.

TONI KROOS

5 There are some higher rated midfielders we could recommend to play in the heart of midfield, but they're not as good all-rounders as Kroos. His passing stats are awesome, he can dribble, he can shoot and he's not too bad at defending if you lose the ball, either.

"WE DON'T THINK FIFA IS GOING TO LOSE ITS TOP SPOT ANY TIME SOON!"

ALSO CHECK OUT ...

PRO EVOLUTION SOCCER 2016

It doesn't have official Premier League teams, but it does have fantastic gameplay that fans will love.

ROCKET LEAGUE

If you want something different, there's no better game than *Rocket League*. It's just like soccer, but you play with rocket-powered cars!

MASTER DRIBBLING

Dribbling isn't all about skill moves (though they do help). Also learn to use feints and the no-touch dribbling (hold L1+L2/LB+LT) ability.

PRACTICE FREE KICKS

It's worth spending some time in training mode to get free kicks right. It means you can punish opponents when you get fouled near the box.

MADDEN NFL

MADDEN NFL

STATS

1988 The year the first *Madden* was released

The *Madden* franchise overall has earned more than
$4,000,000,000

Over
100 game testers work on each game

Over
1.5 BILLION
minutes have been played in Madden Ultimate Team

33 games in total (as of December 2015)

THE ONLY NFL GAME YOU NEED

If you enjoy football and video games, there's no way you haven't played at least one match in *Madden NFL*. One of EA's biggest sporting games, it's proven itself as *the* go-to experience when digitally replicating the drama and the impact of the National Football League. It has led the field since 1988, and the latest entry in the series is quite simply one of the best football games in existence. As close to what's seen on TV week in and week out as you could hope for, *Madden NFL 16* allows an unprecedented amount of depth, from what you can do on the field to the extensive manager mode that takes you into the dressing room. Even if you don't know anything about football, you'll love *Madden*.

DID YOU KNOW?
Even though famous NFL commentator John Madden retired in 2009, he still works on every *Madden NFL* game released.

"THE LATEST ENTRY IS QUITE SIMPLY ONE OF THE BEST FOOTBALL GAMES IN EXISTENCE"

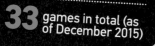

TIME LINE

TRY THE SKILLS TRAINER
Unless you play *Madden* yearly you may not be aware of the changes, so make sure to try out the Skills Trainer.

PLAY SOME PRACTICE GAMES
There's no point playing a real game and getting beaten, so try practice matches to get your skills up to scratch.

LISTEN TO THE COACH
Madden's formation screen can be pretty intimidating, so use the "Coach's Suggestion" option until you feel more comfortable choosing your own.

TOP 5 QUARTERBACKS

AARON RODGERS
GREEN BAY PACKERS

1 With an overall rating of 99 in *Madden NFL 16*, Aaron Rodgers is not only the best quarterback in the game, but also one of the best players, period. He also boasts a throwing power of 95, meaning he can whip the ball to his receivers with impact and ease.

TOM BRADY
NEW ENGLAND PATRIOTS

2 Arguably one of the most famous NFL players of the modern game, Tom Brady has won multiple Super Bowls with the New England Patriots. This is why he comes with a 97 overall rating and the best "throw accuracy short" and "throw accuracy mid" stats.

DREW BREES
NEW ORLEANS SAINTS

3 While not as good as our two frontrunners, Drew Brees still comes in strong with an overall rating of 95 in *Madden NFL 16*. His real skill is in his "play action," though, when he fakes a running play before throwing the ball downfield.

ANDREW LUCK
INDIANAPOLIS COLTS

5 Indianapolis Colts' quarterback Andrew Luck may be last on this list with an overall rating of 94, but he's still a huge force to be reckoned with in the game. With pinpoint accuracy and a powerful throw, he can easily hold his own and is an asset to any team.

BEN ROETHLISBERGER
PITTSBURGH STEELERS

4 Although Ben Roethlisberger has the same overall rating as Drew Brees—an impressive 95—his strength is in different areas, as he has *Madden NFL 16*'s best stats for his "strength" and "throw on the run." This means he's incredibly hard to take down, so he's the best choice for those who are often sacked by the defense.

ALSO CHECK OUT...

NFL BLITZ
Like your football a bit more arcade-focused? *NFL Blitz* scratches that itch, and even lets you explore what happens off the field.

NCAA FOOTBALL
If you prefer college football over the NFL, *NCAA Football* gives you a similar experience but with college teams taking the limelight.

PICK THE RIGHT TEAM
We all want to play as our favorite team, but if you're a more defensive player, make sure to pick a side that matches that approach.

LEARN THE PASSES
Madden has numerous pass types, each of which has pros and cons depending on your situation. Make sure to learn which one works best.

MOST STRESSFUL GAMES

THE WITNESS

WHY: You can't even go two minutes without having your brain challenged in *The Witness*. Once you're a few hours into this huge puzzle, just forget it! Even developer Jonathan Blow has confessed that some tasks are almost unsolvable. Expect it to take everything you have.

#IDARB

WHY: When you're up against a skilled opponent, it's almost impossible to know how to compete. They keep tackling you, they score from distance to earn more points, and they have all the angles figured out ... argh! What am I supposed to do?!

FIFA 16

WHY: Multiplayer battles in *FIFA 16* can become heated affairs and there's nothing worse than having to defend a tight 1-0 lead when the other team is putting you under continuous pressure with shots, corners, and clinical passing again and again. There's a certain feeling of relief when the final whistle blows, though ... phew!

6 WAYS TO STAY CALM

1 DON'T OVERPLAY
You're going to stress yourself out more if you keep hammering away when stuck on a game. It's best to just walk away and try again later. You'll be more likely to succeed after a break.

2 REMEMBER IT'S JUST A GAME
When the fun stops, so should you. It keeps stress down and ensures that smile stays on your face.

3 LEARN THE INS AND OUTS OF THE GAME
Once you start to understand a game, the easier it becomes. Use this approach and you'll remain calm.

4 ASK FOR HELP
If you really can't get past an area—and it's leading to unnecessary stress—ask a friend for help. Share your problems—you don't lose points by asking for help.

5 GO AND DO SOMETHING ELSE
This only applies to some titles, especially open-world games. Just go do a new quest and return later.

6 DON'T GET STRESSED!
Who's in charge? The game, or your brain? Just stay calm and you'll be the winner whatever the hurdle.

DID YOU KNOW?

The Witness broke $5 million worth of sales in its first week of release! Gamers clearly love puzzles.

ORI & THE BLIND FOREST

WHY: It's a pretty game, but don't be fooled by the art style. *Ori & The Blind Forest* looks amazing, but some levels require such precision and "twitch gaming" that you'll be questioning if it's possible every now and then. Stay the course, but be ready for some frustration!

SUPER MEAT BOY

WHY: How can a game where you play as a piece of meat be hard? We're not sure, but we do know that this PS4 platformer is tough as nails! Challenging you to get to the end of the level without even thinking about making a mistake, your hand will start to hurt due to your tight grip of the controller.

THE EXPERT SAYS ...
KENWORTHGAMING
Minecraft YouTube videos

The most stressful game I have ever played is *Until Dawn* on the PS4. Not only was the game filled with jump scares left and right, but it also had many different outcomes depending on quick actions and choices you made during the game!

"THERE'S A CERTAIN FEELING OF RELIEF WHEN THE FINAL WHISTLE BLOWS, THOUGH ... PHEW!"

FOOTBALL MANAGER 2016

WHY: Managing a football team is hard. *Football Manager* gives such a good representation of what it's like to be in charge of a club that you start to blur the lines of reality. A goal down to Hull? You might get sacked in the morning.

SUPER MARIO 3D WORLD

WHY: *Mario* games are not easy. You've made a jump like the one that you've been stuck on a hundred times before. But this time, it's just a little too hard and that's when you start to get stressed. Stay calm though, as you'll get there eventually.

GRIM FANDANGO REMASTERED

WHY: With the remastered version coming back to the PS4, you'll need to go online when you play *Grim Fandango*. The game is confusing, and you'll soon start to run out of ideas for each task—online hints are definitely needed here.

MARIO KART 8

STATS

48 Tracks to race

The maximum challenge is **200cc**

36 drivers to use and unlock

24 items to help you win!

Create karts using **37 different bodies**

MARIO KART 8
PUT YOUR FOOT DOWN

Mario Kart is a classic franchise that never fails to deliver on one promise: this is a great game to play with friends. The ultimate multiplayer title will eternally bring family and friends around the same console to battle out across the crazy tracks that Nintendo dream up—mostly because it's so fun!

With *Mario Kart 8* on the Wii U, the game series took a new step, adding antigravity into the mix. For the first time you can race up walls and across ceilings, into the sky, or down deep underground. The result is a mind-bending marathon down mountains, through castles, and even into space. It's quite a ride.

Of course, it also packs in all your favorite *Mario* characters, from Yoshi to Rosalina, and you can even play as your own Mii character in a selection of awesome outfits.

TIME LINE

1992 **SUPER MARIO KART**
Nintendo's first kart racer took the world by storm thanks to its brilliant two-player multiplayer racing.

1996 **MARIO KART 64**
Mario Kart went 3D for the first time, with some of the most iconic tracks in the series' history.

2003 **MARIO KART: DOUBLE DASH!!**
Two characters per kart meant twice the fun in this game. Up to eight people could play together locally.

TOP 5 TRACKS

GBA RIBBON ROAD

1 When you race your friends on this incredibly inventive remake of a classic retro track you'll feel like you're stepping into a *Toy Story* movie. The whole thing is set in a children's playroom, with board games and other toys holding up the track as you race past enormous presents and over wooden floorboards. Ribbon Road is an amazing location that adds a whole other layer to your karting experience, and ramps up the fun.

GCN YOSHI CIRCUIT

2 We're sure that when Yoshi was designed he wasn't drawn with a racetrack in mind, but in *Mario Kart 8* that's exactly what he has become. From above, this track is instantly recognizable. When racing, it's a frantic battle around chicanes and long bends.

SHY GUY FALLS

3 With the addition of antigravity, there are no rules saying where you can and can't race. On Shy Guy Falls, you can expect to be zipping straight up a waterfall, looping over the top, and then flying down the other side using your kart's built-in paraglider.

SUNSHINE AIRPORT

4 It's hard to accurately recreate the excitement of going on vacation, but if any game does it, it's *Mario Kart 8*. From the summery theme to the sound of an airplane taking off above your head as you race, this is a perfect mix of racing thrills and summer fun.

MOUNT WARIO

5 No *Mario Kart* game is complete without a winter-themed track, and Mount Wario provides the perfect setting. From the downhill slalom to the enormous ski jump, this is icy, skid-filled fun. The control needed to master this track makes it a favorite.

"FOR THE FIRST TIME, YOU CAN RACE UP WALLS AND ACROSS CEILINGS"

2008 MARIO KART Wii
With the Wii came motion controls for *Mario Kart*, meaning you could steer by tilting your controller for the first time.

2011 MARIO KART 7
This entry in the series appeared on Nintendo's 3DS, and it offered an astonishing 3D mobile experience.

ALSO CHECK OUT ...

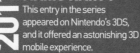

SONIC & SEGA ALL-STAR RACING
Take to the tracks as Sega's biggest names use a series of crazy power-ups to take victory.

LITTLEBIGPLANET KARTING
Sackboy and friends take to the tracks. The twist is that you can create your own tracks and customize your racer.

A-Z OF EASY ACHIEVEMENTS & TROPHIES

ALL DECKED OUT
Costume Quest | Xbox One, Steam

COLLECTED ALL CREEPY TREAT CARDS

A A very simple effort, this one: make sure you defeat all the monsters, bob for all the apples, and trade with every kid you see. You'll do most of this as you go through the game—getting another easy 985G in the process!

BREAKSHOT
Rocket League | Xbox One, PS4

HIT YOUR OPPONENT INTO THE BALL TO SCORE A GOAL

B You may end up doing this by accident after a few games of *Rocket League*, but here's one piece of advice—don't hit full boost speed while trying to get this achievement. If you do, the opponent will explode when you crash into them!

COW TIPPER
Minecraft | Xbox One, PS4, Steam, Wii U

HARVEST SOME LEATHER

C Everyone loves *Minecraft*—not just because of its LEGO-like play, but also because it has easy achievements! After you've played through the simple opening sections and seen the world unfold before you, simply walk up to a cow and use your axe on it to pop this one.

DENDROLOGIST
Never Alone | PS4, Xbox One, Steam

YOU FOUND ALL CULTURAL INSIGHTS IN THE FOREST

D The word for this achievement means "a person who studies trees" and that's exactly what you need to be in The Forest level. You'll hear an owl cry when you circle back to the start of the level: it looks like you need to go down to continue, but ignore that and hop across an icy gap to find the owl when you hear the hoot.

ESCAPIST
Unmechanical: Extended | PS4, Xbox One, Steam

FINISH THE GAME BY ESCAPING

E Don't be put off by the "finish the game" condition—this is an incredibly simple game, and one that is actually quite fun to play through. If you get stuck, you can always watch a guide to the puzzles online. Anyway, there are *two* ways to finish the game, and you get a good trophy/gamerscore for both—so just get to right before the end, save, finish, and reboot. Easy!

FALLING STAR
Brothers: A Tale Of Two Sons | PS4, Xbox One, Steam

MAKE A WISH

F At the beginning of Chapter 3, go through the woods and to a graveyard. The path leads you left, but bear right and you'll eventually hit a statue in the middle of a quiet and deserted graveyard; examine it to trigger a shooting star. Watch it fall for an easy achievement/trophy.

G GOATS 'N' STUFF Goat Simulator | PS4, Xbox One, Steam
HOLD YOUR OWN CONCERT

1 HEAD TO GOAT CITY BAY
Get yourself to the Goat City Bay map (you'll unlock it as you play through the game). Once there, scan the skyline for the highest building on the map—located to the right of the amusement park. There's a concert taking place on the roof.

2 GET UP THERE
To reach that rocking concert, you can either use the elevator inside *or* get another achievement/trophy by climbing up the planter of trees at the back of the building and ragdolling onto a mattress you find there to bounce up after five or six jumps.

3 SPILL BLOOD ON THE DANCEFLOOR
Once on the roof, walk up to the turntable and you'll see someone who looks suspiciously like Deadmau5 on the decks. Headbutt him. You'll net yourself the achievement/trophy, plus the DJ's trademark mask!

THE BEST GAMERS IN THE WORLD?

Pro players might be the best when it comes to winning, but it's not all about points. A select few gamers have pushed their Gamerscore and trophy count well beyond anyone else.

In 2014, Raymond Cox—aka Stallion83 on Xbox Live—became the first player in the world to pass the 1 million Gamerscore mark. Since that incredible milestone, he's added another quarter of a million Gs, bringing his total Gamerscore to over 1,250,000.

On PlayStation, Hakoom is the most prolific trophy-hunter, amassing around 50,000 trophies worth over 1,400,000 points on the PlayStation network. These guys are the real deal.

IN THE BEGINNING
Pneuma: Breath Of Life | Xbox One

COMPLETED THE PROLOGUE

This is the easiest 100G you'll likely get in this list – all you need to do is start up the game and finish the prologue: it's not tricky, the puzzles are really simple and it'll take you less than five minutes. Continue with the rest of the simple game and you'll get all 1,000G in no time.

HOOPER Shovel Knight | PS4, Xbox One, Steam

BOUNCE ON HOOP KID'S HOOP FOR 5 SECONDS

Once you get access to the village (after clearing the first level), you'll encounter a girl running around with a stick and a hoop. Simply bounce on this for as long as you can—it might seem tricky at first, but once you learn how to react to the hoop changing direction, you'll quickly get the trophy/achievement.

KEEP DEFENDING
Massive Chalice | Xbox One

DEFEND YOUR FIRST KEEP

K You're going to want to start up the game and choose some bloodlines—the best tip here is to make sure you have as many beneficial traits running through your blood as possible! Once you're happy with the setup of your family, you'll be thrown directly into your first fight of the game. It's pretty easy to bluff your way through this one—you'll get the achievement as soon as you're done fighting!

DID YOU KNOW?
Contrast's developer was heavily inspired by the *Portal* series—they even named some achievements/trophies after Valve's hit puzzle game.

JUST LIKE HARRY
Contrast | Xbox One, PS4, Steam

UNLOCKED WHEN THE PLAYER MAKES IT OVER THE CROCODILES ON THEIR FIRST ATTEMPT IN THE SHADOW THEATER

J *Contrast* is a very generous game when it comes to trophies/achievements anyway, but this is incredibly simple. In Act 2, you take a visit to the shadow theater. When the crocodile part begins, wait for the first croc to shut its mouth, then jump. And hey, if you do fail, just quit out the game and try again!

LET'S DO THIS! Guitar Hero Live | Xbox One, PS4
COMPLETE THE GH LIVE TUTORIAL

L As soon as you start up the game, you'll be taken backstage at a live gig. Here, a friendly (and hairy) roadie will talk you through the basics of *Guitar Hero Live*—from making chord patterns with your fingers to strumming in time. Complete all of these tutorial sections properly and you will unlock the relevant Trophy or Achievement.

MARKING THE WAY Ori & The Blind Forest | Xbox One
RESTORE YOUR FIRST MAP STONE

1 GET EMOTIONAL

The scene-setting introduction to *Ori & The Blind Forest* is pretty brutal—you get to watch your main character go through some horrible and devastating life changes before you are then taught how to play the game in a tutorial zone.

2 PLAY THROUGH THE OPENING

The game takes the form of a Metroidvania-type action platformer—you can revisit areas and find bonus levels once you unlock more abilities. But, to begin with, you're locked into a tutorial zone. Complete it.

3 FIND THE MAP STONE

Once you start the game, after completing the tutorial, one of the very first things you will be told to do is to activate a Map Stone—the achievement will pop here and you can use this as a waypoint when navigating the rest of the levels. Done!

TOP 5 HARDEST ACHIEVEMENTS EVER
THE REAL BADGES OF HONOR

SHENANIGANS!
CLOUDBERRY KINGDOM

Cloudberry Kingdom is already a pretty tough game, but this achievement requires you to complete Chapter 7. Sounds easy, right? Well, unfortunately this chapter contains level 319, which is a near-impossible mess of fireballs and lasers.

IMPOSSIBLE BOY
SUPER MEAT BOY

The PSN/Steam release of *Super Meat Boy* came with a rejigged set of awards—one of them asking you to get through the "dark world" variant of the secret bonus level *without dying*. The trophy's called Impossible Boy for a reason ...

LOW SCORER
SPELUNKY

You need to be gifted with an unlikely mix of luck and skill to grab this one—the randomly generated levels of *Spelunky* aren't forgiving at the best of times, so completing the game while picking up *no treasure* is unlikely to happen.

THE SILENT
DON'T STARVE

For this one, you need an insane amount of luck—the trophy pops when you complete all four stages in the game (not an easy task in itself) *and* locate the bonus character Wes. And Wes is *not* easy to find. Trust us, we've been searching for ages.

IS THERE ANYTHING YOU CAN'T DO?
TRIALS FUSION

For this one, you need to complete all 120 unique challenges across 40 tracks in *Trials Fusion*—no laughing matter. Some of the challenge requirements are simple enough, but others are pure evil, and within an awful, horrible time limit. Good luck.

NEW RECRUIT
Star Wars Battlefront | Xbox One, PS4, PC

COMPLETE ANY MISSION

N A lot of the rewards you'll get in this game rely on you outperforming teammates, so you need a lot of practice. Luckily, though, the very first award you'll get is for finishing a mission. You don't even have to win an online match to nab this one; just sit back and watch the action.

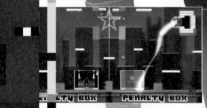

OVER "THE AIR" ACHIEVER
#IDARB | Xbox One

SUMMON THE ACHIEVEMENT BOT

O You'll need a Twitch account for this (age 13 +). Boot the game and stream it online (you can do this through the Xbox One!) Find your live stream; in the comments box, type "#achievement". You'll see a huge robot; the achievement pops after a few seconds.

Ultimate End

Restores HP

NAME		HP	MP	LIMIT	WAIT
Cur	Cure2	Cure3		MP needed 5/584	
Life	Life2	Regen		All: 5×	

PACKING A PUNCH — Final Fantasy VII | PS4, PC

LEARN FINAL HEAVEN—TIFA'S LAST LIMIT BREAK

P From disc 2 onwards, you'll have the ability to visit Tifa's house in Nibelheim. Once there, there's a piano you can play. With Tifa in your party, input [X], [Square], [Triangle], [R1/Triangle], [R1/Square], [X], [Square], [Triangle], [R1/X], [Circle], [X], [Square], [Triangle], and voila!

QUANTITY OVER QUALITY
Street Fighter V | PS4, PC

LEVEL UP FIVE CHARACTERS!

Q For this Trophy, just complete the game with five different characters. Here are the easiest to get this Trophy with:

DID YOU KNOW?
Want more *Street Fighter V* characters? You can download Alex, Ibuki, Balrog, Guile, Juri, and Urien if you have earned enough Zenny in the actual game.

RYU
You can play a simple fireball game from a distance with Ryu, using the odd EX fireball (do the normal fireball motion but press two buttons rather than one).

KEN
Although Ken's fireballs aren't quite as good as Ryu's, you should still keep your distance with him, looking to dragon punch if the opponent jumps at you.

LAURA
You need to stay up-close with Laura, as she has almost no range. Her slow fireballs also work really well to protect her from her opponent's attacks.

ZANGIEF
The AI struggles to deal with Zangief's spinning clothesline, which is executed by pressing all the punch buttons at the same time, so stick with that move!

KARIN
Karin is blessed with one of the best "normal" moves in the game, Fierce Kick. Use this over and over from close range to chip away at your opponent's lifebar.

R | RISING VANGUARD Destiny | PS4, Xbox One
COMPLETE A STRIKE

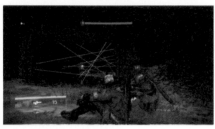

1 CREATE A CHARACTER

Jumping in at *Destiny*'s *The Taken King* expansion instantly allows you to level a character to level 25—so create whichever class of character you want and skip ahead to a good level.

2 JUMP IN!

You'll need to complete a few missions before unlocking a Strike, but don't worry: you'll net about 100G/five trophies' worth of awards in the process. They're super-easy missions, too.

3 STRIKE OUT!

You'll unlock the Earth Strike within 30 minutes of playing—with your character above level 10, it'll take you *minutes* to run through the Old Russia level and take out the boss at the end.

SIMPLY WALKED INTO... METROPOLIS

LEGO: Dimensions | Xbox One, PS4, Steam

COMPLETE PAINTING THE TOWN BLACK

S This one is directly tied to the story (the Batman portion). All you need to do is build the LEGO portal, play through the opening sections of the game, and complete all the Batman-related levels— which won't take you too long at all. Make sure you follow the LEGO building instructions closely.

TUNE UP Rock Band 4 | Xbox One, PS4

CALIBRATE YOUR AUDIO/VIDEO SETUP FOR THE OPTIMAL ROCK BAND 4 EXPERIENCE

T You can get this as soon as you start up the game—just go into the settings, find the Calibrate option, and do what the menus tell you. Not only will this get you an easy trophy/5G, but it'll also make the game perform *much* better on your TV than it would have before. Everyone's a winner!

VANITY OF VANITIES

Terraria | Xbox One, PS4, Steam

WEAR A SET OF VANITY CLOTHES

V The easiest way to get this is right at the start of the game, when you're beginning to cut down trees: just chop away *everything* you can. You'll need to harvest 60 pieces of wood and make a piece of "Wood Armor" for your head, your chest, and your legs. Just equip wood to each slot and this reward will pop.

URBAN OUTLAW Need For Speed | Xbox One, PS4, PC

BEAT MAGNUS'S PERSONAL CHALLENGE

U The main story of *Need For Speed* won't take you too long if you know how to play basically any racing game ever made. That's good news when it comes to this trophy/achievement, which is totally unmissable and part of the story itself. Good luck—you probably won't need it.

W WAX ON, WAX OFF
Trials Fusion | Xbox One, PS4, Steam
COMPLETE TRAINING PROGRAM 2

1 GET YOUR BEARINGS
The first tutorial level is there to get you used to the way *Trials* works—you've got to balance your bike to get over obstacles using the analogue sticks, and time your hops to clear gaps. So, if you've never played a *Trials* game before, this is all very handy.

2 UNLOCK THE SECOND LEVEL
Once you've learned how to play, focus on getting over nine medals in the first set of levels—the easiest way of doing this is getting gold rewards on three tracks. This will unlock the Arctic Open.

3 CLEAR THE FIRST TRACK
Once you have managed to open up the second set of tracks to bust your mad tricks on, all you will then need to do is clear the first track (with *any* type of medal) and the trophy will pop for a nice, easy 25G or a Bronze trophy.

X'TABAY-BYE
Guacamelee! Super Turbo Championship Edition | PS4, Xbox One, Steam
REDEEM X'TABAY-BYE

X X'tabay is one of the harder bosses in the game, but with the right tactic, she's a cakewalk: simply uppercut to knock her off balance, punch her in the air, then grab her and throw her to the floor. This will do *huge* damage, so keep repeating this tactic while avoiding her projectiles.

YOU KNOW THE MIDNIGHT CHANNEL?

Persona 4: Arena | PS3, Xbox 360

TUNED IN

Y Everyone loves these trophies—ever since *The Simpsons Game* had one back in 2007, us gamers have done our own little fist-pumps of joy whenever we boot up a game and get given a trophy for the pleasure. *Persona 4: Arena* does that for you: open up the game and get a Bronze Trophy or 5G.

ZOMBIE DEFENSE

Plants Vs Zombies: Garden Warfare | Xbox One

BUILD THREE ZOMBOT TURRETS IN GARDENS & GRAVEYARDS

Z You'll need to select the Engineer when you play this mode, then hurry to the teleporter build site, marked with a purple wrench. Once there you'll see three scrap piles—run up to each one and hold down the B button to build the turrets. Incidentally, each one of the turrets also counts as "raising a zombie," so you should get the I'm Lonely achievement at the same time. Bonus!

THE EXPERT SAYS ...
RYAN KING

Games writer with over 175,000 gamerscore and 2,700 Trophies

After talking to Achievement and Trophy hunters over the years, it's clear the main thing they all have in common is planning. They check sites like Xboxachievements.com and Trueachievements.com and they keep an eye on new releases to see which games are easy and which ones to avoid.

Don't be afraid to purchase older, cheaper games if you want to get more Achievements and Trophies in a short space of time, either.

Finally, get a group of you together! Not only does the competition make it more fun and keep you all engaged, but you can all help each other out with multiplayer Achievements and Trophies, which can be difficult to unlock if playing with random people online.

BEST GRAPHICS

BEST GRAPHICS

ROYAL RUMBLE
Super Smash Bros. For Wii U
WHY: As well as being the greatest celebration of all things Nintendo that money can buy, *Smash* is also the perfect game to silence those who think Wii U can't do great graphics. Characters, items, and stages all look incredible and the action is smooth as can be—it's probably the best-looking game on the system, all in all.

A WHOLE NEW WORLD
No Man's Sky
WHY: With a practically infinite universe, it's mind-boggling that *No Man's Sky* looks so good especially when you consider that there are barely more than ten people in the development team!

MOVIE QUALITY
Ratchet & Clank
WHY: Sony's daring duo have always looked superb, but in their PS4 debut, the graphics are almost on par with the CG work for the tie-in movie! From Ratchet's glorious coat to the creative and entertaining tools of destruction he wields, it's a real visual feast.

WHAT MAKES GAMES LOOK GOOD?

1 CHARACTER MODELS
The more polygons, the smoother edges will be and the more details it can feature. The best-looking games are those with high polycounts.

2 ANIMATION
You could have the best model in the world, but if it stutters and jerks, the effort is wasted. Fluidity is key—just compare 2K's slick basketball games to the studio's own *WWE* titles!

3 LIGHTING
Good lighting can make a scene pop, creating beautiful shadows and bathing areas in glows. If a game looks real, then it's likely that the lighting is doing most of the work!

4 TEXTURES
In older games, walls, floors, and other surfaces tended to turn into a mess if you got too close. Today, textures are better and you can even read individual words on book covers!

5 ART STYLE
Games can look great even without being technically impressive. The likes of *Minecraft* and *Limbo*, while not hugely impressive on paper, really stand out due to their unique visual styles.

6 RESOLUTION
Bigger numbers aren't always better but generally, a game running at 1080p (or higher) is going to look sharper and crisper than one running at 720p or less.

DID YOU KNOW?
Lara Croft's model in the first *Tomb Raider* was made of just over 200 polygons. In the 2013 reboot, over 40,000 were used!

PLAYABLE CARTOONS?! Cuphead

WHY: Now this one *really* blew our minds when we first saw it. You might be thinking that it looks like a classic Thirties cartoon, and there's a good reason for that—the artists behind the game hand-drew every level in just the same way as the old cartoon animators used to. As you can see, the results are absolutely stunning.

THE EXPERT SAYS ...
DOM PEPPIATT
Senior Staff Writer, 3D Artist magazine

Ratchet & Clank is one of the best-looking games around. It's like if Pixar made a game—all the shiny surfaces reflect things how they're supposed to, all the enemies move really stylishly, the attention to detail on your furry hero is *phenomenal*. The game released alongside a film of the same name, and those expensive Hollywood graphics managed to sneak their way into the PS4, too: some of the cutscenes are the best-looking cinematics we've ever seen, and we're not just being dramatic: they're like *Toy Story* meets *Guardians Of The Galaxy*. When you're in a firefight (turning people into sheep or making them dance with the Groovinator), the on-screen mayhem is enough to make your vision swim.

INK-REDIBLE!
Okami

WHY: While it really pushed the PS2 hardware on its original release, the HD remaster on PS3 is the best way to play this stunning adventure. Perfectly capturing the Japanese sumi-e art style in a colorful 3D world, fans of *Zelda* will adore *Okami*.

"EVERY BATTLE LOOKS LIKE YOU'RE PLAYING A SCENE FROM THE MOVIES"

A FORCE TO BE RECKONED WITH Star Wars Battlefront

WHY: DICE managed to capture the look and feel of *Star Wars* perfectly with this enjoyable shooter. Whether you're fighting off rebels over Hoth's gleaming icy wastes or blasting stormtroopers in Endor's dense forests, every battle looks like you're playing a scene from the movies. It's one of the most beautiful games we've played.

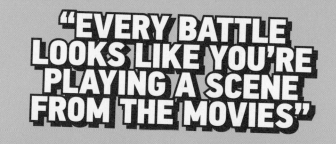

RIGHT IN THE FEELS
Ori And The Blind Forest

WHY: This mesmerizing adventure relies on its stunning visuals to draw players into its curious world and make them care about its strange characters. In this respect, it does a sterling job and this fantasy world is like nothing you've ever seen or experienced before. Keep the tissues close, though ... as gorgeous as it may be, it's also quite an emotional rollercoaster.

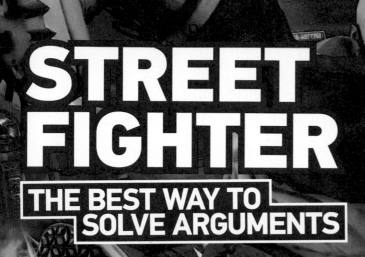

STREET FIGHTER

THE BEST WAY TO SOLVE ARGUMENTS

There's nothing more satisfying than winning a game of *Street Fighter*. Here's a game where you pick a character with unique fighting abilities and play against another player (or the computer) and try to lower their health to zero. It sounds simple, but it takes skill to pull off elaborate combos or to outplay your opponent—which is what makes it so rewarding. That's why it can be so fun to play, because the more practice you get, the better you become—until eventually no one can stop you! At that point, you can settle any argument you have with a game of *Street Fighter*, which is much more pleasant than shouting. People even play the game at tournaments and can earn thousands in winnings, which might give you a bit of an incentive to start improving your skills.

STATS

67 playable characters throughout the series

9 films based on the videogame

7 main titles released in the series

$500,000 in prize money tournaments

35 million copies sold

TIPS & TRICKS

LEARN DISTANCES
The most important thing you can do is know the range of your opponent's attacks, and at what distance you'll be safe.

PRACTICE YOUR MOVES
While you'll be able to win with basic attacks, you may want to take a look at your favorite character's unique moves to do even more damage.

REMEMBER BLOCKING
You're bound to get hit by your opponent's attacks at some point, but if you block then at least you will reduce the damage taken by your fighter.

TOP 5 SECRET BOSSES

AKUMA

1 This redheaded fighter's name means "devil" in Japanese, and is supposed to represent his strength and ferocity. He has a similar fighting style to the popular characters Ken and Ryu, though his attacks are often stronger. He's actually the younger brother of Gouken, another secret boss.

EVIL RYU

2 The evil version of Ryu has been in the *Street Fighter* series for years, but he's still interesting to play against and beat. He generally uses a mix of abilities from the normal, non-evil Ryu and from Akuma, giving him a lot of options when in battle. He's a very aggressive character, which means he's not very good at defending.

GOUKEN

3 As a master martial artist, Gouken— which means "strong fist" in Japanese— is an unsurprisingly powerful warrior. He's the martial arts trainer for both Ryu and Ken, as well as the brother of Akuma. He's a bit more defensive than his brother, though, and is good at looking for weak spots within his opponent's attacks.

Q

5 This character is one of the most mysterious in the whole series. No one knows his real name, what his face looks like, or even what he does. He's been spotted in photos of unsolved murders and when disasters happen, but is he connected? As a fighter he's extremely defensive since he is slow and has a lot of health.

DID YOU KNOW?

The idea of using combos was actually created by accident in the original game, but Capcom expanded on it over the years.

ONI

4 Akuma's search for the most powerful martial art leads him to being taken over by a demon, making this boss one of the hardest you'll ever find and fight. He's quick and powerful and has many more abilities to use than most other characters. However, he relies on getting up close to his opponent to hit them, meaning he can be defeated with longer-range attacks.

ALSO CHECK OUT...

TEKKEN 7
Whereas *Street Fighter* is 2D—you can only move left or right—*Tekken* has 3D environments, letting you move in all directions when fighting.

KNACK
Rather than one on one battles, *Knack* has you fighting swarms of enemies of different sizes. The idea is similar, though, as you use combos to attack.

GUACAMELEE!
Want to play as a Mexican wrestler fighting hordes of the undead? Using combos and unique abilities, you can defeat the skeleton enemies you meet.

USE PROJECTILES
Most characters can shoot fireballs, or other things, at opponents. Find the right buttons you need to press and practice!

COUNTERACT
If your opponent misses an attack—or you successfully block it—then make sure you punish them by aiming to hit them back immediately.

Boutique Hotel

STATS

million copies
sold across
the franchise **44**

Each character
has a number of
stock 10-hit combos

59 Tekken Tag 2
playable
characters

Bazillionaire
Trophy in
Tekken Tag 2
is won by
earning over
10,000,000G

22 years since the
series started

TEKKEN

GET READY FOR THE NEXT BATTLE!

It was one of the pioneers of the 3D fighting scene and *Tekken* has grown and evolved massively in the two decades since it first punched its way into arcades. The concept was so simple, it was a wonder nobody had done it before—rather than have different buttons for varying attack strengths, Namco instead plumped for a four-button setup where each button corresponds to one of the character's limbs. The great thing about this is that it means if you see a move or combo you like, it's usually easy to find... simply hit the buttons for the correct limbs in sequence! While each game in the series has added its own mechanics—from Rage that bolsters your attack power when your life is critically low, to Bound, which lets you extend combos by slamming opponents to the ground—the core combat engine remains one of the best in the business.

TIME LINE

TEKKEN (1994)
The first game launched in arcades before being ported to the original PlayStation with additional characters and modes the following year.

TEKKEN 2 (1995)
The sequel improved gameplay in every way possible, with *Tekken 3* taking this even further. Both are fondly remembered as classics.

TEKKEN 4 (2001)
This series misstep featured a number of broken design decisions, such as sloped stages that allowed for infinite combos.

TOP 5 CLASSIC CHARACTERS

KING

1 Many of *Tekken*'s fighters have been there since the beginning, but few are as iconic as King. Between the jaguar mask that never seems to come off and a varied arsenal of strikes and grapples, he's certainly one of the tournament's more interesting entrants.

PAUL

2 Think you've seen some ridiculous hair in gaming? Check out this dude's 'do! Don't let it fool you, though—Paul Phoenix is a powerful judo master with lots of neat combos and brutal special attacks. Oh, and he's friends with a bear, too. Yeah, *Tekken* isn't your standard beat-'em-up...

HEIHACHI

3 Boss of the Mishima clan and father to some rather demonic upstarts who want to replace him, this old chap can still hold his own in a fight and is even surprisingly nimble. Fun fact: he was once thrown into a volcano by one of his sons, but he apparently got better.

YOSHIMITSU

4 This wandering swordsman changes his look for every single game—over the years, he's been everything from a traditional samurai, to an alien, to a clockwork robot. That still doesn't really explain why he's allowed to bring a sword to a fistfight, though. That's clearly cheating.

LAW

5 It doesn't take a genius to spot that Marshall Law is inspired by martial arts hero Bruce Lee (just as *Tekken 2* addition Lei appears to be based on Jackie Chan), but the connection runs deeper—Marshall's son Forest, who takes his place in later tournaments, bears a striking resemblance to Bruce Lee's son, Brandon.

ALSO CHECK OUT...

SOULCALIBUR V
Another great Bandai Namco 3D fighting series, with a focus on weapon-based combat rather than hand-to-hand showdowns.

VIRTUA FIGHTER 5: FINAL SHOWDOWN
The best in the Sega series, *Final Showdown* is one of the most versatile and balanced 3D brawlers around.

STREET FIGHTER V
The original fighting titan returned in 2016 with some incredible graphics, a selection of all-new fighters, and some pretty awesome special moves.

TEKKEN TAG TOURNAMENT 2 (2011)
With the largest roster and some versatility in its tag battle system, this is one of the series' best outings.

TEKKEN 7 (2016)
It might have fewer characters than previous games, but with several brand-new fighters, it's the most interesting series shake-up in while.

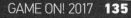

FINAL FANTASY

HEROES, ANCIENT EVILS, AND MAGIC!

STATS

86 different games, spin-offs, and sequels

265 playable characters across the series

highest character level in the series **99**

11 million copies of Final Fantasy 7 sold

58 million: highest boss hit points

With 15 main releases in this series, plus even more sequels, spin-offs, and remakes, you're probably wondering why it's called "*Final*" *Fantasy* when it never seems to end! Well, way back when the very first game in the series was released, the game's developer Square Enix wasn't doing very well. As the story goes, the company called it *Final Fantasy*, believing it would be the last game it ever released.

The game was a huge success, though, and the developer made lots of money from it. Nowadays it's the biggest role-playing game available, with awesome graphics, fantastic stories, and interesting combat systems. The most recent game—*Final Fantasy XV*—features a main character called Noctis who goes on an epic journey with his three best friends.

TIME LINE

FINAL FANTASY 1987
The very first game was released on the Super Nintendo Entertainment System, and kick-started the franchise's long-running success.

FINAL FANTASY VII 1997
This was the first *Final Fantasy* game to appear on PlayStation, and the first time the series had 3D graphics!

FINAL FANTASY X 2001
Thanks to the new PS2, the tenth game featured the best graphics the series had ever seen, along with a great combat system.

TOP 5 SERIES CHARACTERS

NOCTIS LUCIS CAELUM
FINAL FANTASY XV

3 The main character in *Final Fantasy XV*—the latest game in the series—is Noctis, a royal prince of the kingdom of Lucis. He has all sorts of fancy powers, such as the ability to magically summon any weapon he wants, and he can even foresee a person's death.

LIGHTNING
FINAL FANTASY XIII

4 Lightning is a bit grumpy, but she's trying very hard to rescue her sister who's been turned into crystal. She's also strong, athletic, and very loyal to her friends and family, so there aren't many more heroic characters than her—so we can forgive her for not smiling too much.

DID YOU KNOW?

Though there are some similarities between games, every *Final Fantasy* game uses a different combat system—so they all play differently.

CLOUD STRIFE
FINAL FANTASY VII

1 This spiky-haired soldier is the star of *Final Fantasy VII*, and is famous for the huge sword he carries. It's called the Buster Sword, and it's as big as Cloud himself! His original graphics have aged quite badly, but thanks to a remake of the game, here he is in all his HD glory.

YOU
FINAL FANTASY XIV

5 In *Final Fantasy XIV*, you don't actually play as a character designed by the game developer, but instead as someone you create yourself. You can be a human, an elf, or even a person with cat ears and a tail.

TIDUS
FINAL FANTASY X

2 It's not enough that Tidus is a skilled warrior—he's also a sport superstar. He's the world's best Blitzball player, a made-up sport that is basically soccer played underwater. After he's mysteriously taken to a different world, he becomes a bodyguard to help defeat a rampaging monster called Sin.

ALSO CHECK OUT ...

XENOBLADE CHRONICLES X
This game is on a massive scale, with a huge open world to explore and some awesome monsters to fight.

VALKYRIA CHRONICLES
The game's unique art style makes it look like a lovely watercolor painting. A truly beautiful RPG.

BRAVELY DEFAULT
This is also made by Square Enix, so you can imagine how similar it might be. It's made for 3DS, so you can take it on the go with you too.

FINAL FANTASY XIII 2009
This was the first *Final Fantasy* game to be released on the PS3 and Xbox 360, and would later go on to spawn two sequels of its own.

FINAL FANTASY XV 2016
The most recent game in the *Final Fantasy* series is set in the same universe as *Final Fantasy XIII*, but many years earlier.

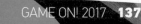

EVERYBODY NEEDS A HERO

SUPERHERO ROUNDUP 2017

Given the phenomenal success that superhero movies have enjoyed over the last few years, it's surprising that we haven't seen more superhero video games. But while gamers may be lacking some quantity when it comes to titles that let you don a costume and gain awesome powers, they still have plenty of quality games to choose from.

Online games like *Marvel Heroes* and *DC Universe Online* offer ever-changing experiences for their players, and games like *LEGO Dimensions* and *Disney Infinity* have fused heroes from comic book worlds with toys-to-life to great effect.

Not only that, but mobile superhero games have never been better. From genre-bending puzzlers like *Marvel Puzzle Quest* to high-quality action games like *Marvel Contest Of Champions*, it's never been easier to become a hero.

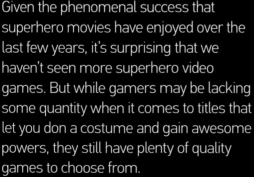

TOP 5 SUPERHERO GAMES TO PLAY RIGHT NOW

DISNEY INFINITY 3.0

1

There are few cooler moments than teaming up characters like Mickey Mouse with Spider-Man and Captain America as they fight against the powers of the evil Hydra. There are lots of characters to try out, and plenty of areas to explore! And with more being added all the time the only limit is your imagination.

LEGO MARVEL'S AVENGERS

2

With a mind-boggling roster of over 200 playable characters, including a brilliant Tony Stark/Stan Lee mash-up—Iron Stan—the latest LEGO Marvel adventure is the most extensive yet. It even makes use of official film audio to authentically recreate the spectacle of the *Avengers* movies we know and love.

MARVEL HEROES

3

This addictive action-RPG might be free to play, but it still packs plenty of polish, modes and playable characters. With a wealth of missions, loot, gameplay types and iconic Marvel superheroes already included, *Marvel Heroes* is becoming more successful. You can expect plenty more great content to come.

ULTIMATE MARVEL VS CAPCOM 3

4

It might be a few years old now, but *UMVC3* (to use its long abbreviation) is still one of the best and most finely tuned fighting games out there. The cel-shaded graphics perfectly capture the comic book feel, and when it comes to ridiculously over-the-top special moves, it can't be beaten.

THE WONDERFUL 101

5

Platinum Games' offbeat Wii U title deserves a mention here because there's no other superhero game quite like it. Not only do its quirky charm, unusual gamepad controls and shape-shifting mob of protagonists make it refreshing to play, it's also great to see a superhero game that shows off Japanese superhero culture!

DID YOU KNOW?

Platinum Games' initial idea for *The Wonderful 101* was a cast of existing Nintendo characters, instead of using their original heroes.

ALSO CHECK OUT ...

SCRIBBLENAUTS UNMASKED

The *Scribblenauts* series' *Unmasked: A DC Comics Adventure* has a great slew of DC characters, vehicles and items.

SUPERHEROES MANIA

Fancy putting your superhero knowledge to the test? This quiz app offers some short and sweet picture-based puzzles to try out. Later levels can get deceptively tricky.

SUPERHERO ROUNDUP 2017

DID YOU KNOW?
To date, *DC Universe Online* remains the highest grossing free-to-play title on both the PS3 and the PS4.

© Mineralblu Photography

KATIE GEORGE

WHO?

Katie is a phenomenal cosplayer who has been lighting up events, conventions, and the Internet with her awesome designs since 2004. Her superhero costumes are particularly brilliant, but she also dabbles in a wealth of different video game, anime, film, and TV characters.

WHY?

Boasting a BFA in Costume and Makeup Design for theater and film from Auburn University, Katie's skills have been honed over many years. She sources, stitches, and assembles every possible aspect of her costumes, and also shares her working process to help other aspiring cosplayers.

DID YOU KNOW?
Fans of The Flash can use his trademark high-speed running when creating their character in *DC Universe Online*.

TIPS & TRICKS

DON'T TAKE IT TOO SERIOUSLY
With occasional exceptions, superhero games are mostly about having a good time and feeling powerful. Enjoy yourself!

KNOW YOUR HISTORY
There are always a ton of references to the comic book universe packed into superhero games that you'll miss if you don't know your stuff.

THE JOKER

Gotham's most notorious villain needs no introduction. He's starred in almost as many games as Batman over the years, from blocky LEGO titles to the crazy action of *Injustice: Gods Among Us.*

GALACTUS

An almost omnipotent being that goes by the nickname 'Devourer of Worlds', Galactus is pretty darn intimidating. He's also the perfect final villain for *Marvel Vs Capcom 3.*

GREATEST SUPERVILLAINS

For every hero, you're sure to find a truly evil supervillain with nefarious plans. Here are some of the baddest baddies!

THE RIDDLER

Batman's trickiest foe remained elusive throughout the *Arkham* series, but his Riddler trophies and challenges provided some of the games' most memorable challenges. We'll admit we never quite got them all ...

DOCTOR DOOM

The long-time nemesis of the Fantastic Four is one of the most iconic supervillains in history. He can currently be found wreaking havoc with the Cosmic Cube in *Marvel Heroes.*

BE THE HERO

The nature of video games means you can put your own spin on established characters through new costume or whole playstyles.

EXPERIMENT WITH CHARACTERS

Everyone has their favorites, but by branching out you might just discover the superhero you've been looking for.

TEAM UP

All-star superhero teams are where it's at, so it makes sense to get a few of your friends in on the action.

HLGMakun

LovelyLovelyLeg [Magic Thistles] chubby panda577
chubby panda577 [Concrete Launcher] choupette1963

90

CAPTURE THIS!

PLANTS VS ZOMBIES: GARDEN WARFARE 2

11-PLAYER VANQUISH STREAK WITH ROSE ON Z-TECH FACTORY

Taking out enemy players in *Garden Warfare 2*'s multiplayer modes is easier said than done, but we managed to get a Vanquish Streak x11 using Rose on Z-Tech Factory. Can you beat our best?

LB   Y   RB

4 Magic Thistles

GIGANTIC

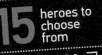
GIGANTIC

JUST ME AND MY MASSIVE GUARDIAN

There are plenty of free-to-play multiplayer online battle arena games to choose from, but *Gigantic* is the only one that lets you go into a skirmish with a giant guardian by your side. While the five-on-five combat is carried out below, the guardians—five stories high—support, boost, and heal the players. So they're not just massive, they're useful! Of course, it matters how you play on the ground too, and fortunately *Gigantic* allows you a lot of choice in how you go about taking on the opposition. Many unique characters are available and each has their own talent, such as sniping from a safe distance or having a large pool of health. Each fighter brings something different to the fray, meaning that while at first you might not select a character you get along with, eventually you're going to realize *Gigantic* does have something for everyone.

TIPS & TRICKS

ACCENTUATE THE STRENGTHS
Pay attention to your hero's strengths. There's no point trying ranged combat if you're using a tank like Lord Knossos.

BUT HIDE THE WEAKNESSES
Be wary of what your hero will struggle with. No one is perfect and everyone has a rival that can take them out.

NO "I"
There are five of you (and your guardian), so work together: there's no point in lone-wolfing. This tip works for real life as well!

TOP 5 HEROES

1 TYTO THE SWIFT

One of *Gigantic*'s nimblest characters, Tyto does sort of give the game away with his name. Regardless, his ability to be always moving, always jinking, always jumping, and always attacking makes him a deadly assailant and terrifying opponent in the right hands. Also, he has a cute little pet. Aww!

DID YOU KNOW?

Players on both PC and Xbox One are able to compete with one another in *Gigantic*—it's a game for everyone!

2 UNCLE SVEN

The rotund Einstein-lookalike might not seem the best choice on the battlefield, but Uncle Sven is a great choice for almost any player. He's mainly employed as a utility player, with his chemical concoctions arcing through the air to help his team or hinder opponents.

3 VADASI

It's always annoying to play as a healer character, only to see your teammates immediately take damage again. *Gigantic* gets around this with Vadasi, who can heal *and* shield friendlies at the same time. Her healing rays *also* damage the opposition—it's a three-for-one!

4 VODEN

A ranged attacker, Voden is a sort of fox-deer-thing who proves very useful on the battlefield. With the ability to poison enemies, confuse them with decoys, and give himself a heal-superjump combo, Voden is a great teammate in the right hands.

5 XENOBIA

This terrifying-looking squid-snake-woman is a tremendous ally to have. Her abilities mainly focus on stripping opponents of their armor, making their attacks weaker, and generally slowing them down. She can slow and weaken enemies, turning the tide of a battle single-handedly.

"GO INTO A SKIRMISH WITH A GIANT GUARDIAN AT YOUR SIDE"

KEEP A DISTANCE

While you're learning, steer clear of intense battles at close range. It's easier to learn how to play *Gigantic* with ranged heroes like HK-206 or Voden.

IF ALL ELSE FAILS

Pick Uncle Sven—his mix of incredible combat ability and usefulness to the team in a support role makes him an ideal choice for most players.

ALSO CHECK OUT ...

SMITE

Another third-person take on the popular MOBA genre, *SMITE* is more technical than Gigantic with a steeper learning curve but every bit as fun.

AWESOMENAUTS

Old-school side-scrolling platform combat with a modern MOBA twist, *Awesomenauts* has a dedicated army of fans—and with good reason.

STATS

$18.5 million
prize pot for The International 2015, the official *Dota 2* tournament

$2 million
earned by *Dota 2*'s highest-earning pro player, Peter "ppd" Dager

111 playable heroes to choose from

2 years
of beta testing before *Dota 2*'s full version was released

Over 1.3 million
videos related to *Dota 2* on YouTube

DOTA 2

IT'S WORTH GETTING INTO

Dota 2, or *Defense Of The Ancients 2*, is a hugely popular MOBA (multiplayer online battle arena) game. However, don't be put off by the acronyms! It has a notoriously steep learning curve, as *Dota 2* punishes players harshly for falling in battle, yet it's one of the most popular games out there based on the fun that can be had.

Taking control of one of over 100 hero characters—each with different strengths, weaknesses, and abilities—you join a team with four other players to take on an opposing five-person team. Simply put, your team has to destroy the base. It's the intense competition and the fine teamplay that makes *Dota 2* something more than just another game.

TIPS & TRICKS

HOLD OFF ON THE CREEPS
If you push too hard you'll be vulnerable. Stay put and wait for the creeps to come to you, trying to bag the last hit for more XP.

TP SCROLLS ARE YOUR FRIEND
They might not seem cheap, but anything to get you automatically back into your lane or others is of great benefit.

PAY ATTENTION TO YOUR ROLE
Each hero has a role, so at least try to play in the style your hero adopts. If you can't, choose a different hero!

TOP 5 HEROES FOR BEGINNERS

LICH

1 An unconventional support character he might be, Lich is nonetheless great for beginners. Not only does he inflict a good deal of damage, his ability to sacrifice friendly creeps gives your team a boost and denies your opponent the XP they would get. And as for his ultimate attack, Chain Frost... wow!

DID YOU KNOW?

Dota 2 can trace its roots back to *Warcraft III: Reign of Chaos*—a real-time strategy game developed by Blizzard.

"LICH CAN SACRIFICE FRIENDLY CREEPS TO DENY OPPONENTS XP"

LIFESTEALER

3 It might look scary—and it is—but Lifestealer is a great "jungler" (ie strays away from main areas to pick off stragglers) for the beginner in *Dota 2*. It's the biggest zombie out there, is immune to magic, is capable of self-healing, and deals a lot of damage given half a chance.

SNIPER

2 There's a mix of combat in *Dota 2*, but Sniper is great for those just starting out—purely because his weapon keeps you away from the front lines, so you'll last a bit longer before falling. While careful positioning is key to getting the most out of Sniper, that's something you can learn ... while away from danger.

WINDRANGER

5 Not everyone wants to be a team player, so the likes of Windranger are perfect for beginners who want to go solo. Her Windrun power allows her to escape tight situations—speeding her up and slowing down enemies—making Windranger the perfect beginner's character for experimenting, figuring things out and finding out just how to win.

LINA

4 Lina stands out as one of the better nuker characters for the beginner. She's capable of dealing heavy damage to the opposition and is a formidable force in the early stages of a match—best grab a Magic Stick to increase her survival rate, though. Lina is a floating fiery maiden who deserves to be mastered for bossing the middle lane.

ALSO CHECK OUT...

LEAGUE OF LEGENDS

Dota 2's main competitor, *League of Legends*, is the most popular game in the world. It's easier to learn than *Dota 2*, as players aren't overly punished for dying.

HEROES OF THE STORM

Blizzard—creator of *Warcraft*—got into the MOBA genre with this game. It's still growing, and people love it.

WATCH OUT FOR RUNES

"Watch out" in the good way—runes are helpful and respawn every couple of minutes, bestowing clone powers, increased damage, and more.

WATCH THE HIGHER GROUND

If you have the lower ground, run away to fight another day. Don't ever attempt to battle uphill.

HEROES OF THE STORM

HEROES OF THE STORM

STATS

66 cosmetic character skins to purchase

47 playable heroes to choose between

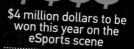

$$$$ $4 million dollars to be won this year on the eSports scene

10 playable maps to choose between

10 heroes in free rotation at any one time

DID YOU KNOW?

While all heroes can be unlocked through in-game play, it would cost you over $370 to unlock them all individually and immediately.

A DIFFERENT KIND OF MOBA

Are you eager to get involved in the MOBA craze, but put off by the steep learning curve that has been established by the likes of *Dota 2* and *League Of Legends*? Then try Blizzard's *Heroes Of The Storm*, the ideal game to help you learn the MOBA ropes.

Heroes Of The Storm has a bigger emphasis on teamwork than other MOBAs—rather than individual players levelling up as they earn kills, the team becomes stronger, so newcomers benefit from playing alongside skilled players. There's also no punishment for dying and unlike *League of Legends*, no need to worry about equipping items. Simply put, you can focus on playing the game without any distractions!

Best of all, *Heroes Of The Storm* retains the competitive thrill of MOBAs, so if you're interested in the genre, give it a try!

TIPS & TRICKS

DON'T GO SOLO
Every time you die, it gives the other team an EXP boost advantage, so team up and stay safe.

KNOW YOUR ROLE
There are four classes to choose between, and it's well worth knowing what each of them can do and are for before jumping into ranked play.

PLAY THE OBJECTIVES
If you want to win games, you'll need to stay focused on the objective. Each map has one to complete, so work with your team to achieve it!

TOP 5 HEROES FOR BEGINNERS

RAYNOR

1 Raynor arrives from the world of *StarCraft* as one of the best entry-level heroes. The hulking marine is part of the Assassin game class, focused on high single-target DPS (damage-per-second), which means you won't have to concentrate on much more than avoiding damage and clicking away at enemy heroes until they die.

DIABLO

2 If you want to jump straight into the middle of the action, you'll want to play the role of a Warrior. Characters in this class are responsible for "tanking", which is to say you soak up damage until the DPS heroes arrive to deliver the killing blow. Diablo not only looks awesome, but he has lots of health!

VALLA

3 One of the most popular characters on the competitive eSports scene, Valla is a simple Assassin class character who's really easy to get to grips with. You'll be able to attack at range, picking off enemies that wander from the pack, and generally have fun without too much worry about abilities and objectives.

ZAGARA

4 This is where game difficulty begins to increase; the Specialist class characters can deliver extreme amounts of damage from range, but are incredibly squishy. Zagara is a good entry-level hero for this role, though you will be expected to provide support during objectives without fail by your teammates.

LI LI

5 Healing in any Blizzard game can be tricky—the role has a lot of responsibility—which makes the Support class a tough role for newbies. Still, if you're committed, you'll find that nearly every one of Li Li's abilities has an auto-targeting system to help you get used to the controls.

STAY ON MINIONS

Ignoring the minions is easily done but they can often drop healing orbs and other buffs that are essential to your survival.

WATCH THE PROS

Heroes Of The Storm has a great online following so if you're the right age to watch YouTube or Twitch you can get tips from the pros.

ALSO CHECK OUT ...

LEAGUE OF LEGENDS

It's the king of the MOBA *and* competitive gaming scene. Existing players don't go easy on newbies!

DOTA 2

Arguably better than *League Of Legends*, it's a tougher and more tactical take on the MOBA genre that features a steep level of entry.

SMITE

Want your MOBA to be a bit more like some other of your favorite games? *Smite* is easier to understand and play than its rivals.

STRANGEST PLOTS

DROPSY

WHY: *Dropsy* is a hugely charming point and click adventure game, but it's deeply weird, too. The clown's quest for redemption after a mysterious fire destroys his circus is filled with quirky characters, surreal locations, and a host of talking animals, all while packing in enough warm and damp hugs to last you a lifetime. It's one of the most bizarre games you will probably ever play, but don't let that put you off. Give *Dropsy* a chance.

GOAT SIMULATOR

WHY: The storylines in *Goat Simulator* are defined by the player, but that doesn't make them any less ridiculous. Whether it's stupid glitches or crazy ragdoll physics, this game has it all. Plus, it lets you crash rooftop parties, summon the undead, fight to the death, and blast off into space—all as a goat (or sometimes an ostrich. Or a giraffe).

GRIM FANDANGO

WHY: The mind of Tim Schafer has produced many crazy video games over the years, but few have been better realized than *Grim Fandango*. A film noir-style adventure set in the Land of the Dead, the game sees players investigating mysterious goings on in the afterlife as skeletal travel agent Manny Calavera. Try your best to save Mercedes Colomar's virtuous soul.

HATOFUL BOYFRIEND

WHY: The dating simulator is a bit of an odd genre to begin with, but *Hatoful Boyfriend* takes it to a whole new level of weird. How? By making you the only human student at St. PigeoNation's Institute—an elite school populated entirely by talking (and entirely eligible) birds. We're not joking. The wait for the English version was totally worth it.

6 WEIRDEST CHARACTERS

TINGLE

The green oddball of the *Zelda* series is one of Hyrule's most recognizable (and unsettling) faces. He first appeared in *Majora's Mask* and has even starred in four spin-off games of his own.

MR. RESETTI

Animal Crossing is usually a relaxing place to spend your time, but turn your game off without saving and you'll have to face the wrath of the series' loudest and angriest mole—Mr. Resetti.

CHOP CHOP MASTER ONION

The smelly sensei of *PaRappa the Rapper,* Master Onion is a kung fu master who is also a rapper, who also has a giant onion for a head. He most recently appeared in *PlayStation All-Stars Battle Royale.*

SEAMAN

Star of the Dreamcast game of the same name, Seaman has gone down as one of the most bizarre video game characters ever. And rightly so: he's a fish with the face of a man!

SUPER MEAT BOY

The hero of Team Meat's hard-as-nails platformer, Super Meat Boy succeeds in being a completely adorable hero, while also being a walking, smiling cube of meat. No mean feat!

THE KING OF ALL COSMOS

Sporting a crown and fabulous ruffle, the King of All Cosmos—from the game *Katamari Damacy*—is an unconventional ruler. And things only get weirder when he opens his mouth ...

LOVERS IN A DANGEROUS SPACETIME

WHY: Intergalactic travel, animals stranded in space, and a quirky love story that spans the universe: *Lovers In A Dangerous Spacetime* is nothing if not unique. The co-op shooter is designed to be played with a friend, but solo gamers can always count on the assistance of their trusty in-game dog or cat.

THE EXPERT SAYS … JAY THOLEN
Designer, *Dropsy*

Dropsy has a history that stretches back to 2004. I was a junior in high school then, working on a small zombie-smashing platformer during my free time. The project was never finished, but I'd always liked a clown enemy I created for the game's circus level. In 2008, I re-used the character in a message board choose-your-own-adventure game and framed him as a kind-but-misunderstood gentle giant. People immediately fell in love with him, and many of his quirks today (including face painting his pets, and hugging people without permission) were from the community that formed around that original little game.

"STUPID GLITCHES OR CRAZY PHYSICS, GOAT SIMULATOR HAS IT ALL"

KATAMARI FOREVER

WHY: This list could easily be filled entirely with *Katamari* games, but the most recent console installment in the sticky ball-rolling series takes the biscuit by including dream sequences and RoboKing—a robotic King of All Cosmos who destroys all the stars in the sky.

OCTODAD: DADLIEST CATCH

WHY: In some ways the story in *Octodad* is very simple. Octodad completes household chores and helps out with grocery shopping. The catch is that Octodad is also an octopus, masquerading as a human, who must evade a sushi chef.

ODDWORLD: NEW 'N' TASTY

WHY: A remake of the classic platformer *Abe's Odyssey*, *New 'N' Tasty* crams in lots of bizarre characters and plenty of disturbing humor. Narrated by its main character, Abe—a floor-waxer enslaved at RuptureFarms, where he is currently employee of the year—*New 'N' Tasty* is a frequently crazy and unhinged adventure set inside "the biggest meat-processing plant on Oddworld."

UNDERTALE
TALKING TO THE MONSTERS

STATS

📅 **2.7 years** in the making

$50,000 raised on Kickstarter from a goal of $5,000

6 hours long, but... ...3 unique endings

48 monsters to fight, or spare

> * (Playfully crinkling through the leaves fills you with determination.)

DID YOU KNOW?

The Annoying Dog that shows up throughout the game represents Toby Fox, the creator of *Undertale*.

What if instead of battling monsters in a game, nobody needed to get hurt? Sounds cool? Or completely lame? Well ... *Undertale* is a unique RPG created, written, composed, and programmed by indie developer Toby Fox. Fight the monsters, or talk to them and befriend them—it's your choice. Fox's project was originally funded on Kickstarter, and now it has sold over half a million copies. *Undertale* takes inspiration from unlikely places: the funny and weird humor of Nintendo's classic *Earthbound*, the web comic *Homestuck* (where Fox has also composed music), and also quirky titles like the *Touhou* shoot-'em-up series and Japanese RPG *Shin Megami Tensei*. But *Undertale* has a personality all its own that reflects its creator, with a wide variety of monsters and characters as you travel through the Underground. With so much hidden content to discover, it's no wonder *Undertale* has an army of loyal fans.

TIME LINE

SHIN MEGAMI TENSEI —1992
This SNES RPG allows you to talk to demons and recruit them to your team, inspiring *Undertale*'s nonviolent battles.

EARTHBOUND —1994
Another SNES RPG classic, known as *Mother 2* in Japan, it has goofy humor and a memorable story.

MARIO & LUIGI: SUPERSTAR SAGA—2003
One of the best and funniest Game Boy Advance games, *Superstar Saga*'s unique battle system makes it special even today.

TOP 5 CHARACTERS

ALPHYS

1 Alphys is the Royal Scientist of the Underground. She is shy and reclusive, but her lab work holds some dark, secret experiments involving other monsters. Although a lizard monster, she loves human culture like anime and manga. Alphys is the only major character you can't fight in *Undertale*.

MUFFET

2 Muffet is running a bake sale in Hotland in aid of the spiders trapped in the ruins, and she won't be pleased if you don't buy something! A spider-like monster with five eyes, she acts as a mini-boss. Muffet was designed by the web comic artist Michelle Czajkowski as a reward for the *Undertale* Kickstarter backers.

SANS

3 Sans is the older of the skeleton brothers. When he's not making puns about skeletons, he's often sleeping on the job or taking breaks from his work. He can teleport, uses a Gaster blaster laser gun in battle, and he knows that he's really in a video game!

"FIGHT THE MONSTERS, OR TALK TO THEM AND BEFRIEND THEM"

PAPYRUS

4 Papyrus is the younger brother of Sans. He's a brash and confident skeleton who dreams of joining the Royal Guard, but his true nature is kind. Papyrus never gives up on anything. Unfortunately this includes his hobby of cooking spaghetti, at which he is terrible. He loves to set puzzles for players.

DOGGO

5 Doggo lives in the Snowdin Forest and is a member of the Royal Guard. He can only see things that are moving—the word doggo means to lie motionless and quiet—a condition known as Riddoch syndrome in real life. His weakness in battle is that he loves being petted.

ALSO CHECK OUT...

XENOBLADE CHRONICLES X
A more traditional RPG: explore a vast and beautiful world filled with dangerous monsters.

MARIO AND LUIGI: DREAM TEAM
Mario teams up with "Dreamy Luigi" to rescue the Pi'illo Folk from Bowser and the bat king Antasma.

MOTHER 3—2006
Earthbound's Game Boy Advance sequel was only released in Japan, but you can play as hero Lucas in *Smash Bros*!

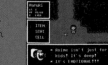

UNDERTALE—2015
While *Undertale* draws inspiration from a weird and wacky selection of games, it's got a style and story all of its own.

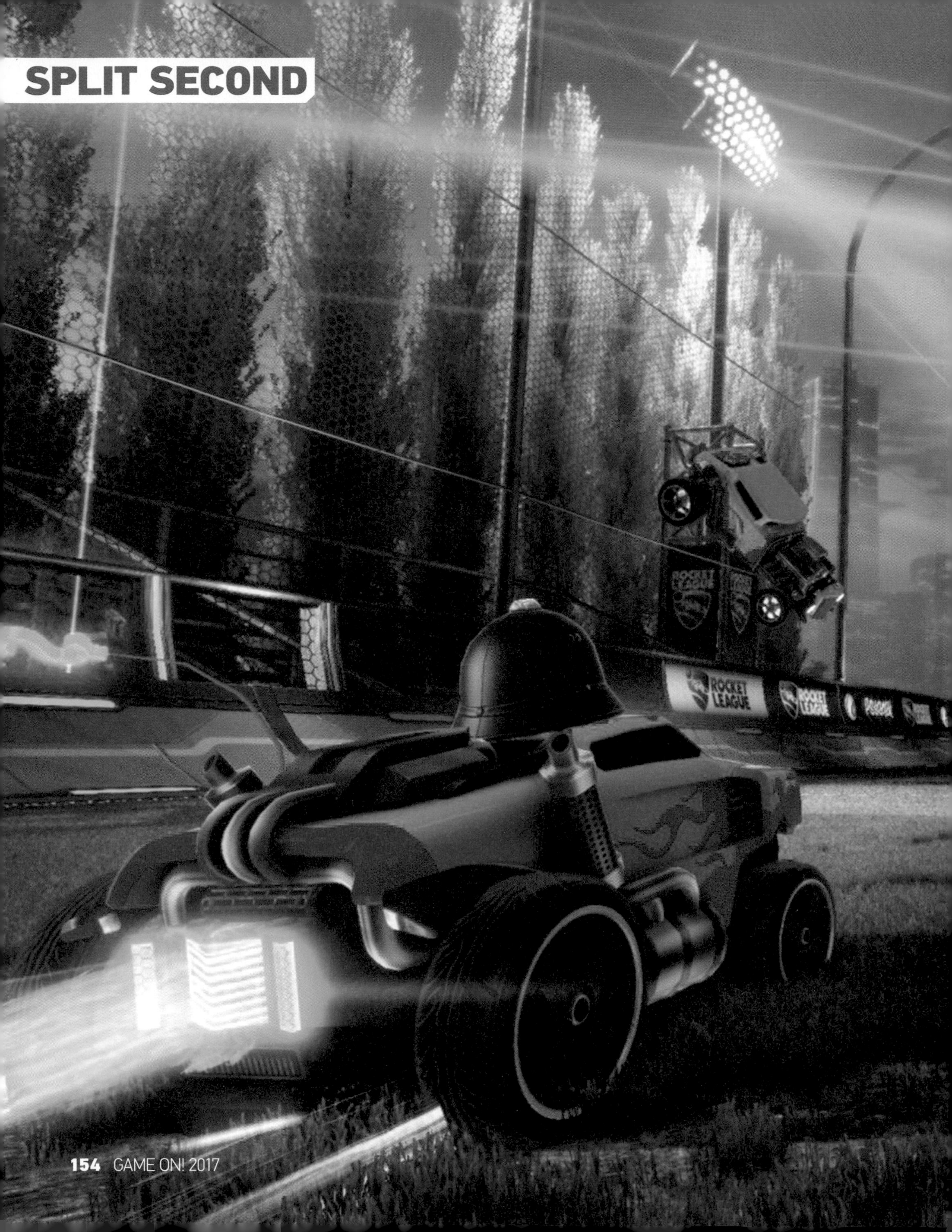
ROCKET LEAGUE
ROCKET LEAGUE
ROCKET LEAGUE

SPLIT SECOND

ROCKET LEAGUE

NITRO-POWERED AWESOMENESS

•

Playing a game of rocket-powered soccer using cars instead of humans is crazy, ridiculous fun, which explains why this is among the biggest games of the past year. Playing a match and having fun is easy, but mastering its advanced tactics is a real challenge.

NO MAN'S SKY

STATS

The E3 2014 trailer on Sony's channel chalked up
4 million views

Assuming a new planet was discovered every second from launch, it would take
585 BILLION YEARS
to see them all

5 people were working on the near-infinite game in the beginning

18,446,744,073,709,551,616 planets to discover and explore. Yes, that's **18 QUINTILLION**

AN INFINITE GALAXY TO EXPLORE!

Most games have a typical structure—a start, a middle, and an end. *No Man's Sky* is not most games. Sure, there's an ultimate goal here (namely getting to the center of the universe) but it's more about the journey than the destination. With a cosmos so obscenely huge that players will never see it all and no idea of the amazing things you'll see and do along the way, this ambitious indie space sim is like nothing you've ever played before. Since its galaxies are all created by the game itself, even the developers won't know exactly what surprises are in store. You can't get closer to the spirit of adventure than that! So hop into your shuttle, set a course for unknown worlds, and blast off—who knows what wonderful things you'll find out there?

TIPS & TRICKS

DON'T GET GREEDY
There's no need to bleed an entire planet dry of resources. Doing so will only net you a bad reputation—there are loads more planets out there to mine!

LOOK AFTER YOUR SHIP
There's no garage or personal armada here—your personal ship is all you have. Keep it in good shape and upgrade whenever you can.

TOP 5 THINGS TO TRY

FLYING

1 As you may or may not have heard, space is pretty big. Since you can't just fast-travel to any old planet, you'll need to hop in your ship and fly between worlds—light-speed travel is all well and good but you're still going to spend most of your time in the cockpit.

EXPLORING

2 Once you touch down on a new planet—possibly one nobody has ever set foot on before—you'll want to take stock of your surroundings. Is it hostile? Are there lots of resources? You'll need to check out each new discovery in order to answer these questions.

DOGFIGHTS

3 Whether battling peacekeepers after doing irreparable damage through mining, or defending your cargo from filthy pirates, space combat is plentiful. The good news is that it's exciting, but the bad news is that doesn't make it any less dangerous!

CHARTING

4 There are plenty of ways to make a name for yourself, and one is by reporting your findings. This way, other players will know if they stumble upon a planet you've already discovered or spot a creature you've already seen—you may even be able to name them!

GATHERING

5 Blasting around the galaxy isn't free, you know. When you find a bountiful planet, you'll need to harvest some of its resources to fund further exploration and upgrades to your ship. Take too much, though, and the authorities will be on your case.

TAKE YOUR TIME
A new planet may *seem* worthless, but spend a little time exploring and you could find that its barren exterior hides an extremely lucrative secret.

PICK YOUR BATTLES
You don't have to shoot your way out of every single encounter, you know. Sometimes, a strategic retreat is your best option.

KEEP LOOKING!
Found ten junk planets in a row? The next discovery could be the one that makes you rich through charting new species or working the land!

NO MAN'S SKY

WHO WILL YOU BE?

THE EXPERT SAYS ...
COBRA TV

A YouTube channel loaded with great *No Man's Sky* videos

Finally there is a game that takes down gaming boundaries that we've all gotten used to: "you can't go here," and "you can't do that." And it doesn't hold your hand through the entire experience: there's a universe of more than 18 quintillion planets; no loading screens; and no story. Your actions in the game will create reactions *from* the game, revealing a personal story of events that will differ from everyone else that plays through it. That's what excites me most about the game—seeing the world of *No Man's Sky* through the eyes and minds of all that play and experience it.

TRADER
By gathering resources from one planet and delivering them to systems where they are rare or even completely unobtainable, you stand to turn a tidy profit. Just be sure to look after your cargo.

ACE
You got skills, kid—and they're gonna pay the bills! Various factions will be on the lookout for skilled pilots to protect their ships and deal with unwanted attention. Keep your friends safe and you can expect to be handsomely rewarded.

PIRATE

Why do all the hard work when you can have others do it for you? Intercept transports and rob other vessels of their commodities and you'll be laughing—assuming you can outrun the long arm of the space law.

EXPLORER

Making it big isn't all about fighting and looting—just by documenting everything you see on your travels, you should still be able to make a decent wage and upgrade your gear that way.

THE EXPERT SAYS ...
65DAYSOFSTATIC
The band that helped Hello Games create the soundtrack

Probably the most exciting aspect of working on *No Man's Sky* for us is the feeling that we're standing on a threshold of a new world of possibilities when it comes to considering the computer game as an art form, and game engines as tools to make art—including music. Our slice of the project is a small one, but nevertheless it's been a great learning experience to be involved with such a talented bunch of people, and to be working with Paul Weir (the audio director on *NMS*) in applying ideas of procedural music generation to our linear compositions and nebulous soundscapes, to build the infinitely-long *NMS* soundtrack.

DID YOU KNOW?

No Man's Sky's universe is procedurally generated, meaning the game's engine creates planets and creatures itself.

ALSO CHECK OUT ...

ELITE DANGEROUS

A much more serious take on space exploration, *Elite*'s long-awaited sequel is perfect for anyone wanting to go deeper into the astronaut fantasy.

STAR CITIZEN

Another straight-faced PC space sim, although one where the aim is ultimately to let players run the galaxy. It's one of the most beautiful games we've seen.

STAR FOX ZERO

At the other end of the seriousness scale is Star Fox Zero, the latest game to follow Fox McCloud's (and his friends') adventures in the Lylat system.

STAR FOX ZERO

STATS

Over **1 million** have watched the trailer

2.1% of Wii U players pick Fox in *Smash Bros*

Falco Lombardi is the tallest of the crew at **6 ft 2"**

23 years that's how long the series has been around for

6 games in the main series

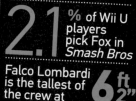

DO A BARREL ROLL!

Strap yourselves into your Arwings folks, because it's time to save the universe, *again*—us gamers tend to do that a lot, don't we … it must be our "thing."

Star Fox Zero brings the series back to its roots, inspired by the excellent *Star Fox 64*, which you may have recently played on your 3DS. What does going back to its roots mean? The emphasis is on combat, as you duck and dive your way through space dogfights. There's a twist, though, as this time you can see forward from your cockpit and behind you thanks to the Wii U's dual-screen capabilities.

Like most *Star Fox* games, you won't be saving the universe on your own. That's right—your wingmen Falco the falcon, Peppy the rabbit, and Slippy the toad are lending Fox McCloud (that's you) a hand, forming the coolest team since *Star Wars' Rogue Squadron*.

TIME LINE

2 BLW (BEFORE LYLAT WARS)—BETRAYAL
James McCloud and Peppy Hare are betrayed on Venom by Pigma Dengar—who is working for the villainous Andross.

0 BLW—TO (LYLAT) WAR!
Andross declares war on the Lylat System and a new Star Fox—this time Fox McCloud—is contracted into service.

0 ALW (AFTER LYLAT WARS)—OUTFOXED
Fox McCloud single-handedly tracks down and kills Andross on Venom. Andross is presumed dead.

TOP 5 VEHICLES!

ARWING

1 The classic, the original, and, obviously, the best. The Arwing has proven to be a versatile and powerful spacecraft and has been the staple of the *Star Fox* squad for years (well, since the very first game, on the Super Nintendo). It's also pretty good at shooting down evil mad scientists, specifically Andross.

WALKER ARWING

2 It's like an Arwing but it stays on the ground! This basically makes it a walking space ship that can wipe out your enemies with ease. Also, there's a significantly smaller chance of you flying into a building if you're using two mechanical legs to move …

DID YOU KNOW?

Do you think the characters talk like puppets? It's because Shigeru Miyamoto is a big fan of the old *Thunderbirds* TV show.

LANDMASTER

3 Well, it's a tank, what's not to like? The Landmaster is a hardy vehicle equipped with a T&B-J2 Laser Cannon and a Smart Bomb launcher. Landmines can't even stop this beast, thanks to the Landmaster's hover ability. We're glad they're on our side!

GREAT FOX

4 Great Scott, it's the Great Fox! This famous bit of tech features prominently outside of the *Star Fox* series, notably appearing as a stage in the *Super Smash Bros* games. In *Star Fox*, though, it's the battleship that serves as a mobile HQ and residence of the *Star Fox* team.

"THE BATTLESHIP SERVES AS A MOBILE HQ"

GYROWING

5 This is Slippy Toad's favored craft in *Star Fox Zero*. While not as agile as an Arwing or as powerful as a Landmaster, this handy little vehicle is useful for moving cargo and debris. Sure, you can go around blasting stuff up, but who's going to take care of all the mess? That's what this thing is for.

ALSO CHECK OUT …

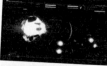

STRIKE SUIT ZERO

This takes the simple, yet effective, gameplay of *Star Fox* and puts it in a mecha game that feels like an anime. It's difficult but it's also great fun.

REZ INFINITE

Rez Infinite is a virtual reality game, which means that the awesome visuals and frantic on-rails gameplay elements are beamed directly into your eyes.

8 ALW—WHERE'S MY ARWING?

Fox McCloud touches down on a dinosaur planet called Sauria, leaving his Arwing behind. Fox meets his future wife, Crystal.

32 ALW—A NEW TEAM

Fox has settled down with Crystal and their son, Marcus, forms a new Star Fox team featuring Peppy's Granddaughter and Slippy Toad's son.

STATS

26 million
copies sold (series-wide)

78.33 Average metacritic
score for the series

14 games in the
franchise

Over 4 million
views for the *R&C*
movie trailer
on YouTube

382 weapons in the
main series

LOMBAX IN ACTION

RATCHET & CLANK

Everyone's favorite Lombax and his talking robot backpack have returned! Insomniac has treated us not only to a film about the dynamic duo, but a new game, too. Well, it's sort of a new game—it's a reimagining of the original entry to the series, with some amazing new graphics. Really, it's the game about the movie that's about the first game!

That sounds confusing but you'll get the idea; it's about time we took *Ratchet & Clank* back to what made the series so great, and where better than the start? The series is best known for its outlandish and kooky weaponry, its hilarious characters and plotlines, and, of course, its crazy, action-packed set pieces filled with explosions and awesome robots. Bring it on!

TIME LINE

RATCHET & CLANK—2002
The first game in the series introduced the two characters, pitting them against the evil Supreme Executive Chairman Drek.

RATCHET & CLANK 2: GOING COMMANDO—2003
Ratchet was taken to another galaxy, trained as a commando, and raced spaceships in the series' second game.

RATCHET & CLANK 3: UP YOUR ARSENAL 2004
This title saw the pair fighting to defeat Dr. Nefarious before he wiped out all biological matter in the galaxy!

TOP 5 AWESOME CHARACTERS

CLANK (OBVIOUSLY)

1 He may be a defective Sentry Bot, but Clank is awesome. He's super-smart, he's pretty much equipped to deal with any situation, and he can turn into a giant robot that fires missiles at everything. What's not to love? Clank was even a secret agent at one point.

TALWYN APOGEE

4 Awesome in every sense of the word, Talwyn is the daughter of a famous intergalactic explorer. Initially she tries to blow Ratchet and Clank out of an airlock, but later on the three become good friends. She ends up helping Ratchet out quite a bit when poor old Clank goes missing.

RATCHET (OF COURSE)

2 This Lombax is quite similar to Luke Skywalker in *Star Wars: A New Hope*. He's a regular sort of guy (sorry—Lombax) who yearns for adventure and, boy, does he get it when Clank comes tumbling down onto his planet. Ratchet is a skilled mechanic and robot/alien smasher and the main hero of the series.

DID YOU KNOW?

1999's *Spyro 2: Ripto's Rage* features an orange creature with a wrench and a tiny robot. Hmm, sound familiar?

SNAGGLEBEAST

5 Qwark's Snagglebeast is *giant*, dangerous, and likes to party by the way of the Groovitron, and, to be honest, any giant and dangerous monster that likes to party has got to be awesome. Just look at those moves! You go for it!

CAPTAIN QWARK

3 Also known as Copernicus Leslie Qwark, this guy is, uh, weird. He's originally billed as a bit of a hero, a guy that Ratchet aspires to be like, but he's anything but—he's hammy, tricksy, and generally quite cowardly. He always gets his comeuppance, though, and the payoff is always *brilliant*.

ALSO CHECK OUT ...

JAK & DAXTER TRILOGY
Do you like all your platformers to star a cool dude and a tiny sidekick? Then look no further.

BANJO-KAZOOIE
Sticking with the theme of duo-character platformers, Rare's *Banjo-Kazooie* challenges you with the task of stopping the evil Gruntilda.

RATCHET & CLANK FUTURE: TOOLS OF DESTRUCTION—2007
Emperor Tachyon tries to capture Ratchet after a trip to the future.

RATCHET & CLANK FUTURE: A CRACK IN TIME—2009
Ratchet must find the lost Clank, while dealing with the threat of a returning Dr. Nefarious in this awesome title.

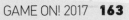

MOST AWESOME HEROES

MARIO

WHY: It doesn't matter if you play Nintendo games or not—everyone knows who Mario is. We don't understand how this chubby, dungaree-ed, mustachioed plumber wormed his way into our hearts, but now he's there, we don't want him—or his brother—to ever leave! There's a reason this guy is the the mascot for gaming and we wouldn't change a thing.

SACKBOY
LittleBigPlanet

WHY: Not only is Sackboy one of the cutest characters we've ever seen, his ability to keep on truckin'—and keep on smiling—through those tricky *LittleBigPlanet* challenges is amazing! Best of all, he now comes with a troop of equally adorable friends to help him out, all of whom we can also dress up in awesome costumes too! Yay!

TOP 6 SACKBOY LITTLEBIGPLANET 3 COSTUMES!

SULLY (Monsters Inc)

We didn't think Sackboy could be any more adorable ... and then he dressed up like Sully! It's our indisputable favorite of the *Monsters Inc.* costumes (although we do love the Boo one too!).

THE TENTH DOCTOR (Doctor Who)

We guess your favorite *Doctor Who* costume will depend upon which is your favorite Doctor, but forgive us if we slip on David Tennant's outfit, grab a sonic screwdriver and shout ALLONS-Y!

OLAF (Frozen)

As gorgeous as Sackboy looks dressed as Queen Elsa or Princess Ana, it's our summer-sun-seeking friend, Olaf, who warms our hearts! Just, uh, keep him away from open flames, okay?!

MARTY MCFLY (Back to the Future)

Few people look as good as Michael J. Fox in that "life preserver," but if anyone call pull off looking like our favorite time-traveller, it's Sackboy! Time to make like a tree, and "get out of here" ...

OCTODAD (Octodad)

Okay, so he doesn't have all the children to look after and he doesn't have all eight arms (boo!), but it's worth checking out this amazing costume just to see that squidtastic moustache!

MALEFICIENT (Sleeping Beauty)

We know it doesn't make sense, but popping on the costume of an evil character just makes Sackboy even cuter, especially when it comes to Disney villains!

LINK Legend of Zelda

WHY: Link is everything a hero should be—courageous, strong, determined, and calm in the face of danger. Time and again Link has stepped up to be a virtuous protector, setting out alone—and in some instances, unarmed!—to save Hyrule and Princess Zelda. No matter what the challenge, you know Link will always do his best.

KIRBY

WHY: It's hard to imagine, we know, but though Kirby looks innocent enough, be careful—looks can be deceiving! Kirby can become pretty much anything he eats, which means he's kind of formidable if he's just munched on a sword or a hammer!

RAYMAN

WHY: Not only do we love Rayman, but we also love all the games he's starred in, too! Although they're, uh, challenging games, they're never dull, particularly as Rayman himself can use those disembodied hands and feet of his to move around the game in very unique and entertaining ways!

PROFESSOR LAYTON

WHY: Unlike other heroes on this list, Professor Layton doesn't need swords or shotguns to demonstrate his heroics. Using his brain where others use brawn, Professor Layton (in his self-titled series of games) solves puzzles to get to where he needs to go, proving there's more to being a hero than just muscle!

PHOENIX WRIGHT

WHY: When it comes to fighting injustice and standing up for the little guys, there's no greater hero than Phoenix Wright, the star of the *Ace Attorney* games. With a brain as sharp as his suit and even sharper hair, we'll never have any "objection!" to spending time with Phoenix!

DID YOU KNOW?

Portal's writer confirmed that although lead character Chell can talk, she simply chooses not to give GLaDOS the satisfaction of saying anything!

THE EXPERT SAYS ...
HEY CHRISSA
YouTube Gamer

My video game hero is Chell. I love that you are thrust into her world, unaware of her past as simultaneously Chell is awakening for the first time from her Relaxation Vault. Together you find out that she is a test subject of Aperture Science and you must work your way through bizarre tests with the aid of a Portal Gun. Even though Chell is a silent protagonist, you feel connected to the character. As the story progresses, it's fun to see Chell become the ever-increasing thorn in the side of AI boss GLaDOS. Remember kids, "the cake is a lie."

CHELL Portal

WHY: Though she never says a word, *Portal*'s Chell is one of gaming's most fearless, determined, and patient heroes of all time. Never giving up on the puzzles—nor giving in to the goading of nemesis GLaDOS—she's the epitome of all things cool, calm, and collected. We don't care how long we're stuck in Aperture Science, providing Chell's there to lead the way!

SONIC THE HEDGEHOG

WHY: Not many characters are as instantly recognizable as this spiky-haired hero. He's fast, funny, and fun, whether he's racing alone or with a pal in a blur of blue and white. There's a reason why he's one of gaming's most famous faces and SEGA's mascot, you know!

DONKEY KONG

WHY: As one of the only video game baddies to change careers and become one of the good guys (remember, it was DK who stole Mario's lady friend in his very first game), we knew it was only a matter of time before Kong had his own starring role!

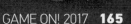

DID YOU KNOW?

Gizzy Gazza's first video was posted in June 2012 ... if you want to be inspired, watch the video to see how much he has developed his style since then!

TOP 10 FUNNIEST YOUTUBERS

PUSHINGUPROSES

WHY: You might not find her must-watch intro video *that* funny, but give her channel a chance—pretty much everything else Roses does involves good quality humor. Covering mainly retro games, PushingUpRoses likes to include some historical information and facts about the games she features. It just goes to show that there is a place for every game to be covered with comedy, and room for lots of different kinds of videos.

GIZZY GAZZA

WHY: With his seemingly endless energy, variety of voices, and creative ideas for videos, it's easy to get swept along for the ride when watching Gizzy Gazza. It's the unpredictable nature of his videos that make you laugh out loud when you least expect it because you never know what's coming next. You don't need to be a *Minecraft* fan to enjoy the humor, just drop by his channel and click away for guaranteed laughs!

IHASCUPQUAKE

WHY: IHasCupquake like to keep things pretty chilled. You won't find any humor that flirts with bad taste here—it's just nice, relaxing, and friendly fun with a lot of laughs thrown in. Cupquake plays a lot of different games, from *The Sims* to *Slime Rancher*, and she is at her best when she's making videos with other folks, bouncing jokes off her family and friends—but even when going solo, she's solidly entertaining.

THEDIAMOND MINECART

WHY: TheDiamondMinecart proves you don't need comedy voices or screeching to provide humor. Despite releasing an insane number of videos, he manages to retain his wit through them all and is great company, too. Our personal highlight? The skit with Dan listening to One Direction ... painfully awkward to watch but hilarious at the same time!

CAPTAINSPARKLEZ

WHY: You probably know Sparklez for his *Minecraft* songs and animations—and rightly so, because they're amazing and he's very talented! There's a vein of humor running through everything he produces that keeps his millions of subscribers coming back for more every day. If you've no interest in *Minecraft*—or *Trials Fusion*, more recently—it might not appeal, but we suggest just giving him a try anyway.

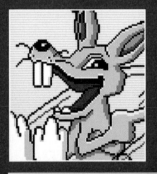

SUPER BUNNYHOP

WHY: An American master of silliness and sarcasm, Super Bunnyhop brings a mix of famous games that you'll almost certainly know, and games you've probably never heard of or played, with a general theme of being very funny across them all. He's got a pretty specific sense of humor, which might not appeal to every viewer, but it certainly appeals to a lot of people!

THINKNOODLES

WHY: A lot of YouTubers rely on being loud to be entertaining, never developing their skill beyond shouting or offering anything with depth or imagination to it. Thinknoodles goes entirely against this ethos, bringing hilarious, cute, funny, clever, and non-sweary videos on all manner of subjects in and around gaming. Some might take it as an insult to be called "kid-friendly," but ThinkNoodles wears that particular badge with pride.

STAMPY LONGHEAD

WHY: Stampy is one of the most popular YouTubers in the world, and there's a good reason for that. He just sounds like he is having *so much fun* all of the time—he's the happiest player we've ever seen. His *Minecraft* videos are great, telling awesome stories in Stampy's Lovely World, and his other Let's Plays are just as fun to watch.

THE EXPERT SAYS ...
HOLLIE BENNETT
Sony UK Digital and Community Manager, PlayStation Access

The best thing about YouTube is that there is something for everyone. It's easy to find YouTubers that you like, that you find entertaining, and who love the same things as you. There is an almost limitless amount of entertainment and there are always new videos and channels to discover! At PlayStation Access, personality is key. It's all about being ourselves and building a community of people who love the same things as we do, and sharing that together. Our absolute main focus is on making videos we feel our community would enjoy.

VENTURIANTALE

WHY: By himself, Venturian is good fun ... but when you put four siblings together, you're destined to get some great entertainment. They know each other so well, and there's the constant need to make each other laugh. Good fun!

PAULSOARESJR

WHY: For something a little different, PaulSoaresJr is an older gamer who has a unique take on everything he plays. Whether it's vanilla *Minecraft* or *Stardew Valley*, Paul's endless stream-of-thought commentary makes for some fantastic moments, which explains why he has over a million subscribers. Even if you don't find him funny, you'll find it hard to disagree that he has the best voice on YouTube!

© Riot Games

THE PROFESSIONAL PLAYERS

ESPORTS HAVE TAKEN COMPETITIVE GAMING TO THE BIG-TIME, WITH ENORMOUS SALARIES AND PRIZES TO BE WON IN FRONT OF STADIUMS FULL OF FANS

Competitive video gaming has been around for as long as people have played games, but eSports are a relatively new phenomenon. With live video streaming services like Twitch, suddenly millions of people can watch gaming tournaments from around the world, making games like *League of Legends*, *DOTA 2,* and *StarCraft* into big business.

Instead of playing at bring-your-own-computer tournaments or at local arcades, today's top competitive gamers practice their craft full-time in team houses, with coaches, analysts, and business managers to help them. That might sound like a dream job, but it's also really hard work. Staying at the top of competitive gaming means that it's rare to get time off, and a workday might consist of eight or nine hours of practice online, plus another three hours of team meetings, strategy sessions, and internal scrimmaging.

Not many people have the ability to play at this level, and even fewer can sustain that amount of work and effort for long. Those that have what it takes, however, can do incredibly well. When the Evil Geniuses' *Dota 2* team won their world championship at The International in 2015, they became millionaires.

The future of eSports looks bright, as card-battler *Hearthstone* and beat-em-'up *Street Fighter V* show that the next eSports hit could come from any genre.

© Riot Games

© Riot Games

FNATIC
FNC

■ **FNATIC HAVE BEEN** around almost as long as eSports themselves. Their *League of Legends* team is also famous for being one of the best in the world and they won the first-ever *League of Legends* championship in 2011. Even more impressive is Fnatic's competitive record under pressure. The team has contested the LCS finals all six times and only lost once, cementing its place as a truly dominant *League of Legends* team.

THREE BIG NAMES
MARTIN "REKKLES" LARSSON: League of Legends
JOHAN "KLAJBAJK" OLSSON: League of Legends
YEONG-JIN "GAMSU" NOH: League of Legends

GAME PICKS
LEAGUE OF LEGENDS
DOTA 2

TEAM LIQUID
TL

■ **TEAM LIQUID ARE** a cornerstone of the English-speaking eSports community. Before Team Liquid were a major eSports organization, their site was the home of pro *StarCraft* fans outside of South Korea. They recruited several top *StarCraft 2* players in its early days, and expanded into every major eSport. To research the history of almost any eSport, their community encyclopedia, the Liqui-pedia, is the place to start.

THREE BIG NAMES
TAEJA: StarCraft
PIGLET: League of Legends
TLO: StarCraft

GAME PICKS
LEAGUE OF LEGENDS
STARCRAFT
DOTA 2

© Riot Games

SOLOMID
TSM

■ **TEAM SOLOMID ARE** one of the most popular teams in the world, and one of the oldest teams in professional *League of Legends*. They have finished in first place in the United States four times in as many years, and are known for recruiting star players from all around the world. Now the team has expanded into newer eSports games like *Hearthstone* and *Super Smash Bros.*

THREE BIG NAMES
YELLOWSTAR: League of Legends
DOUBLELIFT: League of Legends
LEFFEN: Super Smash Bros.

GAME PICKS
LEAGUE OF LEGENDS
HEARTHSTONE

© Riot Games

LGD GAMING
LGD

■ **LGD ARE ONE** of the best and most famous Chinese eSports organizations in the world, with world-class teams in both *Dota 2* and *League of Legends*. Their *Dota 2* team is almost always a big contender to win The International, while their *League of Legends* team was the 2015 Chinese champion. However, success eludes them at major international tournaments, as they have yet to win a title on the big stage.

THREE BIG NAMES
JANG "MARIN" GYEONG-HWAN: League of Legends
MMY: Dota 2

GAME PICKS
LEAGUE OF LEGENDS
DOTA 2

THE BIGGEST ESPORTS TOURNAMENTS

Major eSports tournaments come in two flavors: the first is the annual festival, where a few different games have brief and intense competitions in front of huge audiences. The second is a seasonal tournament, like in soccer or basketball, where teams compete for months just to make the playoffs, then are slowly eliminated until only two remain to compete in an epic final. As eSports become more popular, demand for the latter type of tournament is increasing.

The *Dota 2* world championship, known as The International, is the biggest and best of the annual festival tournaments. In just over one week every year, more than a dozen of the best teams in the world play a gruelling number of games in a packed sports arena. BlizzCon lasts two days and features the *Hearthstone*, *StarCraft*, and *Heroes of the Storm* championships all happening at once.

In the seasonal tournaments, the *League of Legends* Championship Series begins play in January each year, continues through until August, and then the World Championship playoffs take several weeks as each stage takes place in a different city of a major competitive region. By the time of the finals, competitive *League of Legends* games will have been seen in sports stadiums around the world.

THE INTERNATIONAL
PRIZE: $18,429,614   VIEWS: 20 MILLION

Dota 2's flagship tournament takes place each year in Seattle, with the best teams from around the world competing for more than a week. In 2015, four of the top five finishers were from China, but the victory belonged to the American team Evil Geniuses, who won in a dramatic surprise attack on China's CDEC in a moment that became known as the Six Million Dollar Echo Slam.

LEAGUE OF LEGENDS WORLD CHAMPIONSHIP
PRIZE: $2.13 MILLION
VIEWS: 36 MILLION

Known simply as "Worlds," the *League of Legends* World Championship brings together the strongest teams from the Chinese, Southeast Asian, North American, and European leagues. Since 2012, a Korean team has won the tournament every year, and SK Telecom became the first team to win twice in 2015.

DID YOU KNOW?
StarCraft 2 players have to be able to sustain 200–300 "actions per minute" and the best can peak at almost 600.

STAT — During the 2015 *League of Legends* World Championship, an average of 4.2 million people were watching at any given time. 36 million people tuned in.

© Marv Watson

MOST AWESOME TOURNAMENT MOMENTS

The first *Dota 2* International in 2011 had a grand prize of $1 million. In the 2015 tournament, Evil Geniuses won $6.6 million for first place.

© Marv Watson

In 2003, fighting game legend Daigo Umehara finished either first or second in four different games at EVO.

© David Zhou

EVOLUTION CHAMPIONSHIP SERIES (EVO)

PRIZE: $303,000
VIEWS: 19 MILLION

EVO may not be the richest tournament in the world, but it is still one of the most important because it is both the World Cup and the Olympics of fighting games. Every major fighting game is featured at EVO, from classics like *Street Fighter* to *Super Smash Bros.* for Wii U. It's very special because many of the all-time greats from the early 2000s still compete there today.

THE SIX MILLION DOLLAR ECHO SLAM
The International 5
AUGUST 8, 2015

After successfully ambushing Evil Geniuses, China's CDEC went to the Roshan pit to press their advantage by getting a huge power-up. Instead, EG caught them in one of the most devastating surprise attacks in *Dota 2* history, and won the tournament.

© David Pham

KANEBLUERIVER BEATS THE ODDS
EVO 2015
JULY 19, 2015

KaneBlueRiver is famous for his unorthodox *Ultimate Marvel vs Capcom 3* team of Hulk, Haggar, and Sentinel. Yet despite his team of characters being considered weak for tournament play, he beat everyone to lift the Evo trophy.

DUEL OF CHAMPIONS: LIFE VS. SOS **BlizzCon**
NOVEMBER 7, 2015

The 2014 *StarCraft 2* champion, Life, had a chance to become the first repeat world champion in the game's history ... but he was foiled by the 2013 champion, sOs. Their seven game series was an amazing clash between two of the game's very best players.

© Blizzard Press

COUNTER LOGIC GAMING

© Marv Watson

COUNTER LOGIC'S AMERICAN VICTORY
NA LCS Summer Playoffs
AUGUST 23, 2015

CLG are one of the oldest *League of Legends* teams in America, but they had never won the regional title in three years of competition. At the LCS playoffs in Madison Square Garden in New York, they finally broke their curse and beat the odds to win their first North American title.

ESPORTS

INTERVIEW
KIM "REIGNOVER" YEU JIN
League Of Legends pro gamer

Reignover was one of the two South Korean players who helped reinvent Fnatic in 2015. Then he went to start a new team, Immortals, in North America in 2016. At first overshadowed by teammate Huni, Reignover is now recognized as one of the best junglers and tacticians in *League of Legends*. Together, he and Huni went on a regular season winning-streak that lasted over thirty games.

HOW DID YOU GET YOUR CHANCE WITH FNATIC?

I was having a tryout at SK Telecom. But the rule was changed so that you could only have 6-7 players on a team at once, so, unfortunately, extra backup players like me could not be part of the team. I had to go home! But while I was playing around my house, I was friendly with Huni. He went to Fnatic first, and he really wanted a South Korean teammate.

He liked me, so he asked me if I wanted to play in Europe. I could speak English, and the team was Fnatic, which is a really famous team, so I said yes! And we went to Europe together.

WHY DO YOU ALWAYS HAVE SUCH A GOOD SENSE FOR THE RIGHT MOVE IN LEAGUE OF LEGENDS?

There's no special technique. We communicate a lot. If everyone is telling me what they need, I decide what the best play is for me, and then tell people what to do. It always looks like I'm in the right position, but it's my team who makes it look like I'm smart!

MOST PLAYED GAMES

LEAGUE OF LEGENDS
DOMINANT TEAM: SK TELECOM

League of Legends is one of the most popular games in the world, with several million people playing every day. With new champions arriving every couple of months, and tons of cool costumes for each champion to wear, *League of Legends* is always evolving. That keeps a lot of players coming back to the free-to-play MOBA.

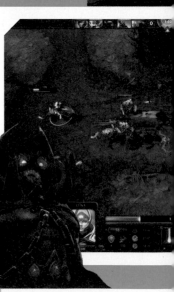

DOTA 2
DOMINANT TEAM:
EVIL GENIUSES

Dota 2 is the successor to the game that started the MOBA genre, the Defense of the Ancients modification for *Warcraft 3*. It's an incredibly complicated game that preserves many unique things about the original mod, which many people love. Perhaps more importantly, it is jam-packed with collectible items, goodies, and special events that keep millions of gamers coming back.

TIPS & TRICKS

LEARN THE ANGLES
Most competitive games involve a lot of geometry that players will memorize so they can always be accurate.

MASTER YOUR PLAY SPACE
Use high-performance monitors and custom settings for your equipment, so that the only variable is your skill, not hardware performance.

PRACTICE THE BASICS
The more you do automatically, the faster and better you'll be. That means repeating and memorizing your fundamentals.

STREET FIGHTER V
DOMINANT PLAYER: INFILTRATION

Street Fighter has been the highlight of annual fighting games showdown Evo since the tournament began back in 2002. It's an unusual eSports series in that the focus is on individual players rather than teams. South Korean player Infiltration is currently edging out the likes of Japan's Mago and the USA's Snake Eyez as the dominant *Street Fighter V* player. Look for this to change, though—new *Street Fighter V* tactics are always being discovered.

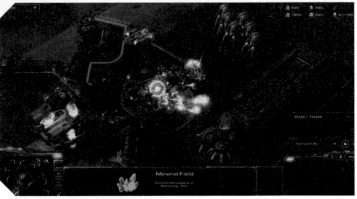

STARCRAFT 2
DOMINANT TEAM: SK TELECOM

StarCraft 2 stood on the shoulders of *StarCraft: Brood War*, which was the game that practically created modern eSports, especially in South Korea. *StarCraft 2* arrived just as streaming video became popular, and that showed the game's incredibly skillful players to brand-new audiences around the world.

DID YOU KNOW?
The fastest game of *League of Legends* was Immortals' perfect game against Team Impulse: 18 minutes and 16 seconds.

HEARTHSTONE
DOMINANT TEAM: NA'VI

Hearthstone is a wildly popular card game that came to prominence partly because so many pro gamers from other games started playing it in their off-hours. *Hearthstone* was embraced by *StarCraft 2* and *League of Legends* players alike, and it wasn't long before it became a great competitive game in its own right.

HIT THE BOOKS
Reading about strategies and item-builds can be more valuable than time spent playing the game.

LEARN EVERY ROLE
Pro gamers become specialists, but first you have to master every role on a team, or every race in a game.

BE COOL
Skill and training are important, but bad teammates and poor sports rarely last in eSports, and are hardly ever recruited.

SPLIT SECOND

OCTODAD

LOVING FATHER. SECRET OCTOPUS.

Indie developers can make some pretty odd games, and this is definitely one. You control an octopus, disguised as a human father, as he attempts to keep his true identity a secret from his family—and the chef next door, who wants to make calamari!

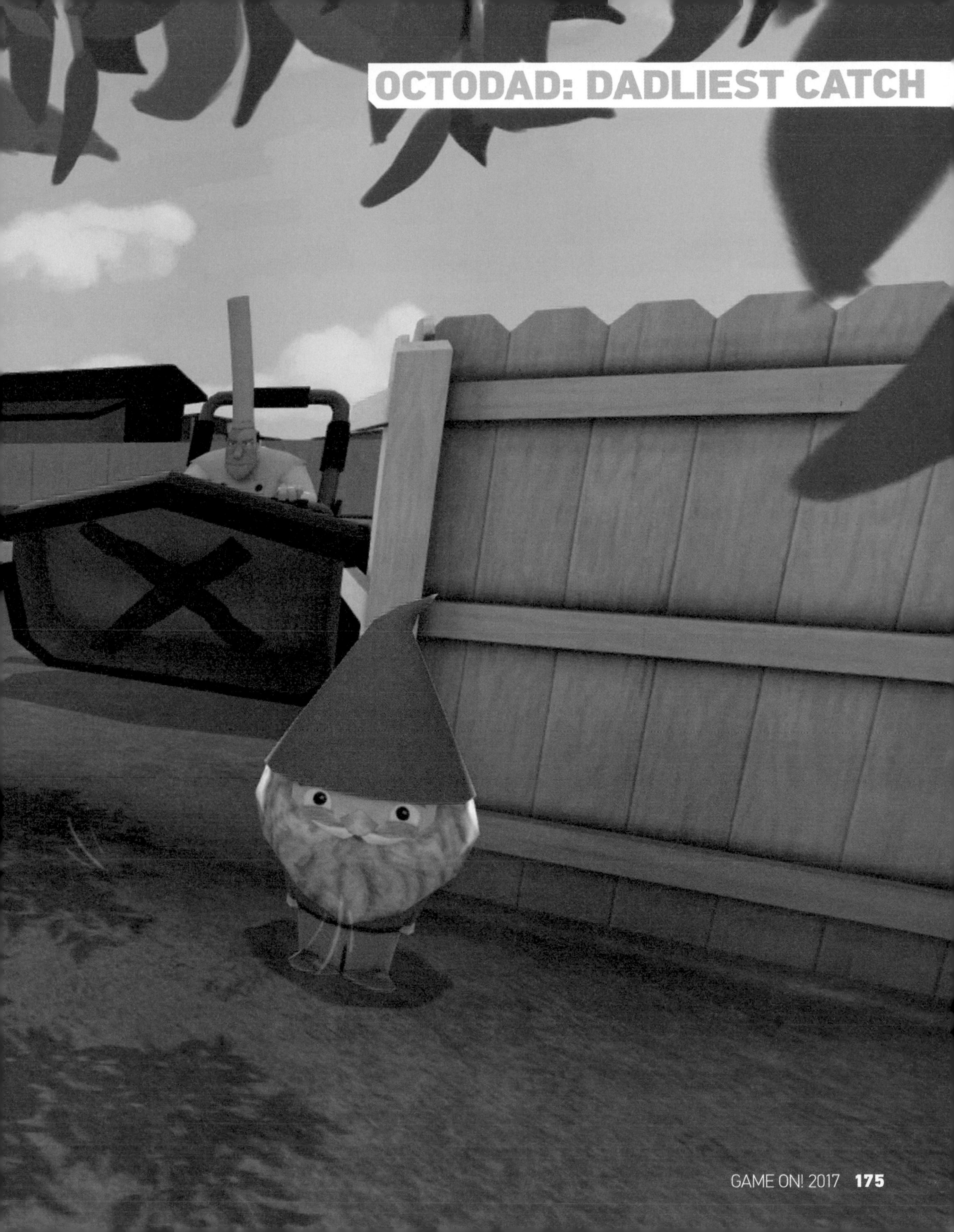

STATS

315 playable songs

Jump into two live

24/7 music channels

Become lead guitarist in 5 different bands

42 playable live-action songs

Jam with up to players locally

GUITAR HERO LIVE

IT'S TIME TO PARTY

DID YOU KNOW?

If you've got a USB microphone handy, you can plug it and start wailing along to your favorite tracks as well.

After five years out of the spotlight, *Guitar Hero* returned in 2015 and, perhaps for the very first time, it truly delivered on creating the ultimate rock star experience. Ditching the cartoon graphics and conventional five-button fretboard, *Guitar Hero Live* combines live-action set lists with an all-new guitar peripheral to make you feel like you're at the heart of a real band. It gives you the opportunity to look out upon sprawling crowds of real people who dynamically react to your skill and accuracy—it's awesome and only a little bit terrifying. And, if that wasn't enough, there are also hundreds of tracks to play through in two scheduled music channels that run 24/7 for players around the world. It's an amazing experience.

TIPS & TRICKS

WORK YOUR WAY UP

Thanks to the new six-button configuration, *Guitar Hero Live* plays more like real guitar than before. Start off on Easy and work your way up to Expert.

PREPARE FOR CHORDS

Get ready for a challenge; songs now demand you switch between White and Black notes, not to mention intricate barre patterns.

LEARN THE SCHEDULE

GHTV has hundreds of songs playing over real-time music channels. Learn the schedules so you aren't stuck playing pop hits from the Eighties.

TOP 5 FUN SONGS

PARAMORE
Now

1 As energetic and catchy as all of Paramore's songs, the difference with *Now* is how it has so many changes of rhythm and fun parts to play. It sounds like a simple song but once you start playing along, you realize how unusual and interesting it is, and it's that challenge which makes *Now* such a joy to play.

BAND OF SKULLS Asleep At the Wheel

2 From one of the hottest new rock bands to emerge in years, *Asleep At The Wheel* represents everything that's great about *Guitar Hero* tracks. It combines a catchy chorus, a driving verse, and a solo that'll tie your fingers together. This will consume your Play credits quickly!

WOLF ALICE Moaning Lisa Smile

3 The grunge-pop band is taking the world by storm, so it's no surprise to see Wolf Alice in *Guitar Hero Live*. This will take some concentration to learn—the switch between beautiful acoustic and driving lead riffs can be tricky—but once you master it you'll have a great time.

MUMFORD & SONS I Will Wait

4 Who knew upbeat folk songs could be so much fun to play? *I Will Wait* picks up the pace throughout and once you get going, the thumping rhythm is infectious. You'll want to stomp your foot in time to the music as you play through this, as will anyone watching! Great fun to play on Expert as well.

RIHANNA California King Bed

5 It isn't all rock and roll. *Guitar Hero Live* also takes on R&B and pop on occasion, and it doesn't get much better than Rihanna in that respect. Better still, get a microphone plugged in and a friend can join you as you nail this absolute anthem.

"THERE'S HUNDREDS OF TRACKS TO PLAY IN TWO MUSIC CHANNELS"

LEARN THE SONGS
Be prepared to learn songs inside out. This way you'll know when to deploy your hero powers and easily move up the leaderboards.

KNOW YOUR GENRE
While it can be tempting to jump straight into the harder tracks, get the basics down on some easier pop and classic rock hits first.

ALSO CHECK OUT ...

ROCK BAND 4
Shifting focus from the guitarist to an entire band experience, *Rock Band* lets you and your friends fill all roles of a conventional group and rock out.

DJ HERO
For aspiring DJs, *Guitar Hero Live* developer Freestyle has you covered with *DJ Hero*, an awesome way to live out your mixing fantasies.

STATS

1700+ DLC tracks

Supports four players

18 million units sold

3,926 dollars to purchase it all

130 million individual track downloads

ROCK BAND
GETTING THE BAND BACK TOGETHER

When it comes to the ultimate in local multiplayer fun, you should look no further than *Rock Band*. It's the game that begs you and your friends to get together, pretend to be rock stars, and play the ultimate form of group karaoke. Between the guitar, bass, microphone, and drum peripherals, there's sure to be an instrument that lets you feel like you're living out your ultimate rock and roll fantasy; unless, of course, you always dreamed of being a roadie, in which case you can be on hand to change the batteries or resync the game controllers if something goes wrong. Still, with thousands of music tracks available across the disk and premium store, there's bound to be something you'll like the sound of; maybe you'll even discover your new favorite band.

DID YOU KNOW?
Harmonix doesn't plan on releasing another full-release *Rock Band* game, just song packs and updated instruments in the future.

TIPS & TRICKS

1 STAY FOCUSED
Keep your eyes on the notes at all times, which is easier said than done in multiplayer. Stay focused or you could derail a song.

2 GET COMFORTABLE
Spend enough time with your instrument of choice so that you don't have to second-guess finger or hand placement during fast color switches.

3 START AT THE BOTTOM
Sure, everybody wants to be a rock star—but if you want to play Expert, start on the lower difficulties and work up.

TOP 5 SONGS FOR EMERGING MUSIC FANS

U2
I WILL FOLLOW

1 U2 are still going strong, but this is from their first album, way back in 1980. Don't let that put you off though, *I Will Follow* is a classic rock song, with the kind of rhythm that will get stuck in your head. Best of all, there are lots of interesting parts to play, whether you're on drums, bass, or guitar. Good luck to whoever ends up being the singer, though—you'd better warm up your voice before trying to hit the song's high notes!

THE MIGHTY MIGHTY BOSSTONES
THE IMPRESSION THAT I GET

2 This song is all about a cool ska punk sound—fast tempo, guitar distortion, and loud vocals. This track comes on the *Rock Band 4* disk and is great to play with your friends. It's energetic, catchy, and above all else, super fun!

MARK RONSON FT. BRUNO MARS
UPTOWN FUNK

3 You've probably been humming this smash hit since it came out 2014, so you might as well learn to play it. It's upbeat, funky—of course—and great to dance to. There's no way this song will be leaving your brain anytime soon.

THE CURE
FRIDAY I'M IN LOVE

4 This song might be more than twenty years old, but it still sounds as cool and fresh as ever. You'll need a few friends to help you perfect the vocal harmonies, but it's worth the effort. Be warned though, you might catch your parents humming along to this one...

R.E.M.
THE ONE I LOVE

5 Find your inner lead singer and grab the microphone from your bandmates to belt out this song at the top of your voice. While your friends play along, see if you can hit the long note on the iconic chorus of "Fiiiiiiiire." If not, just keep practicing until they beg you to stop!

"YOU KNOW WHAT'S GREAT ABOUT ROCK BAND 4? IT CATERS FOR EVERYONE"

ALSO CHECK OUT ...

GUITAR HERO LIVE
Putting the spotlight on the lead guitarist of various fictitious bands, *Guitar Hero Live* is a score-focused experience for the wannabe rock god.

AMPLITUDE
This rhythm action game from Harmonix is a frantic assault on the senses (and fingers). The electronic music is thunderous and it's lots of fun.

4 DON'T RUSH INTO THINGS
It can be easy to forget, but remember to go into Options and calibrate instruments for accuracy—you won't regret it.

5 FREESTYLE SOLO TIP
If you're struggling to nail the timing of those freestyle solos, listen out for when your drummer hits the bass pedal: that's when you should strum.

TOUGHEST ENEMIES

ENDER DRAGON
Minecraft

WHY: There's plenty to be wary of in *Minecraft*, but none are so tricky as the Ender Dragon since you'll need the best weapons and enchantments to kill him. He'll recharge health from the towers by his nest if they aren't destroyed.

DID YOU KNOW?
World Of Warcraft once had a boss so difficult that even groups of 40 people together couldn't beat him. Blizzard had to make it easier!

SLIG Oddworld

WHY: From the original *Oddworld* to the recent *New 'n' Tasty* release, sligs feature early on in the *Oddworld* games and don't pose much threat. But it's the variety and number of them as you progress that gives you grief—Popper sligs, Flying sligs, Bouncer sligs, and Big Bro sligs with armor ... ouch.

LONG GUI Final Fantasy XIII

WHY: Once you reach the Gran Pulse area of this game there's plenty of tough beasties you'll need to take on—called Titans, in fact—but once they're all dead you can then fight an optional enemy called the Long Gui, and this is the toughest fight you'll have in the game!

6 WAYS TO OVERCOME A TOUGH ENEMY

1 KEEP TRYING
Don't worry if you don't beat something the first time, that's what games are all about. Simply pick up the controller and try again.

2 LEARN FROM YOUR MISTAKES
If an enemy defeats you a lot, stop to think about what they are using to beat you. If you remember it for the next time you fight, then you can avoid it completely.

3 ASK FOR HELP
It's okay to ask for help from time to time. Sometimes getting help from someone else will also show you new strategies or tactics that you didn't consider before.

4 UPGRADE YOURSELF
Some games will let you improve certain aspects of your character—such as your health or the damage you deal. If you're struggling, go back and level up.

5 TRY DIFFERENT ABILITIES
In some games you can get enemies that are strong or weak against particular abilities and weapons. Try different items and you may discover a weakness.

6 JUST TAKE A BREAK
If you keep struggling against a certain enemy then you're going to start feeling frustrated. Take a break and come back once you've relaxed.

THE LICH KING World Of Warcraft

WHY: Okay, so if you have a max level character in *World Of Warcraft* then the Lich King isn't going to be so difficult for you, but if you play him at the level appropriate range then you'll find that this frozen warrior is a mean opponent. And that's kind of fair, considering he's one of the central bad guys to the whole *Warcraft* universe!

GOOMBA
Super Mario Bros
WHY: You'll probably laugh at this. How can a tiny Goomba be so difficult? You'll be surprised how many people get caught out by the famous enemy simply because they're not paying attention! These guys have taken more of Mario's lives than any other baddie.

TURRET
Portal 2
WHY: The main reason these little fellas are on our list is that they're the only things that can actually kill you in any of the *Portal 2* test chambers. The gun turrets are also super cute thanks to their despairing robot voices, but don't be fooled—they're dangerous!

DARTH VADER
Star Wars: Battlefront
WHY: As you sprint around Hoth trying to take down an AT-AT, there are few moments that make you panic more than seeing this all-black figure striding toward you with his deadly lightsaber.

PLAGUE KNIGHT
Shovel Knight
WHY: Plague Knight is more like an end-of-level boss than a run-of-the-mill enemy, but he is without a doubt one of the toughest in the game. There's so much happening on the screen at one time that it's incredibly difficult to stay alive, let alone keep track of the tricky enemy as he leaps and teleports across the level. He's an absolute nightmare to defeat!

THE EXPERT SAYS ...
HANNAH WESTLAKE
Games writer

It's not easy being bad. And it's not easy being good at being bad. There are so many carbon-copy villains out there, that when you come across a truly dastardly bad guy it's actually quite a thrill. A good villain needs to have motivations you can understand and some human qualities (deep down inside). It's boring when a villain is evil just because that's the way they are. Give them a backstory, some depth to their character and a challenging weakness for me to try and discover and that's how you'll get me hooked and coming back for replays. And make them tough for a reason, and give that context, not just because it's the end of a level.

DARKNUT Zelda: Twilight Princess HD
WHY: These huge, armored knights are almost as tough as some of the game's bosses. Cutting off their armor is only the first challenge—once it's gone, they'll pull out another massive blade. Don't think that makes them easier, though; without armor they're faster and can block almost any attack, so you better be ready to use those jump attacks. These guys are rock hard!

CAPTURE THIS!

SKYLANDERS SUPERCHARGERS

FULLY UPGRADE YOUR CHARACTER

Skylanders SuperChargers is the first game in the series that adds vehicles to the mix, but this challenge is all about your character. Can you unlock all the upgrades for your Spitfire while choosing the lower upgrade path? It's much harder than it sounds!

FUEL INJECTED

Constant exposure
superheated your
melee damage.

Back

997

4% discount 2

WS

rnadoes have

causing you to do more

MOST AWESOME UNLOCKABLES

BIG DADDY'S PLUSHY
Costume • PlayStation All-Stars Battle Royale

WHY: Although the Big Daddy might look slightly intimidating, when he's wearing this costume he looks a lot more friendly! *PlayStation All-Stars Battle Royale* features a wealth of iconic characters, and playing as each one is tremendous fun.

DARK LINK Costume • Super Smash Bros.

WHY: Dark Link is a complete double of the Link we've grown to love, except he's dressed entirely in black and stares at you through red, glowing eyes. Thought to have been created by Ganondorf (the evil tyrant intent on ruling Hyrule), his every move closely mimics that of his lighter self. You'll unlock him at the same time as unlocking the traditional Link.

BATTLETOADS
Boss Fight • Shovel Knight

WHY: On the Xbox One version of this retro platformer, the old-school heroes make a surprise appearance as a boss battle. They're not easy to find unless you're looking for them, though—head to the Hall of Champions and smash a block on the far-right to find a map, then follow it to these amphibious dudes.

TOP SPLATOON UNLOCKABLE WEAPONS!

1 TENTATEK SPLATTERSHOT

This gun is, hands down, one of the greatest and most balanced weapons in the game. It may not always have the range you need, but it has pretty much everything else—it's the perfect all-rounder!

3 .52 GAL DECO
These shooters have fantastic range and excellent damage, and are useful whether you're in Splat Zones or Turf War. The Sub and Special weapons are good when it comes to claiming turf!

5 SPLATTERSHOT PRO

When it comes to the Splat Zones, few weapons have the damage and range of this gun. It's pricey and not the most efficient, but it'll clear out a bunch of enemies quickly.

2 BLASTER/ CUSTOM BLASTER

We wouldn't recommend this for Turf War, but when it comes to Splat Zone warfare, the Blaster is a deadly weapon, particularly if you're a good shot! Pair with the Bubbler to keep enemies at bay.

4 SPLAT CHARGER
You'll need to be at least Level 3 and have a modest 1,000 spare, but we think the Splat Charger is the best charger available. We particularly love the Bomb Rush Special Weapon.

6 KRAK-ON SPLAT ROLLER

While at first glance this Roller might not seem great, it's the Special that makes all the difference! Using the Kraken makes you invincible and highly destructive.

"LINK'S MASK IS AS FIERCE AS THE NAME SUGGESTS"

FIERCE DEITY MASK
Weapon/Mask • The Legend of Zelda: Majora's Mask

WHY: If you collect every mask available as Link traverses Termina (and this is tricky, we know!) you'll unlock the Fierce Deity Mask. Believe us, it's every bit as fierce as the name suggests. With it, you'll be able to shoot super-powerful Sword Beams and clear enemies with ease. It's worth the effort.

THE EXPERT SAYS...
LAURA DALE
Games Critic

The Fierce Deity Mask is an incentive to fully explore the small, emotional stories in a game about the impending end of the world. With a clock constantly counting down to the destruction of the planet, the stories of a postman lacking purpose or a pair of separated friends might seem insignificant or unimportant.

The Fierce Deity Mask is your reward for going out of your way to collect every other mask, and it grants you as a player the most powerful, heroic version of Link, wielding a sword whose double helix blade stretches up into the sky. That's a pretty great reward for being nice to people.

MR. GAME & WATCH
Character • Super Smash Bros.

WHY: Although *Super Smash Bros.* ships with a load of characters, to really have a smashing time, you're going to have to earn some of the cooler fighters. Take Mr. Game & Watch here—he's been in every *SSB* game since *Melee*, but to unlock him you need to either play 250 Brawl mode matches and beat him, complete Classic Mode with all characters, or complete Target Smash with 30 characters. Phew!

LEVEL STAR-S
Level • Yoshi's Woolly World

WHY: This hidden level can only be unlocked by collecting the smiling flowers in every world and special stage. Once you've collected them all, this new, extra-long level will appear in Craft Island. Cool!

STAN LEE
Character • LEGO Marvel Superheroes

WHY: Stan Lee (co-creator of Spider-Man, Iron Man, Thor, and more) has appeared in every Marvel movie since the first *Iron Man*, so it makes sense for him to be in this game. Find Stan in every level to unlock him as a playable character, then try hulking out!

LUIGI Character • Super Mario Galaxy
WHY: Mario gets all the fun, doesn't he? After all, he gets the lion's share of games named after him. But did you know that in *Super Mario Galaxy* you can play as the other brother? Collect 120 stars, defeat Bowser, and you too can play through the entire game as Luigi! He's better at running and jumping than Mario, too. Sorry Mario, Luigi for the win!

TRANSFORMERS: DEVASTATION

30 YEARS IN THE MAKING

Okay, so we've had some *Transformers* video games in the 30 years since the *Transformers* cartoon series first came out, but it's taken until now for there to be a game that really captures how awesome that original TV show was. Enter *Transformers: Devastation*.

You take control of one of five heroic Autobots—including leader and the best robo-truck-man ever, Optimus Prime—and proceed to journey around, doing your best to foil the evil plans of Megatron and the Decepticons. And you do this mostly by punching things. Not only is *Transformers: Devastation* a lot of fun to play, but it looks *incredible*, too. All of the robots in disguise (even if they're not in disguise) look exactly how they did back in the classic 80s cartoon, and that adds so much to *Devastation*—and helps make it an amazing experience, even if you're too young to remember the TV show or toys.

STATS

32 Years since Optimus Prime first appeared on TV

More than
65,000
Let's Plays on YouTube

7 chapters to play through

7 Autobots feature **5** are playable

31 Achievements/Trophies to unlock

TIME LINE

THE TRANSFORMERS
The very first *Transformers* game, this was released on the super retro C64 and Spectrum computers in 1986—you can still find vids on YouTube, though.

BEAST WARS: TRANSFORMERS
By the 90s, *Transformers* love had waned—all we were left with were games like *Beast Wars*, which weren't great.

TRANSFORMERS
This surprise release on PS2 in 2004 showed us all that, actually, *Transformers* games could be great. It's still fun, even today.

TOP 5 AUTOBOTS

BUMBLEBEE

2 He's the smallest of the Autobots, but Bumblebee proves that it isn't the size of the 'bot in the fight, it's the size of the fight in the 'bot. Often the plucky underdog, Bumblebee battles his way through *Devastation* by taking advantage of his diminutive size and incredible agility.

DID YOU KNOW?
Many characters in *Transformers: Devastation* are voiced by the original actors from the 80s TV show.

OPTIMUS PRIME

1 The heroic leader of the Autobots, Optimus Prime—when he's not transformed into a huge truck—is busy making plans to defeat the nefarious Decepticons. Not just an incredible leader, he's also a fearsome combatant—as you find when taking Prime into battle. This 'bot hits hard, and looks awesome doing it, too.

SIDESWIPE

3 If there's one thing Sideswipe takes advantage of in *Devastation*, it's his incredible speed. Easily the fastest of the Autobots, he's able to dance and dart around the battlefield. Fortunately, there's not just one thing Sideswipe takes advantage of—he has a rocket launcher and flaregun too.

GRIMLOCK

5 The strongest of the Autobots, Grimlock—leader of the Dinobots—uses his size and power to annihilate everything in his way. While Grimlock's speed and agility is lacking compared to his counterparts, he more than makes up for it through the fact that *he's a Tyrannosaurus Rex.*

WHEELJACK

4 One of the oldest Autobots in existence, Wheeljack uses his many years of knowledge to invent gadgets and gizmos for his pals to use against the Decepticons. In *Devastation*, while he's more at home inventing for the others, he does sometimes bring his wrenches into battle, battering the baddies when needed.

"YOU TAKE CONTROL OF ONE OF FIVE HEROIC AUTOBOTS"

TRANSFORMERS: WAR FOR CYBERTRON
While the games based on the films were poor, this series—from 2010—was fun, and created its own wing of robotic fiction.

TRANSFORMERS: DEVASTATION
The most recent of the *Transformers* games, *Devastation* nonetheless goes all the way back to the 80s for its inspiration.

TRANSFORMERS: DEVASTATION

FOUR TOUGHEST BOSSES

DEVASTATOR

1 Putting together a bunch of Constructicons to form a giant killing machine should be a perfect strategy for victory for the Decepticons. And it works ... at least until the different bots start arguing with each other.

DID YOU KNOW?

Transformers: Devastation is developed by Platinum Games. It's the studio's second game based on an original animated series after *Legend Of Korra*.

CHRIS SPANN

WHO?

Chris Spann has been learning about the Transformers since the first animated movie was released back in 1986. Since then he's amassed a plethora of merchandise—including the toys that kicked the whole Transformers movement off—seen everything there is to see of the show and built up the kind of knowledge to rival even the dedicated Transformers Wiki.

WHY?

Chris fell head over wheels for the cars (and planes and tanks and everything else) that are also robots thanks to the power of the 1986 animated movie. Since then he's owned five different versions—*of the same film*. And it's not just because—in Chris's words—"they're *robots* that *transform* into things," it's also because there's depth to the universe. Take Tailgate—one of the series' most interesting characters and Chris's favorite. His lack of knowledge about the Autobots/Decepticons war and his ability to see the point of view of Megatron's army—despite being on Optimus Prime's team—marks him, for Chris, as something that shows just how cool Transformers can be. Plus, thanks to the games, he gets to play as his favorite characters, too.

MENASOR

2 Similar to Devastator, Menasor would be a lot more dangerous if his different parts worked better together. As it is, though, this giant combination of Stunticons is still a huge challenge.

SOUNDWAVE

3 It's less the incredible intelligence and bot-to-bot combat ability of Soundwave you have to be wary of, and more the army of cassette tape mini-robots he can launch your way.

DID YOU KNOW?

Transformers: Devastation is written by Andy Schmidt, a former writer and editor of the *Transformers* comic books.

MEGATRON

4 As the leader of the Decepticons, Megatron is a fearsome opponent. Powerful and intensely cunning, the boss of the bad guys is not someone to mess with. Except you *have to* in *Devastation*.

THE EXPERT SAYS …
SOOOMUNGRY
Covers Transformers on his YouTube channel, which has 80 million+ views

I've been waiting for this all my life, and I'm happy to say it was worth the wait. The game is *Transformers: Devastation*— that's enough to get you on board if you're a fan, but if you are new to the franchise or are not convinced, just play the game for ten minutes and you won't want to put it down. The action is explosive, fast, and smooth.

Each character brings their own fighting style to the battlefield and offers rapid, fast combos and the ability to fight, transform, and fight some more. The story makes it feel like you are part of the show as you face off against a bunch of iconic characters.

Oh yeah, and you go toe-to-toe with giant combiners like Devastator, which is *freaking amazing* and challenging at the same time! If you are a fan of action—hey, if you are a fan of video games—*Transformers: Devastation* is a must-play!

ALSO CHECK OUT …

THE LEGEND OF KORRA
Based on the Nickelodeon cartoon of the same name, this action-adventure game is also created by *Devastation*'s developer, Platinum Games. It's not quite as awesome as the *Transformers* title, but it's good fun anyway.

HYRULE WARRIORS
Devastation lets you fight lots of baddies, so *Hyrule Warriors* is the next logical gaming step, especially for *Zelda* fans. You play as Link (and other warriors from *The Legend Of Zelda*) and fight a *lot* of enemies.

MIGHTY NO. 9

HE'S MEGA, MAN

DID YOU KNOW?

If you're looking for more *Mighty No 9*, check out the brand new animated series too: it's packed with robo goodness.

Mighty No. 9 might be a new game but it actually has a history stretching back nearly 30 years. It was created by Keiji Inafune, a Japanese game designer who also created the *Mega Man* series. When game publisher Capcom cancelled *Mega Man Legends 3*, Inafune left to work on his own game, putting it on crowdfunding site Kickstarter and asking *Mega Man* fans for help.

It's no surprise then, that *Mighty No. 9* looks and plays just like the *Mega Man* games. You play as Beck, a robot lad (and the titular Mighty No. 9) who can run, jump, and shoot at enemies. That might not seem like much but he's got one special ability: he can take the weapons from any bosses he beats and use them himself—just like *Mega Man*.

TIME LINE

MEGA MAN—1987
Mighty No. 9's ancestor was born nearly 30 years ago. It looked basic, but the gameplay was surprisingly similar.

MEGA MAN X—1993
After six *Mega Man* games, Capcom rebooted the series with this 16-bit game. It was the first big graphical evolution.

MEGA MAN LEGENDS—1997
Ten years after the original, this PlayStation game brought the *Mega Man* series into 3D for the first time, and starred a new Mega Man character called Volnutt.

TOP 5 MIGHTY ROBOT BOSSES

COUNTERSHADE

1 There are eight other Mighty robots, who are the game's bosses. Countershade is the eighth, and is the coolest of the bunch: he's dressed like a cowboy and can disappear into the background to hide from you, shooting at you with his sniper rifle or his hidden machine gun leg.

PYROGEN

2 Pyrogen was the first Mighty robot ever built, and, in case you can't tell by the picture, his special ability involves fire. His entire body is covered in gas burners, which lets him shoot out fire from all directions whenever he wants, for a special flame armor. He won't go out easily!

SEISMIC

3 Seismic is Mighty No. 4 and is designed to look like the sort of machine you'd find at a construction site. His special power is raw strength: he can crush metal with his hands and slam onto the floor to create earthquakes. Punching Seismic would be like punching a truck ... not that we've ever actually punched a truck.

BRANDISH

4 Otherwise known as Mighty No. 7, Brandish looks a bit like a robot ninja. Instead of having a special power, Brandish is highly skilled in close combat, thanks to the two massive swords he can use like a large pair of scissors. Be extra careful, because they can block projectiles, too.

DYNATRON

5 Mighty No. 3, Dynatron, is one of two female robots in the game. She looks a little like a lightbulb and that's no accident: her special power is the ability to control electricity. Get too close and she'll give you a nasty zap, firing out little spiked balls that can buzz you.

ALSO CHECK OUT ...

MEGA MAN LEGACY COLLECTION
If you want to try out *Mighty No. 9*'s ancestors, this digital collection includes the first six *Mega Man* games.

MEGA MAN 9 & 10
These may look like the old *Mega Man* games, but they were only released a couple of years ago. They've got the same addictive gameplay and famous difficulty.

SHOVEL KNIGHT
Want to play something similar that isn't *Mega Man*? *Shovel Knight* is a brilliant example of games like it, with fantastic old-school, 8-bit graphics.

MEGA MAN BATTLE NETWORK—2001
Imagine *Mega Man* as an RPG and the result is *Battle Network*, a series of fun Game Boy Advance and DS games.

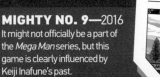

MIGHTY NO. 9—2016
It might not officially be a part of the *Mega Man* series, but this game is clearly influenced by Keiji Inafune's past.

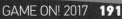

UNRAVEL

YOUR CAT WOULD LOVE TO PLAY THIS!

Yarny, the adorable character made of rolled up yarn that you play as in *Unravel*, might not seem like the most talented of platforming heroes, especially when you compare him with the variety and customization of *LittleBigPlanet*'s Sackboy. Yet as he travels the gorgeous 2D landscapes he leaves a trail of wool behind him... useless, you might think? Well, not so. The plucky yarn-boy can tie this trail to objects in the world, helping him swing across large gaps, climb, and—most interestingly—use it to pull objects and create trampolines. This means there's plenty of puzzles you'll need to figure out to make the best use of Yarny's unique abilities. Just don't let his yarn run out, or Yarny will unravel.

STATS

34 real-world Yarnys retweeted by EA on Twitter

16 countries that these Yarnys have visited

1.2 million views on YouTube

Yarny is 8.6" tall

4 E3 awards won when it was revealed to the public

DID YOU KNOW?

Yarny represents the love between a parent and their child. No matter how far Yarny travels he's still tied to the thing he loves.

TIME LINE

JUNE 2013
Development on the game begins in secret, and continues for two years before the game is even announced to the public!

JUNE 2015
The game is officially unveiled at EA's E3 conference where all the visitors—and those watching online—instantly take to Yarny's charming platform adventure.

AUGUST 2015
A full-length gameplay video is released of *Unravel*, showing everyone the type of puzzles you might encounter during the game

TOP 5 YARNY SKILLS

TRAMPOLINE

1 Creating a trampoline isn't difficult for Yarny, all he needs to do is tie a piece of wool between two points and suddenly he's created a bouncy trampoline. You'll need to be smart about where you build these though, since many will be needed for reaching higher places!

SWINGING

2 It's the simple things in life that are often the most fun, but don't let that make you believe that swinging in Yarny is simple. It's one of the first things you do, but as the game rolls on you'll discover far more challenging and entertaining ways to swing.

PULLEY SYSTEMS

3 Okay, so this probably sounds pretty boring, but it's not! The idea is easy: tie some yarn to a weighted object, tie another end to the edge of a plank then push the weight off an edge. Then watch as your object tied is propelled high into the air!

GO FISH

4 So far all we've talked about is the way Yarny can interact with stationary objects, but what about moving items... or even animals! As you explore there will be all sorts of things to attach to, even fish that will pull Yarny's tiny sailboat across a stream.

FLY A KITE

5 Since our hero is only made of wool he weighs practically nothing. He's light enough that if you were to attach him to a tiny kite he would easily be pulled along, soaring on the air like a bird or a plane!

"THIS PLUCKY YARN BOY CAN TIE THIS TRAIL OF WOOL TO OBJECTS"

JANUARY 2016
The game's developer, Coldwood, releases a tutorial on how to make your own Yarny, which fans of the game have been doing ever since.

FEBRUARY 2016
Unravel is released for both PC, PS4, and Xbox One as a digital download. Hopefully there will be more adventures for Yarny in the future.

ALSO CHECK OUT ...

LITTLEBIGPLANET 3
If puzzle platforming is your thing, then you'll definitely want to take Sackboy and friends for an adventure. You can even learn to make your own levels too!

SUPER MARIO 3D WORLD
Mario makes his Cat Suit debut in this adventure and he's almost as cute as Yarny is in *Unravel*... almost!

RAYMAN LEGENDS
Rayman is another old school face for fans of platforming, and his most recent game—*Rayman Legends*—has music-themed levels too.

DID YOU KNOW?

The Witness has one puzzle that's so hard, its creator expects only one percent of players to be able to solve it!

INDIE GAMES

THE BEST OF THE BEST

It's a great time in gaming for companies outside of the biggest ones. They can find ways of being more original and innovative, and there's an indie game for everyone. Indie games are getting bigger and bigger, with recent hits including the treasure-hunting of *Spelunky*, the fiercely difficult combat of *Shovel Knight*, and the sheer insanity of *Goat Simulator*. There are moments of beauty too, such as *Beyond*

Eyes, a game that gives you an idea of what it's like to be blind with some truly unique gameplay and a heartwarming story.

This success should come as no surprise either given that *Minecraft*— arguably the biggest game in the world— started from similar beginnings. Give at least one of these great titles a try. It might just be the next big thing.

TIPS & TRICKS

THINK OUTSIDE THE BOX

The Witness is not an easy game— but that's the point. Explore to make sure you know all there is to know.

LOOK THEN LEAP

Always take your time in *Spelunky*. The most valuable move you have is looking down by holding down on the D-pad for a few seconds. Use it often.

WITH FRIENDS

If you're struggling to control more than one character in *Kalimba*, get a friend to jump in with you and help you out.

TOP 5 INDIE GAMES

THE WITNESS

1 Coming from Jonathan Blow—the man who was also responsible for indie smash *Braid*—*The Witness* is a 3D puzzle game where nothing is fully explained. Not only do you have to figure out how each puzzle works, you also have to figure out why you're on this island and where to go next.

HYPER LIGHT DRIFTER

2 Paying homage to some of the classics from yesteryear (*The Legend Of Zelda* and *Diablo* to name but two), *Hyper Light Drifter* is an action-RPG that wouldn't look out of place on the SNES! With a bird's-eye perspective and a whole host of bosses to defeat, it's well worth a look.

COBALT

3 When a game comes from the same guys that created *Minecraft*, you know it's probably going to be good. This, though, is totally different to *Minecraft* in pretty much every way—it's a side-scrolling action platformer with some seriously crazy multiplayer. It's all about doing backflips while firing your weapons in every direction, which is awesome fun.

NO MAN'S SKY

4 This huge space-faring adventure might have more than 18 quintillion planets (yes, that's a *lot*), but it was actually put together by just 16 people—and that's a *tiny* team for a video game! It's one of the most epic adventures ever, so if you haven't climbed into your ship already, now is the time to do it.

ROCKET LEAGUE

5 It's the simplicity that makes *Rocket League* so much fun. It's soccer with cars. Anyone can pick up the pad and understand that. Despite a later release on Xbox One compared to PC and PS4, it's proved just as popular on Microsoft's console, and delivers hours of fun.

ALSO CHECK OUT ...

TITAN SOULS

Sharing a similar art style to *Hyper Light Drifter*, all *Titan Souls* asks of you is to defeat its many bosses, which are also a bit like mini-puzzles. It's great.

ROGUE LEGACY

Rogue Legacy is one of the greatest indie games ever made. Although the aim is simple—explore a castle and best its bosses—it's fiendishly difficult to achieve.

USE YOUR BRAIN

Hyper Light Drifter is constantly teaching you as you play. Remember all the tips as they will make the bosses easier.

FORGET THE GLORY

Everyone wants to score in *Rocket League*, but you can be just as effective focusing on defense, too. Keep an eye on your own goal.

COOLEST VEHICLES

HOT STREAK Skylanders SuperChargers

WHY: With a body forged from magma rock and wheels that literally ignite when it's speeding through Skylands, Hot Streak is our pick of the many great vehicles available in *Skylanders SuperChargers*. Throw in Spitfire as its supercharged driver and some awesome customization options, and you've got one powerful racer.

WARTHOG
Halo 5: Guardians

WHY: The *Halo* series has a host of fantastic vehicles, but if we have to pick just one then the M12 Warthog is a clear winner. The staple of the UNSC army is quick, handles sharply, and is incredibly versatile. To put it simply, *Halo* multiplayer just wouldn't be the same without it.

KART
Mario Kart 8

WHY: *The Mario Kart* series has expanded to include everything from gliders to motorbikes of late, but the humble kart will always be at the heart of Nintendo's frantic racing games. Even with recent bells and whistles like anti-gravity wheels we're thankful that the classic kart design remains intact.

6 THINGS THAT MAKE A GREAT VEHICLE

1 SPEED
If you're in a race then speed is always going to be king. Lightning acceleration and an enormous top speed are the best things a player can ask for.

2 ARMOR
Speed is important, but it's all for nothing if your ride falls apart at the first sign of trouble. A solid layer of protective armor is a must for seeing off aggressive competition.

3 HANDLING
Whether you're rounding hairpin bends or flying through tight corridors, you need to have a ride that handles smoothly.

4 FIREPOWER
What's better than a fast, strong vehicle that handles well? A fast, strong vehicle that handles well *and* can blast opponents away with a laser cannon.

5 COMFORT
An underrated aspect of video game vehicles, a plush interior, especially one that you can view in first-person, goes a long way toward making a your ride feel spectacular.

6 STYLE
Winning is one thing, but winning in style is something else entirely. You might have dominated the battlefield, but make sure that you look good doing it.

MILLENNIUM FALCON
Star Wars Battlefront

WHY: *Star Wars Battlefront* is here to make our dreams of flying the Millennium Falcon come true. X-Wings are cool, but nothing beats grabbing the Hero power-up and rocketing around the battlefield blowing TIE fighters out of the sky with Han's ship.

LIGHT CYCLE
Disney Infinity

WHY: Few vehicles have captured imaginations as completely as *Tron*'s light cycle with its distinctive neon design, so it was incredibly exciting when the bike was finally added to *Disney Infinity*'s Toy Box mode. As you'd expect, it's nimble and powerful.

ARWING
Star Fox Zero

WHY: The iconic *Star Fox* spacecraft has been our fighter of choice since the SNES days, and its latest incarnation is hands down the best yet. Not only can it dominate the skies, but the new Arwing can also now transform into a walker for land missions in the blink of an eye.

KING OF RED LIONS
The Legend Of Zelda: The Wind Waker HD

WHY: Easily the vehicle with the most personality in this list, the King of Red Lions isn't just Link's means of traveling across the Great Sea, he's the hero's guide and friend. The King also hides the series' greatest secret ...

THE EXPERT SAYS ...
JEREMY DUNHAM
Vice President, Psyonix (creators of *Rocket League*)

The key to a great video game vehicle is to treat it as an extension of the player; it has to do exactly what the driver expects it to do or you risk disappointing them. As a result, you can't overcomplicate how your vehicle handles complicated tasks like drifting through a tight turn or shifting into lower or higher gears—it just works, even if that's not the case in real life, because being able to react to your world in an immediate and dramatic way is fun—and having fun is the whole point!

VENOM Rocket League

WHY: Okay, so in terms of stats like speed and handling, pretty much every vehicle in *Rocket League* is the same. They're all rad, but picking your favorite ultimately comes down to personal preference. We've gone for Venom here though, for its excellent mix of old-school box car aesthetics and awesome supercar modifications. You won't find a gnarlier set of vents and exhaust pipes any time soon.

REGALIA
Final Fantasy XV

WHY: *Final Fantasy* fans can get very familiar with this vehicle in the fifteenth—and latest—entry in the series. The Regalia is the main mode of transport for Noctis and it's a suitably regal ride given his princely status. All-black paint, a luxurious leather interior, and chocobo-inscribed hubcaps.

ROCKET LEAGUE

ROCKET LEAGUE

JOIN THE FUN

If you are someone who has managed to miss this word-of-mouth hit that has taken the gaming world by storm, you're also missing out on a lot of fun. It's basically soccer played with rocket-powered cars instead of players—see, told you it was fun. The great thing about *Rocket League* is that even once the novelty silliness of flying a car around, trying to hit a giant ball into the other team's goal has worn off, the game doesn't get boring at all. That's because there is a wealth of depth to *Rocket League*, meaning you can score spectacular goals and pull off amazing saves as you develop your *Rocket League* skills. The game does have single player, but is much better when played locally or online with your friends.

TIPS & TRICKS

LEARN TO FLY
The most difficult but most effective skill to learn, controlled flying with boost lets you get to high balls first.

ROTATE POSITIONS
You shouldn't all chase the ball at the same time. It's important that you sit back to cover your goal when your teammates are attacking.

USE THE WALL
You can drive up the wall and leap off it to snatch the ball away from opponents near the edges of arenas.

TOP 5 MUTATORS

MOONBALL

1 By adding low gravity, a light ball, and fast rechargeable boosts, this mutator places all the focus on one of *Rocket League*'s most difficult skills: flying through the air using boost. It's not only lots of fun soaring through the sky, but might actually help you get better at flying when you return to the normal game.

PRESS △ TO TOGGLE

DID YOU KNOW?

You can get the iconic DeLorean from the *Back to the Future* series as downloadable content. Sweet!

PINBALL

2 With a tiny ball that bounces all over the place at speed, it isn't hard to work out why this mutator mode is called pinball! The chaos that little ball causes can be good for a few laughs, but goals are really satisfying because the ball is so hard to control!

SNOW DAY

3 This mode, which has its own online playlist, transforms *Rocket League* from a game that's like soccer to one that's more like ice hockey. You've got a puck to deal with instead of a ball and you have to get used to sliding around on the icy playing surface.

BEACH BALL

4 This mutator makes the ball you are playing with huge and bouncy, to the point where it becomes less like a soccer and more like—you've guessed it—a beach ball! It's actually quite hard to get this gigantic ball in the goal, but this mode can be pretty funny because of that.

PURE CHAOS

5 To create a crazy custom game, we recommend these settings: super-fast, light weight, small size, cube type ball with high bounciness, unlimited x10 boost, low gravity, and friendly fire demolition. You'll spend more time laughing than you will scoring.

"YOU CAN DRIVE UP THE WALL AND LEAP OFF IT TO SNATCH THE BALL"

RUN INTERFERENCE

When you see an opponent tending the goal line, make yourself a nuisance by knocking them out of position when your friends shoot.

FLIP FOR SPEED

If you've run out of boost and need to get somewhere quickly, successfully pulling off multiple flips in a row will give you a similar kick.

ALSO CHECK OUT ...

SPORTSFRIENDS

If you love weird sports, then you've got to play *Sportfriends*. The highlight is Barabariball, which plays like a cross between volleyball and *Smash Bros.*

MARIO KART 8

Rocket League asks: what would soccer be like with rocket cars? *Mario Kart* says: what would racing be like if the racers could fire turtle shells?

FORZA MOTORSPORT

STATS

There are **450+** cars in *Forza Motorsport 6*

161,000 Videos on YouTube about *Forza Motorsport 6*

280mph+ Fastest speed recorded in a *Forza* game

22 million Copies of *Forza* games sold

5.49 million Number of copies sold of *Forza Motorsport 3*

AND THEY'RE OFF!

The *Forza Motorsport* series has hit its stride in recent years, with the main *Motorsport* series joined by the excellent (but very different) *Horizon* series, which took the driving open-world. Between the two series, players have been invited to take part in some of the most gorgeous and fun simulation racing out there.

While the *Motorsport* series has focused on accurate driving and car simulation, it's never been to the point where less experienced players can't take part. There are always help and tweaks available to make sure anyone can have fun. The same is also true of the *Horizon* games, but these are made to be much more open and less of a hardcore racing simulation. As such, they're better for the less obsessive player. Whichever you pick up, though, you're guaranteed a thrilling ride.

TIPS & TRICKS

FULL CONTROL
Brake in a straight line before the corner, start turning then accelerate out of the bend. It's the simplest, most important advice in a racing game.

CHOOSE YOUR RIDE
Not every car suits every driver—you'll have to experiment to find the ride that fits your style the best.

SOUP IT UP
Don't forget to work on the engine underneath, and fit new tires. Tweaking the performance is important.

TOP 5 CARS IN FORZA 6

2017 FORD GT

1 It's costly, but there's a reason the 2017 Ford GT is the poster child for *Forza Motorsport 6*: it's amazing. With 630 horsepower under the hood and the ability to handle corners without any trouble, your spending will be rewarded with one of the game's best cars.

DID YOU KNOW?

The *Forza Motorsport* series turned ten years old in 2015, and every Xbox console had a game from the series on it.

ULTIMA GTR

2 It won't win out against the best of the best, but the Ultima GTR is affordable and more than holds it own on the track. You can expect high speeds alongside some sweet handling with this nippy little supercar, and with the right tweaks under the hood it will last you a while.

DODGE VIPER ACR

3 The Dodge Viper is a car you should always get in any driving game. It's not the easiest to control, but once you master it you will be in possession of one of *Forza 6's* most impressive road-faring beasts.

CORVETTE Z06

4 An American classic reborn for the modern era, the Corvette Z06 benefits from being both a very solid car to tear around the track in, and surprisingly cheap. It's another car that won't be with you in the latter stages of the game, but for the early days you can't go wrong with a Corvette.

TVR SAGARIS

5 If you want the ideal vehicle to set yourself up with early on in *Forza Motorsport 6*, go for the TVR Sagaris. It's affordable, powerful, and—with due care—handles like a beast. Use it in your early days and you'll very quickly be on the road to affording a whole garage of hypercars.

"SOME OF THE MOST GORGEOUS SIMULATION RACING OUT THERE"

ALSO CHECK OUT ...

GRAN TURISMO 6

The *Gran Turismo* series is PlayStation 4's answer to *Forza*, which is an Xbox One exclusive. The gameplay is pretty similar.

HAUNTED RACETRACKS

Make sure to use your best lap ghost to improve your skills as you replay each track.

SPEND BIG

Don't just keep your pile of money forever—use it to buy bigger, better, faster cars; even if you only use them once.

PROJECT CARS

Even more sim-based than the super-accurate *Forza* or *Gran Turismo*, *Project CARS* treats its subject matter very seriously.

STATS

89 The highest score for N4S on Metacritic

Developers responsible for all the games: **16**

51 cars can be customized in *Need For Speed*

150 MILLION copies in the franchise sold

26 N4S games as of 2015

DID YOU KNOW?

Need For Speed was turned into a movie in 2014 and made more than $200 million at the box office.

NEED FOR SPEED

THE RACING GENRE KING

Need For Speed has been a standout racing series for over 20 years. With the first game released way back in 1994, the franchise has gone from strength to strength with each passing entry, with some iterations even considered the best the genre as a whole has to offer—and that's no small feat.

Publisher EA continued this run of arcade racing success with 2015's reboot of the series, simply entitled *Need For Speed*. Taking elements from the games that came before it, the PS4, Xbox One, and PC game offers an open world to race around, incredible customization, a whole heap of different vehicles to drive, and some of the best visuals that have been served up to date. If you've ever wanted to live out high-octane fantasies in gaming form, *Need For Speed* is for you.

TIPS & TRICKS

DON'T FORGET: YOU CAN FAST TRAVEL

Need For Speed's (2015) open world is huge—thankfully, if you can't be bothered to drive, you can fast travel to a location.

LEARN THE MAP

Each part of the map offers something a little different, so make sure to learn what's where in order to suit your particular playstyle.

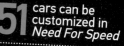

PRACTICE ALL DISCIPLINES

There are five different gameplay types in *Need For Speed*, including the awesome drift mode.

TOP 5 N4S GAMES

NEED FOR SPEED: MOST WANTED

1 Released in 2012, *Need For Speed: Most Wanted* is still one of the best racing games that money can buy. Police chases are a staple here, and are huge fun to take part in. Completely focused on fast-paced, arcade action, it still holds up when pitted against modern racers, even though it came out on the Xbox 360, PS3, and PC. Not even time itself can slow it down!

NEED FOR SPEED: HOT PURSUIT

2 Every franchise needs a refresh every now and then and *Need For Speed* pitched that perfectly with *Hot Pursuit*. Focusing the action on cops vs robbers, you can choose to either chase or be chased by the police. It's non-stop, adrenaline-fueled action that rarely lets up.

NEED FOR SPEED

3 EA's 2015 reboot of the series, *Need For Speed* takes everything the franchise has achieved and fits it all into one absolutely beautiful package. Its biggest draw is the huge open world that you can drive around, be it just for fun or to compete in dozens of races and other competitive modes.

NEED FOR SPEED: CARBON

4 While this came out in 2006, *Need For Speed: Carbon* deserves a mention as you can play it now on your Xbox One thanks to backwards compatibility. Plus, it boasts a mode called "Canyon Racing," which takes place at night and is absolutely exhilarating to play.

NEED FOR SPEED: RIVALS

5 Cops, racers, open worlds, customization, power-ups, unlocks, and multiplayer. It's hard to imagine a *Need For Speed* game with more options. Throw in some amazing visuals thanks to the Xbox One and PS4, and it's a racing game you won't regret playing!

"THE FRANCHISE HAS BECOME MORE SUCCESSFUL"

ALSO CHECK OUT ...

FORZA HORIZON 2
The Xbox One's *Forza Horizon 2* not only looks great, but plays great as well. It's a must for anyone who considers themself to be a fan of fast cars.

THE CREW
Open world racers don't get much bigger than *The Crew*. It has a persistent online world, which means that other players are always inhabiting the experience.

SEARCH FOR LOOT
Lots of collectibles are scattered around the world and finding these will open up more options for you to customize your car.

TWEAK YOUR HANDLING
Need For Speed lets you play around with your car's settings. Try out different setups to see what works best for you.

STATS

 Two-player co-operative action

1930s The decade of inspiration for *Cuphead*'s rather unique art style

30 Unique bosses

900,000+ E3 2015 trailer views on YouTube

13 Layers of hand-painted backgrounds

CUPHEAD

A MUG'S GAME

DID YOU KNOW?
Cuphead's animations and watercolor backgrounds are all painted by hand. Even the text was drawn by a professional sign painter.

Cuphead and Mugman bet against the Devil and lost, and now they must repay their debt. Lucky for us, the game itself is actually a lot of fun: relentless battles against a selection of bosses so large they can't even fit on your screen.

Although the art style is inspired by Fleischer and Disney cartoons of the 1930s, like *Popeye* and *Steamboat Willie*, beneath the surface it's closer to classic run-and-gun action games like *Contra* and *Gunstar Heroes*. This means you can expect a wide variety of action: one minute Cuphead and Mugman are fighting a giant potato in a field, the next they're flying fighter planes and facing off against an angry bird that's flying around, despite still being in its birdhouse. One thing's for sure, *Cuphead* will provide a stiff challenge for anyone.

TIPS & TRICKS

PAY ATTENTION
Every boss's attacks have a unique pattern—keep an eye out to learn when to dodge them.

MASTER THE "STRAW SLAP"
Cuphead can slap objects like train carts to move them, but with perfect timing you can parry pink bullets too.

BRING A FRIEND
Cuphead was made for two. Team up with a buddy for a better chance against the rogue's gallery of bosses..

TOP 5 BOSSES

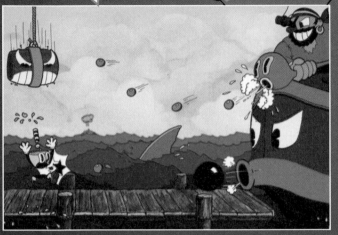

THE PIRATE

1 This guy looks a lot like Popeye's arch nemesis Bluto, but there's not a can of spinach in sight. As well as the usual ship cannons, he summons sharks and giant squid to attack Cuphead—aren't they meant to hate pirates?—and uses an octopus as a makeshift rifle. A tricky foe, but certainly an entertaining boss to battle.

PSYCHIC CARROT

2 When he's not opening his third eye to summon mystical energy blasts, he uses psychokinesis to uproot carrots and fire them at you like rockets. Thankfully, these are just regular carrots—he's not using his friends and family as weapons.

BOXING FROG TWINS

3 One of these twins throws fireballs that would make Ryu and Ken cower in fear, while the other spits flaming homing bees at Cuphead, and whirls up like a desk fan. Be careful to dodge them rolling across the screen as they try to surround you.

IN THE BIRDHOUSE

4 Cuphead takes to the skies in a dogfight with a bird that's using its own house as a suit of armor, eggs as explosive missiles, and feathers as bullets. If that wasn't enough, it also recruits budgies to charge at you with nails strapped to their backs.

TRAIN GHOST

5 This particular ghost has a collection of eyes, which he throws at Cuphead like bowling balls of destruction. Watch out for his skeleton friend who's waiting furt her up the train, hiding in the carriages. A spooky boss who is not easy to overcome, you may find that you need a few tries to beat him.

"BOSSES SO LARGE THEY CAN'T EVEN FIT ON YOUR SCREEN"

BE PATIENT
Save your charge attack for when you're guaranteed to hit an enemy—don't waste it on thin air.

PRACTICE!
It's supposed to be difficult! You might die a lot, but there are plenty of cups in the cupboard. Don't give up!

ALSO CHECK OUT ...

GUNSTAR HEROES
A classic run and gun platformer, with amazing boss battles against weird and wonderful robots. Made in 1993, but feels fresh on 3DS!

EPIC MICKEY
This take on Mickey Mouse builds on the same cartoon heritage as *Cuphead*. It's a loving tribute to the mouse mascot, and great fun.

BEST GAMING LEVELS OF ALL TIME

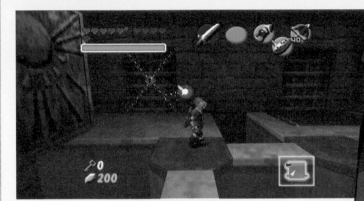

SPIRIT TEMPLE
THE LEGEND OF ZELDA: OCARINA OF TIME

■ It should come as no surprise that one of the most celebrated 3D games of all time would also happen to feature some of the most celebrated levels. *The Legend Of Zelda: Ocarina Of Time* has some absolute wonders, though none compare to its Spirit Temple. This gorgeous desert dungeon is built around a series of clever puzzles that utilize the Mirror Shield; the symmetry of battling through it as both young and adult Link is a stroke of Nintendo genius.

DID YOU KNOW?

A sequel to *Psychonauts* is finally due to launch in 2017 after games company Double Fine raised enough money to make it via a crowdfunding (online donations) campaign.

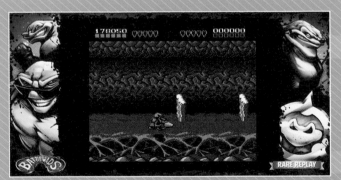

TURBO TUNNEL
BATTLETOADS

■ *Battletoads* is often thought to be amongst the most difficult games of all time, and a lot of that is due to the level Turbo Tunnel. The thing is, it's also sort of the reason we love it. It forces you into an intricately designed tunnel where you—as a walking, talking toad on a speed bike—are forced to dodge obstacles throttling at you at a simply insane speed. It's burned into our memories forever as the level despised by a generation. Check it out on YouTube and see how difficult it is!

THE MILKMAN CONSPIRACY
PSYCHONAUTS

■ *Psychonauts* is one of those brilliant games that almost nobody played—something you should change now that it's been made available again on PS4. It's one of the most creative games of the decade and that shines through in the level The Milkman Conspiracy. A twisting puzzler that's heavy on the humor, what really stands out is the eccentric design, showcasing more dazzling creativity in a few streets than most games do across entire levels. Memorable and genius.

WORLD 1, STAGE 1
SUPER MARIO BROS

■ This is without question one of, if not *the* greatest video game level ever created. The first level of *Super Mario Bros* is a master class in game design, with the geniuses over at Nintendo using 1-1 to teach players every single basic aspect of the seminal platformer within 30 seconds. Every part of the level—from the blocks, to the Goombas, pipes, and death pits—is expertly placed to teach you something you need to know. There's a reason *Super Mario Bros* began one of the most successful franchises in video games and it all starts with this level; revisit this classic on Wii U and 3DS!

AREA 5
REZ

■ *Rez* is a incredibly strange game that also happens to feature some of the most wickedly cool levels ever. Area 5 was always a definite fan favorite, though, an adventure in action that also happens to include thunderously thumping music to catapult you through the chaos. Area 5 is a gem in a killer selection of levels. Revisit this classic on PS4—time hasn't dulled any of Area 5's edges.

GREEN HILL ZONE
SONIC THE HEDGEHOG

■ There's so much to love about the Green Hill Zone that it's difficult to know where to begin. There's that music that forces its way into your brain, the hyper-satisfying sound of picking up a ring and, of course, the super thrills to be found in tearing Sonic through one of the coolest levels ever designed at eye-watering speeds. If you've never played it before, you can grab *Sonic The Hedgehog* for iOS and Android.

WALK THE CHOMP
YOSHI'S WOOLLY WORLD

■ Yoshi's adventure is already one of the cutest games we've played this year, but the smart and intricate design here will ensure this level stands the test of time. To complete it 100% you'll need to store up wool so you can spit them at the chomp and push him around the level, opening up new areas as you go.

DID YOU KNOW?

Level designers from *Yoshi's Island* and *New Super Mario World*, which explains why the levels are so much fun!

LEVEL 7-4
BRAID

■ *Braid* is one of the games credited for starting a fantastic new wave of great indie games, and that's partly due to its little genius moments—like the ones found in the final moments of the game in 7-4. It isn't the most challenging level in this time-manipulating puzzle game, but it does put your skills to the test and brings the story full circle—ensuring you'll experience a rollercoaster of emotions.

LOST VALLEY
TOMB RAIDER: ANNIVERSARY

■ It's funny: at the beginning of *Tomb Raider* you might find yourself taken aback by the eerie sense of peace that permeates its isolated caves and caverns. That all changes once you get out into the sprawling jungles of the Lost Valley. The level showcases some great design but once again (and most importantly) reaffirms that there's nothing cooler in video games than going toe-to-toe with a dinosaur.

BEST GAMING LEVELS OF ALL TIME

THE AQUARIUM
OCTODAD: DADLIEST CATCH

■ *Octodad* is already a really odd game (the main character is an octopus pretending to be a human, for goodness' sake!) but this area takes things to a whole new level. As Octodad and his family take a trip to the Aquarium, you must navigate your way carefully past marine biologists who will see through your disguise and make your way back to your family, who have mysteriously gotten lost …

LIGHT CITY RUN
TRIALS FUSION

■ Light City Run is the final summit all *Trials Fusion* players have to conquer, an intricately designed level that pushes your patience and reactions to their absolute limits. There's no way you can stumble through this level—you have to be perfect with every rev of your bike. This extreme ranked level burns itself into the memory, mainly because you will have to play it so many times!

MIDWAY ARCADE
LEGO DIMENSIONS

■ Toward the end of the *LEGO Dimensions* story you'll come across this level packed with awesome retro gaming references and some pretty awesome level design. By this point you'll know exactly what you're doing, meaning you can sit back and enjoy the side-scrolling 2.5D design while your favorite characters from worlds like DC Comics and Doctor Who run around doing your bidding on screen.

OVERWORLD
MINECRAFT

■ Want to know what makes *Minecraft*'s Overworld one of the greatest levels of all time? Well, its biggest strength is that it's a completely blank canvas! You can do and construct pretty much anything you want to with Mojang's creation tools, thanks to the basic building blocks provided by the Overworld. The level itself may change each and every time, but that's because only your imagination is the limit. It's a wonderful exercise in creativity and playing around.

CHAPTER 7-5
PORTAL 2

■ While this whole game is a series of incredible levels, there's one that has really stuck with us, and that's the test chamber in Chapter 7-5. It's without question one of the tougher tests in the game. Featuring dizzying leaps of faith and free falls, you'll have a wild time trying to scale the giant structure that towers above you. But the pay-off is huge, as you get to see just how far you've come in a single level.

CASTLE ROCK
RAYMAN LEGENDS

■ One of the most entertaining and imaginative levels ever, *Rayman Legends* had the totally ingenious idea of taking real-world rock songs and pairing them up with its platforming greatness. The resulting level, Castle Rock, is a frantic scramble as you look to not only complete every level, but keep in perfect sync with the classic rock song *Black Betty*—it's pretty awesome!

SUMMONER'S RIFT
LEAGUE OF LEGENDS

■ In case you haven't heard of this one—in which case, where have you been hiding?—Summoner's Rift is the go-to game map for the monstrously popular MOBA *League Of Legends.* This is the map that players have won millions of dollars on in tournaments by dominating the three lanes. This is the map where you can easily sink *hours* of your time into. Simply put, Summoner's Rift is an excellent example of how far a simple design can take a game. It's the only map anyone cares about in *League Of Legends*, and it will be remembered for *many* years to come.

RAINBOW ROAD
MARIO KART 8

■ One of the greatest racing tracks of all time got a remake for Mario Kart 8, making it better (and more frustrating) than ever! It's a co-op classic.

HALF THE LENGTH

Nintendo drastically cut down the length of Rainbow Road, ensuring laps don't devolve into boring, monotonous runs. Now it's all about the fast and frantic racing, so just be sure to keep your eyes on the road!

WATCH THOSE CORNERS

Rainbow Road is still one of the most frustrating racing levels ever, which is mainly due to how it doesn't include any barriers. That means it's way too easy to fall off the edge ... or push a friend who's inching ahead.

BLUE SHELL NIGHTMARE

One of the best things you can do on Rainbow Road is save that Blue Shell for the final lap. Wait until your friends take that last corner, make a dash for the finish line, and then use it to destroy them at the last second!

ALL THE OBSTACLES

One of the reasons Rainbow Road is so beloved is because of how excellently it is paced. Just when you've managed to gain some speed, you'll find it throwing tight corners, crashing obstacles, and chokepoints; pretty sneaky.

TOY TIME GALAXY
SUPER MARIO GALAXY

■ He might not have changed his clothes much in decades but that energetic plumber sure does love a bit of video game innovation. *Super Mario Galaxy* felt like a revolution when it launched on the Wii thanks to its intriguing, mind-bending design, but it's Toy Time Galaxy that remains a solid favorite. It throws you into a literal toy box, and navigating its gravity-defying platforming puzzles is an absolute treat.

THE MANSION
GONE HOME

■ A level doesn't need to contain action and theatrics to be considered great— sometimes it can contain nothing but everyday household items and still blow our minds. *Gone Home* is a game that revolves around one expertly-crafted level and the items you find within it; this indie treat has a thoughtful story to be found, but it's also a testament to how much intrigue you can pack into a small, homely space.

DID YOU KNOW?
A major update to *Rocket League* in 2016 introduced different arenas for the first time, including a tiered level and one featuring four goals.

THE ARENA
ROCKET LEAGUE

■ *Rocket League*'s most basic arena is a perfectly designed level. It will stand up as one of the greatest levels in video games for years to come, because it's built in such a way that its fun will never fade. From the curvature of the sides to the placement of the boost pads and height of the goals, everything about it ensures that every wild play you make for the ball keeps your heart-rate going strong.

BEST GAMING LEVELS OF ALL TIME

CHINA
STREET FIGHTER IV

■ Sure, it might look like you're just moving left to right and hadoukening anything that nudges toward you, but there's actually a subtle genius to the design of the *Street Fighter* locations. China is one of the best, not only providing one of the busiest and best backdrops in fighting games—the perfect blend of crazy going on in the background without immediately drawing the eye from the fight—but it also perfectly represents its hero, Chun-Li.

SCHOOL
TONY HAWK'S PRO SKATER HD

■ *Tony Hawk* may have wobbled in recent times, but the HD remaster of some of his finest *Pro Skater* pursuits brings us back to the glory days of the franchise. School has stood the test of time thanks to its perfectly-placed rails, insane challenges, and pretty radical selection of quarter-pipe combo opportunities.

PALACE DEFENCE SYSTEM
PRINCE OF PERSIA: SANDS OF TIME

■ *Prince Of Persia: Sands Of Time* is one of those ageless classics; a fine combination of sublime platform puzzles, awesome time-rewind mechanics, and a level design that'll leave you scratching your head in amazement. That shines through perfectly on the Palace Defense System level, requiring not only your keenest of senses but unwavering patience to work out how to beat this tricky puzzle—once you figure it out, prepare for your mind to be blown.

COLOSSUS 13: PHALANX
SHADOW OF THE COLOSSUS

■ *Shadow Of The Colossus* doesn't contain levels, at least not in the traditional sense. It charges you with wandering a giant desert wasteland to slay behemoth monsters and, as it turns out, each of the Colossus are actually incredible levels themselves. You'll need to work out how to approach, scale, and eventually kill each one, and one of the most exciting of these is Phalanx, the flying Colossus that will pull you into a breathtaking journey.

DID YOU KNOW?

The train wreck sequence in *Uncharted 2* was voted as the best in the series by game fans in an official Sony poll.

A ROCK AND A HARD PLACE
UNCHARTED 2: AMONG THIEVES

■ There are two completely jaw-dropping levels involving a train in *Uncharted 2*, but the best—and one of the finest levels to feature in a video game in the last decade—has to be A Rock And A Hard Place. This tense and breathtaking opening to *Uncharted 2* sees Nathan Drake trying to delicately climb off a train suspended over the side of a mountain. Every moment of this ascension to safety will have you on the edge of your seat. It forces you to consider every slight motion and movement; you'll be in constant fear that one step too fast and the train car will plummet— it's exhilarating! You won't soon forget it.

THE EXPERT SAYS …
ROSS HAMILTON
Games writer

It's tempting to pick the entire interwoven overworld of *Ori And The Blind Forest*, but if forced to choose a specific level I'd go for the Forlorn Ruins. Arriving late in the game, the Ruins are a marked departure from anything that comes before. While much of the forest of Nibel is made up of verdant woodland and overgrown caves, here the environment is cold and hostile, rife with mysterious glowing architecture and icy stalactites. The tragically frozen figures of the Ruins' former inhabitants, the Gumon, heighten the unsettling atmosphere. But not only is the Forlorn Ruins one of the most evocative levels in recent memory, it's also one of the most ingenious. The perpetually moving platforms and gravity-shifting mechanics deliver some of the most creative moments in the game. Challenging, different, and engaging, Forlorn Ruins is easily the highlight of the game.

STATS

Winner of 7 gaming awards

0.7 % of Steam players completed the game without dying

2 new areas in the Definitive Edition

88% Metacritic score

9 skills to learn as Ori

ORI AND THE BLIND FOREST

FROM THE DARKNESS COMES LIGHT

Before you even make your first running jump with little Ori, it's clear that *Ori and the Blind Forest* is a special game. The world in which this tiny white guardian spirit roams is absolutely stunning, with incredible backdrops and some of the most beautiful graphics we've seen in years. The Blind Forest feels expansive, alive ... and also a little dangerous. That's because, in this side-scrolling platformer, you must help Ori return light and life to the dark forest after a cataclysmic event withered the plants and food, forcing Ori to head out and explore.

While it might look fantastic, don't be fooled—*Ori and the Blind Forest* is tough. Difficult jumps and challenging enemies mean you'll always have to be on the lookout for the next threat ... but if you can overcome them, you're in for an amazing treat.

TIPS & TRICKS

SAVE OFTEN
Don't be afraid to use your blue orbs to save the game—you will regret not saving if you die.

BASH!
Ori's bash attack isn't only useful for traversal, it can also help a lot when fighting enemies.

PAY ATTENTION
When cutscenes play, keep paying attention. If a bird flies off in a certain direction, that is probably your next area.

TOP 5 AREAS

ORI'S HOME

1 The start of the game is actually quite sad. Prepare yourself for some heartbreak as a cataclysmic event wreaks havoc on the forest, and forces Ori to leave the home that the spirit shared with his protector, Naru. The start of the game shows how beautiful the world can be, and will make you want to fight to get that beauty back.

DID YOU KNOW?

The Definitive Edition of *Ori and the Blind Forest* features new areas to explore and new difficulty levels to try.

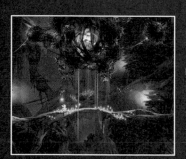

SUNKEN GLADES

2 After the huge event that causes Ori to be forced from his home, it is here that the light of the Spirit Tree, a powerful tree that protects the forest, revives the little spirit. This is the first area you are able to properly explore, and it's here you'll learn the basic techniques.

FORLORN RUINS

3 The Forlorn Ruins were the Gumon, a race of inventors who used the Spirit Tree's light in their creations. After the event, the Forlorn Ruins were frozen, and the Gumon couldn't escape. Ori must find the last Gumon and discover the Element of Wind.

GINSO TREE

4 This tree sits in the Forest of Nibel, and it was responsible for purifying the forest's waters as they passed through its trunk. The huge event caused the tree to go rotten and dry, so Ori must search for the Element of Waters inside the tree to restore its powers and bring life back to the forest.

MOUNT HORU

5 This volcano will not be accessible to players until late in the game—it is the final challenge faced by Ori as the spirit attempts to save the forest. Lava flows inside, so tread carefully as you look for the Element of Warmth, the final element needed.

"SOME OF THE MOST BEAUTIFUL GRAPHICS WE'VE SEEN IN YEARS"

ALSO CHECK OUT ...

LITTLEBIGPLANET 3

Take the cute little Sackboy through a whole range of incredible levels, and when you're finished with the game, start building your own. A lovely game that is so much fun to play.

RAYMAN: LEGENDS

If you want a beautiful-looking game as well as a great platformer, *Rayman Legends* ticks all the same boxes as *Ori and the Blind Forest*. It's fun, has a great learning curve, and features awesome music levels.

LEVEL SMART

If you're struggling to survive, make sure you use your experience points to level up Ori's survival skills.

LOOK EVERYWHERE

There are dozens of secrets and lots of hidden ability points around the world.

MASTER GAMING JARGON

ACHIEVEMENT
An unlockable virtual trophy that can be won by completing a specific action in a game. Popularized by Microsoft's Xbox platform.

AI
Stands for "artificial intelligence." Usually when you're playing against an opponent controlled by the computer, it's referred to as playing against the AI.

BETA
A select bit of the game made available to a small group of players before development is finished. Unlike a demo, a beta isn't supposed to represent the finished game, as developers want to fix any problems or glitches that are found.

BOSS
A much larger and tougher enemy that usually appears at the end of a level. Often beating a boss will result in the player learning a new skill, unlocking a new area, or becoming more powerful.

CAMPING
A technique used by online players, which involves staying in one area and killing any other player that approaches. This strategy is generally frowned upon by other players.

CHAT
A COMMUNICATION METHOD THAT ALLOWS TEAMMATES TO SPEAK TO EACH OTHER DURING A GAME. COMMUNICATION IS KEY, AND PRO PLAYERS ARE CONSTANTLY IN CONTACT WITH THEIR FELLOW PLAYERS.

MASTER GAMING JARGON

CASTING
A shortening of the term "broadcasting," used as a way of describing a livestream. Can also be used as a shorter form of "shoutcasting"—the term used to describe live eSport commentaries.

CHEAT
In older, single-player games this was often a code or secret that gave players hidden weapons or access to locked areas. In online games, cheating can take many forms and if the developers notice, this could even result in a ban.

CLASS
This is a specific set of abilities tailored toward a certain playstyle, such as healer (can heal other players) or tank (acts as a "shield" for the other players).

CLUTCH
Used to describe a successful play at a critical moment in competitive gaming, usually determining the outcome of the game.

COMBO
This is an unbreakable combination of attacks, most commonly seen in fighting games. Doing a jumping attack followed by a sweep before the opponent can block, for example.

CO-OP
Short for "co-operative." A game where you can play alongside other players to achieve your goal.

COSPLAY
Contraction of "costume play," which sees cosplayers dressing up as fictional characters, usually from games or anime.

COUNTER
A STRATEGY, CHARACTER, OR UNIT, THAT DOMINATES ANOTHER STRATEGY, CHARACTER, OR UNIT. ALTERNATIVELY, CAN BE USED AS A SHORTENED FORM OF THE WORD "COUNTERATTACK" TO REFER TO A STRIKE BACK AGAINST AN ENEMY.

DLC
Short for "downloadable content," which is extra content made available for download after a game's release. *Street Fighter 5*'s extra characters like Guile and Alex are examples of DLC.

EASTER EGG
This is a hidden item in a game that serves as a fun extra with no obvious gameplay benefit.

ESPORTS
Professional gaming competitions in which expert teams face-off to win huge prize money on stage, watched by millions of people on livestream.

MASTER GAMING JARGON

EXPANSION
Short for "expansion pack" and is usually significant in size, offering a wealth of new content. *Mists of Pandaria* for *World Of Warcraft* is an example of an expansion pack.

F2P
A short form of the term "free to play," referring to games that are free to download. However, they often contain extra purchases within the game itself for new weapons, abilities, and so on.

FPS
Stands for first-person shooter. Games like *Destiny* and *Halo* are popular FPS games.

FRAME-RATE
THE NUMBER OF FRAMES THAT THE CONSOLE DISPLAYS PER SECOND, MEASURED IN FPS. THE HIGHER THE FRAME-RATE, THE SMOOTHER THE GAMEPLAY.

G
Stands for gamerscore. Every time you unlock an achievement on an Xbox game, you are awarded points that count toward your gamerscore. The higher your gamerscore, the better a gamer you are.

GENERATION
A term to distinguish between the console eras. PS3 and Xbox 360 are referred to as last generation while PS4 and Xbox One are current generation.

GG
Good Game. Used extensively in online PC games after each round, but can be used in any game.

GRIEFING
When players annoy or harass other players by using game mechanics in unintended ways. An example of this would be trapping teammates or stealing players' kills.

HACKER
A player who downloads mods to change the game, usually giving them a major advantage in competitive play—for example, invincibility or unlimited ammunition mods.

INDIE
This is short for "independent." Refers to games made by smaller teams without big publishers backing them, such as *Rocket League*.

JUNGLER
In MOBAs, junglers are players who roam the "jungle" areas between the lanes, killing the mobs there to level up.

KICKSTARTER
A website where projects are pitched and people put money towards them being made. *Shenmue III*, *Mighty No. 9*, and *Elite: Dangerous* are examples of games funded on Kickstarter

KITING
In an MMORPG, kiting is grabbing a mob's attention before leading them in a certain direction. In MOBAs, kiting is attacking from a distance so an opponent can't easily retaliate.

L2P
Learn to play. This is something that is often shouted at noobs.

LAG
THE TERM USED TO DESCRIBE A DELAY BETWEEN THE PLAYER'S COMMANDS AND THE ACTIONS OCCURRING ON-SCREEN— USUALLY CAUSED BY A POOR CONNECTION. SOME PLAYERS CAN USE THIS TO THEIR ADVANTAGE, BUT IT IS CONSIDERED UNFAIR.

LANE
MOBAs are based in battlegrounds that feature one or more "lanes", through which computer-controlled minions attack. Think of lanes as pathways through the map. In most games, teams divide their players up between these lanes to defend and attack from all angles.

LEADERBOARDS
Leaderboards are scoreboards that rank highest scores or fastest times starting with the best.

LINEAR
Games that focus on narrow pathways and story over exploration are often described as "linear." *Minecraft: Story Mode* is linear, for example, while *Minecraft* is not.

MASH
A term for pressing buttons as fast as you can without any real thought process or strategy.

MIA
Missing in action. The term originated in *League Of Legends* and means that an opponent has disappeared from their "lane" and therefore could be a danger to the rest of the team elsewhere.

MMORPG
Stands for massively multiplayer online role-playing game. These are RPGs that thousands of people can play online at the same time such as *World Of Warcraft* or *DC Universe Online*.

MOB
Short for "mobile," this term is used for computer-controlled monsters. The term is most commonly used to describe computer-controlled enemies in MMORPGs and MOBAs.

MOBA
Stands for multiplayer online battle arena. These are games between small teams on a top-down map such as *Dota 2* or *League Of Legends*.

MASTER GAMING JARGON

MOD
A piece of software that modifies how a game functions. This can include everything from graphics mods that change the basic look of the game, to mods that add new characters, skins, or weapons into the game.

NO-SCOPING
Killing someone with a sniper-rifle without "scoping" (or aiming down the sights). This is one of the toughest skills to master in competitive shooters.

NOOB
A term used to describe someone new to a game, which has been shortened from "newbie."

NPC
Non-playable character. A computer-controlled character in the game.

PARRY
This is a move in combat games that, when timed perfectly, lets you deflect your opponent's attack and leaves them momentarily open for a counter-attack.

PERMADEATH
When death in the game wipes out all of your stats and progress, forcing you to start the game again from scratch.

PLATINUM
This is awarded to players who have unlocked every single Trophy in a PlayStation game.

POINT-AND-CLICK
Games genre where you collect objects to solve puzzles by pointing the cursor and clicking on them, as seen in *Dropsy* or *The Secret Of Monkey Island*.

PVE
Player Versus Environment. Most typically used in MMORPGs, this means players versus computer-controlled enemies rather than versus other players. Usually, PvE can be played alone and contains some sort of storyline.

PVP
Player Versus Player. Most typically used in MMORPGs, this pits players against one another.

RAGEQUIT
When someone quits an online game early, usually out of frustration at losing.

REBOOT
A term used to describe new entries to dormant gaming series that start the storyline and gameplay from scratch, often taking it in a whole new direction. *Need For Speed* and *SimCity* are recent examples of reboots.

RE-SPEC
When you reset the stats of your character to build him or her in a different way.

RHYTHM-ACTION
Games genre where the objective is to press buttons in time to music, as seen in *Guitar Hero* or *Rock Band*.

ROGUE-LIKE
A genre of games that typically feature 2D pixel graphics, permadeath, a high degree of difficulty, and randomly-generated dungeons. These games are inspired by the 1980s game *Rogue,* hence where the name comes from.

RPG
Stands for role-playing game. Games like *Final Fantasy* and *Ni No Kuni* are popular RPGs.

RTS
Stands for real-time strategy. *StarCraft* and *Civilization* are famous real-time strategy series.

MASTER GAMING JARGON

SALT
A term for when players take defeat poorly. This was originally shortened from "salty tears."

SANDBOX
A TERM USED TO DESCRIBE GAMES THAT ARE OPEN AND FOCUS ON CREATIVE AND EXPLORATION ELEMENTS MORE THAN STORY AND COMBAT. *MINECRAFT* IS THE MOST FAMOUS EXAMPLE.

SCRUB
A derogatory term for a player who is overconfident and boastful despite not being very skilled.

SHERPA
An experienced player who helps noobs beat games. Most commonly seen in MMOs such as *Destiny*.

SPAMMER
This is a derogatory term for someone who uses the same moves over and over again. You will usually get "spamming" from inexperienced players in fighting games.

SPEEDRUN
Completing games as fast as you can is known as a speedrun, with the community of players who participate in this known as speedrunners.

STREAM
Playing games live for an audience is known as streaming, which is commonly done through Twitch or YouTube Gaming.

TOWER DEFENSE
A term used to describe games where the purpose is to build towers to stop enemies from reaching your base.

TOYS TO LIFE
Games genre where you use real figurines to unlock characters and powers in the actual game.

TROLLING
The act of deliberately upsetting or provoking someone else. This can be as simple as shouting through a chat headset, being rude on social media or constantly following and killing one player over and over.

TROPHY
Every PlayStation game has a series of in-game objectives ("Complete the tutorial," "Finish top of the leaderboards") that award you with a Trophy when completed.

TWITCH
An online platform dedicated to streaming games. PS4 and Xbox One both have Twitch apps that let players stream their gameplay.

UPDATES
A term for small, obligatory downloads for certain games. Updates will usually fix any glitches and bugs or correct balance problems (one character or weapon being too powerful, for example).

VANILLA
Used to describe the original or base version of a game, without any expansions, add-ons, or sometimes even patches. For example, a vanilla server in *Minecraft* is one without any mods or expansions.

WHIFF
An attack that misses and does no damage. Although this is usually accidental, some players deliberately whiff attacks for tactical reasons, such as building up meter in fighting games to spend on powerful moves.